NOT JUST a COOKBOOK

**L'ECRIVAIN RESTAURANT
DUBLIN**

NOT JUST

a

COOKBOOK

L'ECRIVAIN RESTAURANT
DUBLIN

Derry & Sallyanne Clarke
with Tom Doorley

Photography by
Mike O'Toole

Foreword by
Hugh Leonard

Published by L'Ecrivain Restaurant
109A Lower Baggot Street
Dublin 2, Ireland
www.lecrivain.com

Design: Aad
Recipe testers: Anne Marie Tobin, Lucy O'Grady
Editing & indexing: Pat Carroll
Printed and bound in Belgium by Snoeck-Ducaju & Zoon

To
Sarah May & Andrew

GENERAL CONTENTS

RECICES

Soups

Starters

Starters {cont.}

Frank Hederman's beech smoked salmon
with quenelle of crab & cauliflower tempura   *114*

Wholegrain mustard & whiskey cured wild
Irish salmon, pink grapefruit couscous,
avocado cream   *116*

Terrine of wild Irish smoked salmon with
crab, Mascarpone cheese & horseradish, crisp
capers & onion ice cream   *117*

Terrine of smoked mackerel, mussels &
salmon with leek & potato, pickled cucumber   *118*

Terrine of red mullet & Mediterranean
vegetables scented with saffron & yellow
pepper, opal basil dressing   *119*

Sally Barnes's natural smoked haddock risotto
with Parmesan & spinach, poached hen's egg
& curry froth   *120*

Seared peppered rare tuna loin, soy & honey
glaze, red pepper escabèche, avocado &
lime purée   *122*

Terrine of teal & swede with confit citrus
fruits, bitter raisin preserve   *124*

Roasted farmyard quail with leg ballotine &
peppered quail egg, truffled Savoy cabbage,
red wine glaze   *125*

Roasted wood pigeon on a tart of caramelised
red onion, madeira jus   *126*

Starters {cont.}

Crisp organic salad Landaise, selection of
farmyard fowl with pommes sautées, sherry &
walnut dressing   *127*

Assiette of duck: Jerusalem artichoke &
smoked duck terrine, duck ballotine, confit
duck & black truffle Pithiviers   *128*

Seared duck foie gras with banana dressing,
spiced brûléed banana, walnut &
raisin brioche   *130*

Pressed ham hock with chicken confit &
roasted shiitake mushrooms, fig compote   *131*

Carpaccio of aged Angus beef with wild
asparagus & horseradish oil   *132*

Boudin of Clonakilty black pudding with
Cashel Blue cheese & cider sorbet, crisp
cured bacon, stout jus   *134*

Roasted veal kidney with a nage of garden
peas, beans & asparagus, parsnip mash, black
truffle jus   *136*

Ravioli of goats' cheese with char-grilled
aubergine, red pepper & courgette dressing,
Jerusalem artichoke froth   *137*

Chilled goats' cheese parfait, pickled pear &
brioche crouton   *138*

Roasted white asparagus wrapped in Parma
ham with garden peas, tomato & Parmesan
butter, poached duck egg, black olive tapenade   *140*

RECIPES

Main courses

Main courses *{cont.}*

Desserts

Basics

L'ECRIVAIN

'within range of the toast'

HUGH LEONARD

Discovering a great restaurant is often the same – only different – as finding oneself locked into either the most intense of love affairs or the bitterest of quarrels. I mean that in either case it is there, and yet you cannot for the life of you remember how it began . . .

I do recall that I was writing a newspaper column called 'Not While I'm Eating', which was both more and less than a food column. Unfortunate is he who chooses to eat alone, and one weeps for the likes of the multimillionaire, Nubar Gulbenkian, who boasted, 'The best number for a dinner party is two: myself and a damned good head waiter.' After all, the most musical words in any language are an ecstatic 'Oh my God, taste that!' uttered to a dining companion. So my requirements for a great meal are not food alone, but the company to go with it.

Two is an ideal number. You can discuss affairs of the soul and, often, of the heart. If I were of a mind to propose marriage, I would do so at L'Ecrivain or not at all. I reckon that a combination of Derry Clarke's cooking and the balm of Sallyanne Clarke's presence would dramatically raise the odds in my favour. If she still says 'No,' then the only explanation can be that she is already spoken for and, as the expression goes, you might as well throw your hat at it.

As for having, say, four people at table, it is perhaps time that a new adage replaced the chestnut that says 'Two's company; three's a crowd.' I would suggest: 'One's a raconteur; three's an audience.' I hold that good food should be a civilised pleasure and not treated as half-way between either a kind of divine service or a profane knees-up. And I should not move on without a word about that most unhappy of combinations: which is that of three persons breaking bread together. Whatever the truth of the matter, to an outsider it must resemble either two persons comforting a miserable third one, or that third party intruding upon a long-suffering couple.

Like Topsy in Uncle Tom's Cabin, L'Ecrivain could probably say that it 'Never was born, I 'spect I grow'd.' I first of all recall a small, box-like basement room where I interviewed the late entertainer, Marty Caine. Next thing, it went up in the world, both in the figurative as well as the literal sense. 'Lowliness', if you can stand another quotation, 'was young ambition's ladder.' Sallyanne and Derry had moved a few doors away, where there were stairs, a terrace and – on occasion, however rare – sunlight. And there were writers, looking out of their frames at the mere mortals who ascended from wine bar to dining room. And good grief! I was and am one of them, seen cradling a cat – my beloved Pooka – and if ever a Burmese mog belongs in cat heaven, it is he.

L'Ecrivain had not yet completed its true ascent; it closed and opened again, far grander than before, but with the old intimacy unchanged. Now, however, it had metamorphosed into a restaurant to which one brought special guests only. On special occasions – at least that holds true for me – perhaps we partook of Derry Clarke's ambrosial tasting menu. There is nothing quite like ordering this Lucullan feast and then, once committed, to sit back and wait for the miracle. And suddenly I recall the experience of two Americans – which was related to me by a mutual friend – who were touring in Co. Kerry recently.

After lunching in a wayside hotel, they came out to find that they had had a puncture. Theirs was a rented Renault car, but it contained a spanner that was the wrong size, and there was not a garage within several miles. But salvation was at hand, for there were two painters beautifying the sign on the hotel roof, and there was a Renault in the car park. One of them obligingly picked the lock of this other car, opened the toolbox and extracted a spanner of the required size.

''Tis all above board,' he explained. 'That car has a Cork registration.' Any Corconian – or Kerryman – will explain that gnomic utterance. In any case and within ten minutes, the afflicted wheel was changed. Of course the American tourist insisted that the two men accept a few euro as a reward for their kindness.

At once the pair put their paint brushes to one side and headed for the hotel bar. One of them lingered, however, to explain their haste. 'We want,' he said, 'to drink to your good health while you're still within range of the toast.' Which to my mind is what this foreword is about:

to celebrate and raise a glass of Grand Régnard – it is my best-loved Chablis, and there is always a bottle at the table before I am – while the best restaurant in Dublin continues to be 'within range of the toast'.

Probably – almost certainly – I am not a special person; perhaps it is part of the magic of L'Ecrivain that it subjects each one of its clients to the same *grande illusion*. I do remember one act of kindness, however, that caused my friendship with the Clarkes to be written in granite and, embarrassing as it will be for them, it must be told.

The first anniversary of my wife's death fell on 13 April 2001. My thought was to mark the occasion – or, to be truthful, avoid the pain of it – by taking my daughter and a couple of friends to dinner and assisting the day to pass quietly. But that date, 13 April, occurred on a Good Friday, and every restaurant in town was shut. I have forgotten how it came about, but on the previous day and according to Sallyanne's instructions, I parked my car outside L'Ecrivain, and members of the staff came out into Baggot Street bearing parcels containing dinner for four, already cooked. So for that occasion, perhaps, I was after all 'special' . . .

Let us not be too fanciful, but a restaurant is more than its *patronne*, its *chef de cuisine*, its service, its Michelin star and the smile one gets from its petite *sommelière*, Martina, and one can add as other ingredients that indefinable quality: its ambience. L'Ecrivain has them all – in spades.

ACKNOWLEDGEMENTS

We would like to thank everybody involved in this project, without whose hard work and dedication it would not have been possible: Scott Burnett, Pat Carroll, Tom Doorley, Johnny Kelly, Hugh Leonard, Lucy O'Grady, Mike O'Toole, Anne Marie Tobin, Mary Weddick, all our suppliers, and the dedicated team in the kitchen and front of house at L'Ecrivain.

INTRODUCTION

MY LIFE WITH

FOOD

& OTHER SUCH STORIES

AS TOLD BY DERRY CLARKE TO TOM DOORLEY

When I was growing up, food was important in our household – if for no other reason than it actually put bread on the table. The family business, John Clarke & Sons, distributed all sorts of food products throughout Ireland back in the days when the Irish palate was notoriously conservative.

Undeterred by the cautious tastes of Irish people, my dad and his brother Joe dealt in everything from proper Continental cheeses and Danish rusks to snails and frogs' legs. In the warehouse on Wellington Quay in the centre of Dublin there was a treasure trove of edibles and drinkables: Huntley & Palmer biscuits, rusks, maple syrup, caviar, chestnut purée, Schwarz spices, smoked salmon, bottles of carrot juice for the health food shops, Sunquick orange squash for the less choosy, bags of whole spices imported from Indonesia, vast wheels of Brie . . .

In a sense the family business was ahead of its time. I often wonder what sort of turnover it would have these days, when every town in the land has several thriving restaurants. John Clarke & Sons was founded by my grandfather at a time when food, for most people, involved simple staples and many people survived on a subsistence diet.

Grandfather John, or Sean as he was called in the family, started life as a farmer near Killucan in Co. Westmeath. He opened a farm shop in Camden Street in 1914. This was not good timing, as it was the eve of World War I and, in addition, Dublin would be plunged into turmoil two years later with the Easter Rising. Nevertheless, he went on to set up John Clarke & Sons under Webb's bookshop in 1916 and in 1923 he built new premises at 51 Wellington Quay.

During my childhood – I was born in 1957 – things had changed, but the Ireland of that time was still a far cry from the prosperous European nation we live in today. The company dealt in some fairly basic foodstuffs, but I suppose the bulk of the business lay in what would have been considered luxuries by many in those days.

I remember Nick Power, the warehouse manager, cutting huge cheeses into convenient weights and carefully wrapping each in greaseproof paper. This was no easy job and it required a skilled eye, especially when dealing with vast Bries, which could be eight feet in diameter.

My dad, whom everyone knew as DJ (for Dermot Joseph), was always ahead of his time. He decided to import the first-ever Danish blue into Ireland, sometime in the late 1950s, I think. The whole consignment was impounded by the authorities down at the docks on the basis that it had gone off and was unfit for human consumption. We have come a long way.

When he brought the first Belgian chocolates into Ireland – only too fit for human consumption – there was a different kind of problem at the docks. Some 35 per cent of each shipment went missing!

John Clarke's customers were many and varied. We tend to forget that, in those far-off days, Dublin had a number of very good food shops: places like Smyth's of the Green (where Habitat is now), Farm Produce in Baggot Street (now transformed into Oddbins), Findlater's with branches throughout the city, and Magill's, which, thankfully, is still with us. Other names I remember include Morton's in Ranelagh, McCambridge's, H. Williams, Five Star, Lipton's and Leverett & Fry.

The family business

My dad refused to be deskbound; if he wasn't travelling to trade shows all over Europe he would be out on the road arranging displays of tins and packages. These days we call it merchandising. As I say, he was ahead of his time and he was, in many ways, always young. I laughed when he told me, in the early 1980s, that Temple Bar could be a great area for restaurants. He always enjoyed the company of young people and he never seemed to mind noise. Maybe this youthfulness was part of the reason that he anticipated what was coming in terms of eating habits. He was the first yoghurt importer in Ireland (our dairy industry had yet to try making it), but without success. It just wouldn't shift. Likewise with pâtés. I don't know whether people associated the word with bald heads but, for whatever reason, it didn't sell. Until, that is, my dad changed the name to 'spreads'. He understood his market – John Clarke & Sons had five or six trucks on the road at any time.

Food was in my mother May's family too. Her father, Nicholas McEvoy, was a fruit importer and his company was the first in Ireland to bypass the London market and bring produce in directly from South Africa after World War II. My mother started her working life in the family business and both she and my Aunt Margie were directors of the company until it was bought over. Ultimately it became part of Fyffes.

My mother did a little cooking at home when I was small (mainly confining herself to great, hearty stews with whole cloves of garlic), but my dad was constantly experimenting in the kitchen, which was highly unusual for a man in those days. He kept up a continuous output of brown soda bread. The larder and the fridge were always packed with unusual stuff: Baxter's tinned soups, jars of olives, tins of anchovies and shark's fin soup (for the Chinese restaurant market), even rollmop herrings, which were never a big seller. All came from Wellington Quay.

Home was a big, rambling country house that had become marooned in suburbia: St Anne's in Clonskeagh. Not surprisingly, it's gone now and the grounds where I used to play have become the Annsbrook development. In the context of Dublin today, it's almost incredible to remember that the house was surrounded by three acres of gardens, including a huge old orchard with apples, pears and plums and a fully functioning kitchen garden. There was even a paddock for Connemara ponies and donkeys. We had a large fish pond stocked with golden carp and two big lean-to greenhouses in the kitchen garden planted with tomatoes and peaches. In the old outhouses, which had originally been the coach house and stables, my father started a mini-factory to produce jams and chutneys.

It was as perfect a place to grow up as could be, but, while we were well off by average standards, we weren't rich. In those days big, old houses with large gardens were out of fashion. People wanted neat, modern, suburban houses with 'all mod cons', including central heating. Even before the oil crisis of 1972 you would have needed your own Texan gusher to heat St Anne's so, naturally, we didn't bother. To this day, my sister Ann, eight years my elder, my brothers Joey, a year younger, and Sean, six years older, and I are completely immune to draughts and I find myself getting hot and sweaty in temperatures that most people think are completely normal. We never got colds when we were children, yet at home in winter you could see your breath condensing in front of your face.

One of the reasons my mother did very little cooking was because we were lucky enough to have a wonderful housekeeper, Breda Dwyer from Wexford, whose brother was one of our two gardeners. We formed a little community of our own.

Early food memories

Even though I was exposed to all sorts of food from a very early stage, I can remember detesting cheese of all sorts until my dad brought home a processed, smoked Austrian version. It took years for me to get to like the olives and hot spices that were an important part of our livelihood.

My early food memories are of the big kitchen at St Anne's where we almost always ate (the dining room was strictly for formal occasions). There were my mother's stews, which I adored, and the big bread cabinet stocked with good old-fashioned batch pan and home-made jam, either our own or the Mellifont Abbey jams (made by the monks), which my father sold.

When I was ten, in 1967, my parents separated. My father was a great enthusiast, an idealist and always at home with young people. My mother was a different character, but very kind. While my father was pretty indulgent, she was scrupulously fair. It is never easy when parents move apart, but the blow was softened for us because, as often happened in those days, they decided to live separately under the same roof. This arrangement continued for three years, at which stage my mother got an apartment in Booterstown where she lived until she died. My father continued to live in St Anne's until he died in 1984.

My mother was a great beauty in her young days and she was always in great demand for dances and soirées. Even in later life she had a very active social life and a huge circle of friends, the full extent of which, as is often the case, I didn't realise until she died. She seemed to know everybody and, until very late in life, she was the life and soul of every party she attended. Mum was Lady Captain of Woodbrook and Captain and Vice-captain of various bridge clubs. She died in January 2001 aged 79.

After primary school at St Conleth's in Clyde Road and a year at Dundrum Tech, it was decided that I would go to boarding school. I wasn't particularly put out about this new departure in my young life; in fact I wanted to be a boarder. I was thirteen at the time – and I suppose I was lucky in that the school was very unusual, small, liberal and, actually, good fun. I remember arriving at St George's in Portroe, near Lough Derg in Co. Tipperary, on a balmy autumn evening in 1970.

I have no idea how my parents found St George's, but they did. It was in a fine old country house and had about forty pupils, all boys, aged between eight and eighteen. It was the personal fiefdom of Commander Earle, ex-Royal Navy, and his wife, who had settled there just after the war.

Not surprisingly, it was very English in tone (we did GCE O and A levels), but it certainly wasn't stuffy. The Earles were kind-hearted and quite enlightened for the times. The Commander treated us with genuine respect and impeccable manners and he expected the same from his pupils.

On my first evening there I got into my only fight, not very willingly, with one of the older boys. This was a bit of a tradition, seemingly, for the new recruits and I acquitted myself well. I was a big lad, even then, and managed to floor my opponent with one kick to his more delicate parts, much to my own surprise. As in the tradition of all the best school stories, we got on well after that.

St George's was, I suppose, a bit like Gordonstoun, the famous Scottish boarding school, except on a much smaller scale and a bit eccentric. It was a real outdoor kind of place and I developed a life-long love of sailing thanks to the fact that the school kept several boats (including an old World War II speedboat) on the lough. Anyone who enjoyed Arthur Ransome's *Swallows and Amazons* books as a child would have felt perfectly at home there.

Sailing through school

Many of the teachers were either retired from other local schools or part-timers. As a result, we often got to spend the day outside, returning to the classroom for lessons at around five in the evening. It was certainly different, but, of course, most of us thought that all boarding schools were like that.

One of the great things about St George's was that the boys came from all over the world. One of my friends there was Henrici Osborne of the sherry family and another, from closer to home, was Anthony Musgrave from Cork.

Anthony and I were partners in my first restaurant venture – a tent in the woods close to the school. The meals at St George's were probably no better or worse than at any other boarding school, but we found that we had a ready market. It's hard to remember exactly what we served, but I recall hoarding tins of ham, sourced from home, and producing thick, doorstopper sandwiches with it.

When we weren't doing fifty knots on the Shannon in the school speedboat, orienteering, riding or sailing on Lough Derg, we would be renovating boats or building model aircraft. Strangely enough, we didn't do science (the emphasis was on English, maths and history), but we had plenty of practical experience of the physical world.

We were encouraged to be ourselves, to express ourselves and to have respect for others. There was no uniform, no corporal punishment and nobody minded what length your hair was provided you had good manners. Older boys were even allowed into Portroe for a few beers on the strict condition that nobody got ossified. It wasn't a very academic school and I suppose it was obvious that very few of us would end up doing nine-to-five jobs.

During my schooldays I always spent my summer holidays in Kinsale with my mother's sister, Aunt Carrie Roche, and her husband Stanley. Uncle Stanley was a great sailor. My brothers and I used to stay with them and my cousins Nicholas and Peter on board his eight-berth yacht and every year we cruised down west to Baltimore or Crookhaven.

When I was fourteen I got my first job – and it was in a restaurant: cleaning the loos in Man Friday's in Kinsale. In time, I was even promoted to the position of waiter, but I found I couldn't handle the people. Indeed, when anyone complained, I would tell them that they had no idea how much effort had gone into their meal. Peter Barry became aware of this lack of diplomacy and shifted me to kitchen duties. It had never occurred to me to make a career in the food business; I had been seduced by the sea very early on and I decided that this would be my future. When I was sixteen, my mother brought me for interview to Irish Shipping and I was offered a cadetship.

With a view to my career on the ocean waves, I decided to try my hand at crewing on a trawler out of Crosshaven and discovered, to my horror, that this was very different from sailing yachts along the coast of West Cork. The work was so hard and relentless that I decided, maybe not very logically, that a maritime career was simply not for me.

The next step was crucial, I suppose. Straight out of school, I had the opportunity to go into the kitchen at Peter Barry's Man Friday's and to work under a great French chef, Xavier Poupel. This was the first half of the 1970s and Man Friday's was ahead of its time, helping to turn Kinsale into a real restaurant destination. My Aunt Carrie was Peter Barry's business partner in Man Friday's. She was a remarkable and wonderful woman, always looking after us and giving encouragement right up to the time she died, aged 72, in 2001.

From the loos, to the tables, to the kitchen

It seems strange now, of course, but Xavier's steak *au poivre* was cutting-edge food in those far-off days. And anyone who wanted their steak really rare, or *à la minute*, knew that this was one of the few places in the country that you could get it. No wonder it was packed every night.

It was tough, but a great place to start. There were three of us in the kitchen: myself, Xavier and Michael Cantwell, who is now a *ki* masseur in Dublin. Xavier opened our eyes to lots of things, including presentation.

The plate of hors d'oeuvres – ratatouille, ham, egg, rollmop herrings, smoked salmon – was plated up with scientific precision. If something I produced wasn't just right, he would say so, but he'd also give encouragement; it was a great way to learn.

The routine was always the same: into the kitchen at nine in the morning for three hours of prep, back at five, open at six, close at 10.30 and then off to The Spaniard, also owned by Peter Barry, for pints. On Sundays, Peter would cook us lunch in his home and we would laze around with the Sunday papers until it was time to head off for the night's service. There was a genuine team spirit and, even though it required lots of energy, it really didn't feel like work at all.

Xavier left to return to France to cook for President Mitterrand for seven years, then went to Australia for a year or two. When he returned home to St Tropez, I sent him chefs from Ireland. Now he's running a restaurant in Vietnam. A new head chef, Eddie Morrison, arrived and expanded the menu. This experience really opened my eyes as to what could be done in a restaurant kitchen.

Whole pan-fried mackerel, straight from the sea, were a knockout. Steaks were now given extra ageing. We made the best prawn cocktails ever – with proper Dublin Bay prawns, of course. There was sole on the bone and baked turbot with an intense clam chowder sauce.

Man Friday's was so called because of the connection with Alexander Selkirk, who, according to the story, landed at Kinsale before being marooned on his desert island. It seemed appropriate, therefore, to give seafood pride of place.

Peter Barry had trained in hotel management and opened The Spaniard, which is still Kinsale's most famous pub. He went on to open Man Friday's in 1968. I was lucky to meet Peter when I did. He was my aunt's business partner and therefore a kind of honorary uncle; he was quite a prophet in his own land as far as the hospitality industry was concerned. Mind you, I don't think we called it that in those days.

It's fashionable now to knock Kinsale and to say that its days as the 'gourmet capital' of Ireland are over. The whole country has moved on and Kinsale has done the same, so it's easy to forget what an exciting place it was, as far as food was concerned, from the 1960s right through to the 1980s. It was the only place in the country where you could find a concentration of good restaurants within walking distance of each other. Peter Barry got the ball rolling with The Spaniard and then Man Friday's, Gerry Galvin, later of Drimcong fame, helped to put Kinsale on the map with The Vintage, there was spectacular food at the Blue Haven and there was even a Scandinavian restaurant. It certainly was, beyond any shadow of doubt, where the Irish food revolution started and people who were in search of exciting cooking flocked there in their thousands. It was a great place to be.

My Kinsale days were happy. I was young – very young – and we were a hard-working group who enjoyed an amazing social life outside the kitchen. But the time eventually came to move on. I was 21 and felt that this was fairly old, so I wanted to explore new pastures.

Blowing up stoves &
joining the Royal Marine

My first billet beyond Kinsale was at the Delgany Inn near Dublin and it was not an entirely happy experience. In fact, it nearly put paid to my hopes of ever cooking again. One night, when I was trying to light an old stove in the kitchen, I noticed that the pilot light had gone out. So, without stopping to think about the laws of physics, I struck a match.

The result was pretty dramatic. Apart from the very loud explosion, the only thing I was conscious of was being thrown violently across the room. Then, slowly, I realised that I was badly singed and generously bruised. It took a few minutes before I noticed that the kitchen was wrecked and that I was very lucky to have walked away.

Later, when I was having a pint in a local pub to soothe my nerves, the barman asked, 'Are you the genius who blew up the kitchen?' My pride was very sorely hurt but, thank God, the rest of me was in reasonable shape.

I don't know if the management of the Royal Marine Hotel in Dún Laoghaire ever got to hear about my explosive time in Delgany, but, a few weeks later, they offered me a job in the grill bar, which was called, in those innocent days, The Gay Nineties. The menu was not exactly advanced – we did a roaring trade in steaks and apple pie – but my stint there did me a world of good.

I soon realised that I was expected to work way beyond my experience and that speed and organisation were essential for coping. Working in that kitchen gave me a great deal – mainly because I was literally on my own and I had nobody to blame except myself if anything went wrong.

Doing two hundred covers in a one-man kitchen is no joke, but I had certain advantages. There was no prep to be done – the main kitchen did all that – and my main task was to keep on top of the steaks and their various timings. Many of the customers were long-term residents who liked their steaks well done, which was a bit of a blessing, but one old gentleman always asked for his fillet to be 'flared', or well done outside and very rare inside. It took me ages to get it right and then, one evening, I was summoned to his table. He got up, danced a little jig, hugged me and kept yelling, 'You did it!' This was pretty exciting stuff for the staid grill room at the Royal Marine. Satisfying as this certainly was, I knew that I had to move on. I had done a brief stint at Les Terrasses in Paris but could not settle into it and I started looking for something a bit more demanding in Dublin.

John Howard had opened Le Coq Hardi in Pembroke Road in 1977 and, by all accounts, he was cooking the best food in Dublin. The Mirabeau in Dún Laoghaire, with its outrageous prices, was attracting the Dublin glitterati at the time, but John Howard was in a different league altogether, as time would ultimately tell.

My father wasn't just a supplier to Le Coq Hardi, he had become a very good customer too. I can see why. He loved good wine, he adored smoked salmon (which was still a delicacy in those days) and he was such a connoisseur of cheeses that he used to judge them at the RDS Spring Show. Le Coq Hardi was the only restaurant in Dublin at that time that did all these things really well. Knowing I was looking for a job, my father arranged an interview with John Howard.

We had a brief chat, I answered a few questions and suddenly John was asking me when I could start. I was a bit taken aback. I was in my early twenties and this was one serious restaurant. 'Tomorrow morning,' I said, and this was the beginning of four of the most formative years in my cooking career. Coming from the grill bar at the Royal Marine, with a brief interlude in Baggot Street, I knew as soon as I walked into the kitchen at Le Coq Hardi that this was different. This was the real thing.

Kicked out of bed at
Le Coq Hardi

John was in his prime then. He was in his early thirties and he was cooking like nobody else in the country. His perfectionism was legendary. He would drive his Merc (he seems always to have had a Merc) to the market at five in the morning and choose the vegetables as if his life depended on it. And, speaking of vegetables, every single order was cooked from scratch; there was no parcooking for John.

He was incredibly patient with me and he was a great teacher, but there were limits. 'I'll show you once,' he would say. At first, I wasn't the best timekeeper. One morning, when I was sleeping soundly in my little flat in Pembroke Road, I thought there had been an earthquake. John had run me to ground and kicked the bed over.

There was no more messing after that. I buckled down. I suppose I knew that I was in a great restaurant kitchen with a brilliant chef at the helm. John's food was absolutely classic, true *cuisine bourgeoise*. It may have seemed old-fashioned in comparison to the other two restaurants that were being talked about in Dublin in those days, the Mirabeau and the King Sitric. But the execution was nothing short of superb and I learned then the lesson that there is simply nothing better than old-fashioned food when it's done well.

A lot of people think of John Howard as being gruff, but he never failed to thank the kitchen crew every single night at the end of service. And on Saturday nights there were pints for everyone until the small hours.

Because of the demands of working at Le Coq Hardi, where John Howard not only bought the best produce but demanded the best of himself and his team, I was approaching burnout after only four years. When Dave Darragh, an old school friend from my days at St Conleth's, approached me with the offer of a nine-to-five job, I jumped at the opportunity.

Dave's father, Dr Austin Darragh, who ran a pharmaceutical trials company in St James's Hospital, needed someone to cook for patients who had volunteered for drug-testing programmes. My task was to upgrade the food generally and to tailor meals for volunteers who needed specific diets. At first, the regular hours were attractive and the challenges involved were quite satisfying, but after less than a year I felt, once again, that the time had come to move on. I spent my twenty-fifth birthday painting the walls of a new restaurant in the basement of the Lansdowne Hotel, right next to Le Coq Hardi, having just got a job there. It was 1983. Philip Duggan, who had been head waiter at Le Coq Hardi, had joined forces with Patsy McGuirk, a chef with whom he had originally worked in Rosslare. Their new venture, the Bon Appétit, needed a deputy to Patsy and I stepped in.

Exciting as it was trying to establish a new restaurant in Dublin, Ireland was in the doldrums at the time. Bumper stickers asked the last person leaving the country to 'Please turn off the lights.' I reckoned that I was still young enough to make a life elsewhere and I set about getting a work visa for Australia, which, in those days, was crying out for trained chefs. It seemed like the obvious thing to do and it was spiced with a bit of excitement.

No sooner had I got my visa and travel plans sorted out than I got a phone call to say that my father was seriously ill. I put everything on hold; he died a few weeks later in July 1984, aged 66. My world had been turned upside down and suddenly the prospect of heading off to the far side of the globe had lost its appeal. I decided to stay at the Bon Appétit, at least for the time being.

It's not a decision I regret. If I had bitten the bullet and gone to Australia, who knows where I might be now. I suppose I could have been head chef in a hotel in Adelaide. Staying here, although I certainly didn't know it at the time, opened up lots of more exciting possibilities.

Life changes

The opening of L'Ecrivain was, of course, coming closer, but there were other things that had to happen first. Like any chef worth his salt, I knew that I wanted my own restaurant some day, but the time had not yet come.

In June 1985 one of the waiters at the Bon Appétit, Michael, a friend of mine, had met an attractive blonde and wanted me to join him to introduce me and his sister to her. We met in the newly opened Westbury Hotel bar. The blonde turned out to be Sallyanne; we got along famously. I asked her to go out with me straight away and every time I met her after that. Although she declined, we met as a group regularly over the next few months. It was a great summer. In September Sallyanne rang me. She needed an escort for a work-related insurance event at the Royal Hospital in Kilmainham. That was our first official date. We had a great night and I asked her to marry me two weeks later. After numerous proposals, she eventually said yes and we married in October 1987.

In the meantime I had moved back to Baggot Street, taking up my first post as head chef in the Ante Room restaurant, which was owned by Annette and Ted O'Sullivan. The head waiter was Ray Hingston; I ended up working with Ray for many years. It was a short stint but an enjoyable one and, in the end, I returned to the Bon Appétit because Patsy made me an offer I couldn't refuse. However, I knew that I would eventually do my own thing.

Ray had moved to the restaurant in the basement of the Fitzwilliam Guest House on the corner of Baggot Street and Fitzwilliam Street. In May 1989 Ted O'Sullivan, who was friendly with Gerry Reddin, the owner of the Fitzwilliam Guest House, called to say that Gerry needed a new operator for the restaurant. I knew in my bones that the time had come to make that decisive move.

I remember coming home one evening months earlier, and Sallyanne telling me that she and a friend had been to a fortune teller. This clairvoyant was convinced that I was a surgeon. 'I can see lots of white, lots of sharp instruments,' she told Sallyanne. Not bad, considering. In the heel of the hunt she told her that we would open our own restaurant within seven months or in the seventh month of the year. Sceptic that I am, I replied by asking whether the fortune teller had supplied a set of keys and an address too?

As it happened, on 7 July 1989, the seventh of the seventh, Sallyanne and I opened L'Ecrivain in that small, cramped basement. The name L'Ecrivain was suggested by Ann, my sister, as we were looking for a name and a theme that reflected our pride in Irish literary tradition. We chose a French name because of my background in classical French cuisine and also, frankly, because you wouldn't be taken seriously as a restaurant fifteen years ago if you didn't have a French name. The top restaurants in Dublin at the time were Le Coq Hardi and Restaurant Patrick Guilbaud. The writer theme was continued with Liam O'Neill's wonderful paintings of Irish writers, which are still on our walls after fifteen years. We first started buying them when Liam was selling paintings in St Stephen's Green.

We got credit wherever we could and the largest bank loan that we could get. Needless to say, we didn't have a business plan as such, so many mistakes were made. A separate book could be written on where we went wrong, but some of the big lessons were: never employ friends; always check deliveries; make sure you get your margin; put money aside for tax; keep upgrading.

Our first customer was Rory O'Byrne, who still eats with us. He was having a drink in Larry Murphy's when he heard Sallyanne asking a barman for swizzle sticks. Hearing that we had just opened a new restaurant across the road within thirty seconds' walk, he brought two friends with him and we served our first meal as fully fledged restaurateurs.

L'Ecrivain is born

Sallyanne continued in her day job and would come into the restaurant after work to write menus, do the cash sheets and, basically, run the business. It was a huge relief to me when she came on board full time six months later, allowing us both to do what we do best: Sallyanne running the business, me cooking. Although Sallyanne had never worked in a restaurant, her family background was in the retail business; apart from that, she had (and has) a very good business head. Working together as a husband-and-wife team has huge advantages, but we realised very early on that you can't bring your work home with you.

Sallyanne and I knew, even then, that the first premises would be too small, but I had to make my mark. There were times when we opened the doors and prayed for customers and the food, to be honest, was often fussy and overworked because I was still at the stage when I wanted to – needed to – show off. I'm mortified when I remember that I used to serve lovely fresh scallops wrapped in rashers! But simplicity and honesty had a place, even in those early days. I'm still proud of the rack of lamb that was such a popular feature of the early L'Ecrivain menu.

My philosophy of food, for want of a better way of putting it, has developed since those early L'Ecrivain days, but its roots go way back. I suppose my upbringing was, in a way, more Continental than Irish in that we were always being brought out to restaurants. We went to the Castle Inn and the Lord Edward up by Christchurch, the Lafayette at the Hibernian for very special occasions, the Gresham in the heyday of Toddy O'Sullivan, the Shelbourne dining room with its unrivalled view, the Oyster Tavern and the Arbutus Lodge in Cork. We were never brought to the Russell Hotel, for some reason, but we would go to the old Clarence with its quota of country bishops and parish priests, and to the Goat Grill and the Lamb Doyle's. We were exposed to good, serious food, but, funnily enough, I never developed a big appetite, something for which I'm grateful now.

When we were small, we Clarke kids were actively encouraged, by our mother as well as our father, to try everything. Even today, I always start tasting with my nose and I notice that my eight-year-old son Andrew does the same. 'Monkey see, monkey do!' However, my fourteen-year-old daughter, Sarah May, is a different story. She doesn't eat fish or meat at all!

My dad believed that good produce was essential for good cooking and that no amount of cheffing was going to change that. Cooks are not alchemists. I grew up thinking that this was a normal viewpoint and on occasional visits to the homes of school friends I was sometimes horrified by the grub. I particularly remember refusing to eat burnt chips, hard as rocks, and realising that not everyone ate like we did at home.

On the other hand, one friend's mum, who was Italian, introduced me to home-made pizza and I thought it was the best thing I had ever eaten. That first taste has never been rivalled by any pizza I've eaten since and I've eaten many. Likewise with yoghurt; nothing compares with my first spoonful – it was magic and I've never recaptured that.

I also remember cycling down to the chipper at the Triangle in Ranelagh and adding salt and vinegar to my fish and chips, then wrapping it all up in the bag and letting the steam infuse the flavours through the whole thing. You have to do this to get fish and chips to taste right; and you have to eat them out of the bag. It's just not the same on a plate. Fish and chips, for me, have to be eaten with Coke. The sweetness, the sourness, the saltiness: it's a form of fusion.

I don't think that we in Ireland have yet developed a real sense of food. We're only a few generations from the Famine and most of us still eat to live, rather than the other way round. Food is fuel.

Food is flavour

Irish people don't eat like the people of the Mediterranean; very few of us spend hours around the table in that sense of communion that comes with sharing a real meal for half the day. Food in Ireland might be an excuse for meeting, but it's the meeting up and the few jars before the meal that seem to capture the Irish imagination. Italians will go straight to the table and get stuck into the food and the chat. And the wine, of course. Is it the weather, maybe? I don't know. The closest we come to that Italian ideal is the barbecue. It's one of the few occasions when we Irish linger over a meal and drink – loads, admittedly – in proportion to the eating. People tend not to get so alcoholically challenged at barbecues.

Great cooking, for me, is about discipline combined with the best ingredients. If the raw materials are great, you need to treat them with respect, keep it simple and don't show off. Complicated food all too often conceals flaws. Chefs in Ireland still need to be brave to cook simply. We're always afraid that people will think that they can do this at home, so why pay good money in a restaurant? Well, of course, customers who don't understand food can be like that.

I don't like 'tall food'. I want to be able to eat spread-out food, taking a piece of this with a chunk of that and a bit of sauce. You blend flavours and textures on your fork.

I hate chopped herbs thrown all over the plate; they're there to hide the smudges. I loathe redundant elements: has anyone actually eaten those sprigs of uncooked rosemary or the deep-fried julienne of leeks? And I detest all-purpose sauces: in other words, one sauce that crops up in all ten main courses. That's just lazy and insulting.

It may seem obvious, but let's be clear about one thing: food is about flavour. Razzmatazz is all very well in its place, but the taste of the meat or the vegetable or the fish is what it's all about.

Organic isn't always better; in fact, it's not always even good. But small Irish producers are really growing for flavour and it shows. I don't think you have to be small to achieve this. Bigger producers have economies of scale and money to invest, but currently it tends to be the small operators who have seized the flavour issue. And people are prepared to pay more if the produce is really good.

This is something that most Irish farmers have yet to grasp, because they don't have a sense of food. Maybe they have lost a sense of pride too. They are in farming as a business, and that's perfectly understandable. But why the lack of emphasis on quality?

There are lots of possible reasons. Farmers, as a rule, don't make a fortune, so depressed prices are one possibility. And being paid to produce stuff that nobody wants to buy is no way to advance quality. But I have another theory. Farmers work bloody hard doing extremely physical tasks from early morning until well after most people have clocked off. Result? The average farmer has an appetite the size of Croke Park. And if you're that hungry when you sit down to eat, you want substance. Taste comes further down the list of priorities.

And it's not just farmers. The Irish male appetite is a strange thing. If I serve a twelve-ounce sirloin and one potato, people think they are being robbed. Give them an eight-ounce sirloin and lots of spuds and they are as happy as Larry. No matter how sophisticated we're supposed to be these days, we really do still have an obsession with potatoes in Ireland. Why else do Chinese and Indian restaurants offer rice *and* chips?

We have failed to develop a distinctly Irish cuisine and – I think this is sadder – in places where Irish food matters, places where the tourists go, what are they dished up? Lasagne. Frozen chicken Kiev. Chicken curry. Toasted sandwiches.

Home grown

Tourists may come to places like L'Ecrivain once or twice on a holiday, but they eat in pubs most of the time. And pub menus, for the most part, are dire. Why not proper Irish stew? And baked Limerick ham? And floury spuds with really good cabbage? Lamb's liver Lyonnaise? Crab? Oysters?

People tend to assume that people like me are a bit sniffy about what we eat. Well, I am in terms of quality raw materials. But I love sausages sandwiched with YR sauce (that's brown sauce to people outside Ireland) between slabs of batch loaf (unknown outside Ireland). My Death Row meal would be this, or possibly a sanger of crisp, salty bacon made with real country butter, the sort where you can sense the crunch of salt crystals.

This may seem like a far cry from L'Ecrivain. But it must have something, however small, to do with the kind of chef I've become.

Anyway, there was no way of knowing, back in 1989, whether L'Ecrivain would last and develop. As they say, it seemed like a good idea at the time and, despite the odd quiet night, the restaurant developed a good and loyal customer base. Without that, it would never have lasted. We had no idea that the 1990s would be a decade of promise, both for us and for the country at large.

As it turned out, thanks to the fact that we managed to strike a chord with our customers, we were able to build not just a restaurant with a strong sense of itself but also a team who are, in a very real way, the true L'Ecrivain. L'Ecrivain is not just about me and Sallyanne and our customers. It's about a group of very dedicated people who share the same passion and the same ideal. This is their story and L'Ecrivain is their creation. I'm proud to have helped to make it happen.

To put it bluntly, this is not the Derry Clarke Cookbook. It is, I hope, a celebration of the hard work, achievements and vision of some very special people who happen to have come together in a restaurant in Baggot Street. If I have left anyone out – and it's quite possible that I have – I apologise. I can assure you that it wasn't deliberate. And I salute you all, whether named or unnamed!

Derry Clarke
Baggot Street, Dublin
September 2004

| Derry Clarke

AND WITHOUT

WHOM

IT WOULD NOT BE POSSIBLE

AN INTRODUCTION TO L'ECRIVAIN'S DEDICATED TEAM

Sallyanne

When I tell people that my dad started life as a farmer, they always think he came from the country. In fact, the farm was in Clondalkin; we forget that the countryside came right into Dublin within living memory. My grandmother thought Clondalkin was right out in the sticks and she missed having neighbours, having been brought up in Blackhorse Avenue, where – another sign of the times – her family were market gardeners only a couple of miles from St Stephen's Green.

She eventually persuaded my grandfather to move closer to the city, so they ended up keeping the farm but buying a house in Kimmage Road West, which, in those days, was on the fringe of Dublin. Dad was brought up there, but he spent a lot of time on the farm, which he eventually took over when my grandfather retired. Grandad was a part-time farmer. His day job was as a cooper in Guinness's, but he managed to keep a dairy herd and I remember a big orchard at Clover Hill in Clondalkin. The Parkers have always been that kind of family: hard workers who don't mind putting in the time because that's the only way to get what you strive for.

My dad, Desmond (Des), had a milk round in Crumlin and this, in a way, was how he met my mum Sarah, better known as Sadie, who lived in Kildare Road in Crumlin. He went to a local dance – maybe there was a business motive, I don't know! – but anyway, that's how they met. Grandad James Malone, my grandfather on mum's side, was a farrier, again self-employed. He had a forge in Malpas Street, Dublin, where my Nana Sarah Malone helped him run the business. Guinness was his biggest customer. Unfortunately he died when my mum was barely eighteen.

Mum and dad married in September 1961. I arrived in September 1962, followed by my brother Tom in September 1963. People forget that Dublin in the 1950s and 1960s was not an easy place in which to earn a living. Despite being hard workers – mum worked in Prescott's, the dry cleaners, as a book-keeper – it was hard to get ahead. Being willing to work was simply not enough.

So, encouraged by both his brothers who had gone out earlier, dad headed off to Chicago in 1963 and found work and accommodation before the rest of us went to join him a few months later. When he went for interview to a big trucking company, he was asked whether he could drive a tractor. Well, dad had been driving tractors since he was a boy, but he didn't realise that a tractor in Chicago was the front bit of an articulated truck with a sixty-foot trailer behind it; we didn't have things like that in Ireland in 1963. Anyway, he got the job and mastered the skills in no time. Mum got a job too, in an insurance office as a book-keeper. Mum worked days and dad worked shifts, as the money was better.

By 1968 Granny Annie Parker, dad's mother, was seriously ill and it was decided that we would all go home to see her. Nana Malone had died shortly after we arrived in America, but we couldn't all afford to go home for the funeral. By that time I had been joined by my siblings Jocelyn in 1964 and Jim in 1966. As soon as the family arrived back in Dublin, mum decided, on the spot, not to go back to the States. Dublin seemed a better place for us as we grew up and, while mum got us settled here, my dad went back to Chicago for a year.

When he returned to Dublin, he got work as an ambulance driver and helped out on my grandparents' farm. My parents had decided that they wanted a house-cum-shop and, thanks to their hard work in Chicago, they were able to pay cash for just that – a shop on Crumlin Road, which became Sallyanne's Boutique, with lots of living accommodation above it. Margaret arrived in August 1970 and Bernard in August 1971. My parents' friends used to joke with them – two children going, four coming back and two more when they resettled – two more trips to the States and they could have had a football team!

Mum ran the boutique and in 1974 dad went into business when he bought a newsagent's off the North Circular Road. My parents have always had a fantastic work ethic. When we were growing up, they always told us that the door to success is labelled 'Push' and that there's no such word as 'can't'. Mum and dad took all six of us everywhere with them – to the races, to plays, on shopping trips for the boutique, out for lunch or dinner. We spent two months every summer in Skerries. Those were the days – swimming, sailing, horse-riding and the carnival every night.

The work ethic and the fairly hectic life involved in running two retail businesses many miles apart meant that eating had to be fitted into the schedule. My mum is a good plain cook and she quickly discovered something that the busy people of France and Spain had known for centuries: one-pot cookery is both delicious and convenient! Coming in from school, there would always be a lovely smell of a stew or casserole cooking away slowly. It was never just the family for meals; anyone who dropped in was always welcome and staff in the shop often stayed to eat.

My dad was a good cook too. On some Sundays we went out to lunch – places like the Downshire Arms in Blessington, the Montrose or the Skylon in Drumcondra, which was close to the newsagent's; but, when we had Sunday lunch at home, dad helped prepare it. Mum would do a roast with all the trimmings. When I first met Derry, I always had to go home for Sunday lunch – mum and dad insisted. Derry would often ask when he was going to be invited and one day mum answered the phone and he invited himself. She wasn't at all put off by the fact that he was a chef. After the event, mum asked what he thought about her fare and Derry duly said how lovely it was, but why did she cook the bejasus out of the meat? Now mum always keeps the rare parts of the joint for Derry.

I spent twelve years in Loreto Crumlin, where I was involved in drama, the choir and the orchestra. Mum always believed that being able to play a musical instrument was something that would stand to you. I played cello and piano. I had a marvellous time there and the nuns and lay teachers were wonderful. My best friends Charlotte and Joan and my other close friends are all girls I went to school with. A lot of the people I meet in the restaurant even today are people I went to school with or their sisters, or were in other Loreto schools, where I would have met them through the choir and orchestra. In 1978, six of us from Crumlin and ten from Dalkey were asked to play the female parts in the Blackrock College production of *The Pirates of Penzance*. We had a ball. The priests were great to us girls, spoiling every one of us, all the while keeping the boys in check. The Boomtown Rats were very big at the time and, as they were all ex-Rock boys, it was an experience to be there and hear the stories. In 1979 I was runner-up in the Young Economist of the Year competition, where I did cooking, sewing and a project on food safety. (I lost points because the dress was a black satin number – very unsuitable.)

As a teenager, I wanted to be a teacher or a lawyer, but, when I left school in 1980, the country was in the grip of a serious recession and there wasn't enough money to send me to university. We are not the kind of family that would see this as a setback, so I knuckled down and did a diploma in marketing at night in the College of Commerce in Rathmines.

For a bet, while I was doing my Intermediate Certificate, I had agreed to go on local radio (this was 1977, when pirate stations were springing up all over the city) and I found myself working as a presenter and DJ for the pirate station Capital Radio during weekends and school holidays until 1981. I also did a spell with Radio Leinster, where I worked with the infamous Vinnie Connell. There was a stint at Radio Nova and a period of three years as newscaster on TTTR, where I had to get the news from the papers and the BBC and rewrite it. But this wasn't my day job. I had been behind the counter in the boutique from the time I was seven and I loved it. My mum used to exhibit at fashion shows, and again I was put on the ramp very young and continued modelling part-time until I got married. I also got work doing voiceovers for radio ads. After school I worked as an accounts clerk, receptionist, telephonist, book-keeper, etc.

By the time I was twenty, I was selling insurance – life, pensions and investments – but within a few years I wanted a change and left to work as PA to the managing director of an alarm company. After that I went into marketing, selling hotel amenities to hotels in Ireland and all over the world, still keeping my insurance agency.

It was at this stage that I went to a party one night and met a guy called Michael, who was working with Derry. I will give Michael ten out of ten for persistence – he got my phone number from a friend and insisted I go for a drink. Eventually I went out with him, his sister and a few friends. One of the friends was Derry Clarke. From the moment we met he asked me to go out with him. They were a fun crowd to be with and Derry's persistence was even more impressive. It was a great summer.

Months later, I was going to an insurance industry reception in the Royal Hospital, Kilmainham, and the person I was supposed to be going with let me down at the last minute. I phoned Derry and said that, as he had been asking me out for three months, this was his big chance.

It was 1985 and I was 22. Two weeks after the Kilmainham reception, Derry asked me to marry him. And, regular as clockwork, he asked me again every fortnight from September to December. Neither of us had a penny, it was early days anyway and my parents thought I was too young to have a mortgage, even though they thought the world of Derry.

Eventually, Derry produced a ring and said, 'If you say no this time, I won't ask again.' Put like that, I had to say yes. We got married in October 1987. Derry's mother didn't really know what to make of me and I think she probably didn't approve of this forceful blonde from Crumlin marrying her son. In the end, however, we got to know each other very well.

I always knew that Derry wanted his own restaurant and we started looking, mainly in the so-called Golden Mile, from Jury's in Ballsbridge to St Stephen's Green. But there was always something wrong. Derry, being Derry, often wanted to jump in with both feet, so I reckon this was a good example of how we make a good team. I'm the business person, he's the creative one.

Of course, wherever we found would have to be affordable and it seemed for a while that the sums just wouldn't add up. Then, one day, I went with a girlfriend to see a fortune teller. She was in the Temple Street flats and the first thing she asked me was whether my husband was a surgeon. 'I see lots of white and sharp blades.' Well, that covers chefs too, I thought. I told her that we were trying to start our own business and she replied that we would get it in either the seventh month or within seven months. When I told Derry this, he asked whether she had given us an address and a set of keys?

As it happens, we took possession of our first restaurant premises on 7 July 1989, so maybe there's something in it. We started with a team of seven doing 36 covers, sometimes over forty on a Saturday night. I was still working full time – there was no choice – but I worked in the restaurant in the evenings, doing the bills and reservations and writing the menus for the next day. Derry and I had done a lot of the painting and decorating ourselves. I even made the blinds.

One of the waiters, Ray Hingston, taught me how to do silver service, how to carve, how to bone a sole. Ray and Craig Smith were both very helpful in showing me what 'service' was all about. Prior to this, I had only ever been in a restaurant as a customer. We would work with Ray for the next ten years.

During the first few months, we had two customers who came every second Saturday. They were lovely, but Mrs X was always very inquisitive. One evening she asked me lots of questions over a couple of hours – 'So you don't do very much, darling?' I replied that I did as much as I could. Then it was 'What experience do you have?' to which I replied, 'None.' Her final question was 'Well, darling, if you don't have any experience, only do a few hours a week and the pay is OK – how on earth did you get this job?' To which I replied, 'I sleep with the boss.' A couple of weeks later she said, 'You never told me you were married to him!' For years after that she always greeted me with 'Still sleeping together, darling?'

I gave up the day job in December 1989 and got even more involved in the restaurant. I'm not a book-keeper, but I thought that running a restaurant wouldn't be all that different from running a shop (how wrong I was!). I found discrepancies in the books and it soon became clear that I was needed to run the business full time.

Our daughter, Sarah May, was born in April 1990. The day she arrived, Derry went back to the restaurant and bought champagne for all the customers – fortunately there were only 36 booked that Friday night.

When Riverdance opened, we had our first taste of being really, really busy. We had two busloads of people going to the show, 99 covers in three sittings. But we never managed to hit the hundred in L'Ecrivain Mark I.

Derry and I never stopped looking for a restaurant, even after we had set up in business. We knew that it was a good place to start, but we also knew that it would never be the kind of restaurant we ultimately wanted. It was just too small. When the Celtic Mews, just round the corner, came up for sale in 1993, we looked at it, but there was a big gap between the asking price and what we could afford. We made an offer, but were turned down. Time went by and the restaurant didn't sell. A year later we came back, with a business partner, but there were problems. The title deeds were in a bit of a mess and there were issues about access. The solution was to rent the premises for a year and just hope and pray that the legal difficulties could be sorted out.

We spent a lot of money refurbishing the restaurant, a big part of which was paid out before we actually completed the deal in 1995. And, of course, we ended up back at square one in a sense. It soon became obvious that the new restaurant, just like the first one, was too small. By now we knew that L'Ecrivain was no ordinary, run-of-the-mill restaurant. We had something special and a lot of people wanted to experience it.

We relocated to the old Celtic Mews in March 1995. Exactly a year later, our son Andrew was born. My father had died very suddenly six weeks earlier, so it was a difficult time. The restaurant was getting busier and we knew we needed more space. Then, as luck would have it, the coffee shop next door came up for sale in October 1998. We bought it and put in a planning application before the year was out.

We thought that it would simply be a case of knocking through the wall and extending, but this was not possible. We were granted planning permission to knock down both premises and build a custom-built restaurant, so we closed – not an easy decision – on 31 July 1999 and planned to be open for business again on 1 November. In fact, we remained closed for six whole months, not three. This was what we eventually christened 'The Nightmare on Baggot Street'. The unexpected delay in opening placed a great strain on our finances, but my cousin Bill Botterill and his wife Elizabeth stepped in to help us financially. They are now our partners, with 25 per cent of the business. Without them, we would have gone under. Bill, who has always been like an older brother to me and my siblings, is a tremendous support. Bill and Elizabeth live in London with their five children.

When we did eventually reopen, with a brand new and much bigger restaurant, in January 2000, we had exactly what we wanted, but not without a lot of hassle and quite a few scary moments. But we did it.

One area I never get involved in is the kitchen. There's strict demarcation: I know where my skills lie and it's not there. But Derry and I make joint decisions on everything else – right down to the crockery – and we all comment on new dishes because they are plated up for the whole team to sample.

Running a restaurant is rather like putting on a show and each service is another performance – some go better than others. I have been able to use all my skills here in different ways. KISS ('Keep it simple, stupid'), the first principle in marketing, always applies in everything I do. I try to keep things as uncomplicated as possible in running the business.

Complaints – and please don't tell me the Irish don't complain – are very important. They help us to correct things and make them better and a complaint handled well is a customer for life. Constructive criticism is always welcome when it is valid. However, we do get some complaints that verge on the ridiculous. One man complained bitterly about our lack of urinals, another about the colour of the walls, another because we had two 'n's in his name instead of one on our table plan. One Valentine's night a lady came out to me in reception and asked me to sort out her husband, as he was being mean to her! Another very well-meaning customer wrote to us to say how wonderful his experience had been in the new premises, but that we were restaurateurs and he, as an architect, felt we should be helped. He enclosed a two-page snag list – a very accurate one – which I immediately sent off to the builder. A separate book could be written on complaints alone.

We are very lucky in that we have a strong and loyal customer base, far too many to mention. However, one group of gentlemen, the GaGas, have been coming into us for lunch every Monday for over fifteen years. They are Terry Sudway, Eoin O'Buachalla, Sean Mac Dermott and Louis Scully. We always thought GGA stood for Geriatric Gastronomic Association. However, the real meaning is slightly different. They sit at the same table every time, and they are wonderful. They are also a great source of information on any changes we make.

There is a great rapport in the restaurant industry. Everyone knows everyone else and we all try to send business to each other as much as possible. The 'bitchy' rumours are just not true. L'Ecrivain is very much a partnership, not just between Derry and me, but with the whole team.

Without that, and despite all our complementary talents, it might be just another restaurant. You can try to analyse what makes L'Ecrivain the restaurant it is – and believe me, I try – but it's just not possible to put your finger on it. L'Ecrivain is not just a restaurant. After all our ups and downs, triumphs and moments of real anxiety, and even disillusionment, I know that, whatever L'Ecrivain is, it's more than just a restaurant.

Sallyanne Clarke

| Sallyanne Clarke

| Martina Delaney

| Mary Weddick

Martina

Martina Delaney, sommelier, has been at L'Ecrivain since 1994. Her interest in wine started, as it has for many Irish people, with the New World. But for Martina it wasn't a case of having a glass of Jacob's Creek and liking the taste; while working in Sydney as a waitress she took a trip up the Hunter Valley and did the usual tasting tour around the wineries.

'One wine really stood out,' she says. 'It was Brokenwood Semillon. The quality really jumped out at me. And then, back in Sydney, I remember tasting Cloudy Bay for the first time and thinking that this stuff was really different.'

Martina grew up in Finglas, north Dublin, with her four sisters. 'My dad works for Dublin City Council and he cycles to work every day. He and both my grandfathers were great vegetable growers and we always had our own spuds and onions when I was growing up.'

Perhaps it was this early exposure to fresh produce that made Martina decide to become a chef. 'I wasn't a sporty person at school,' she says. 'I was more interested in the Girl Guides and in fashion. I did think of taking up fashion design, but I went into a sewing factory when I was sixteen and I hated it. The money was terrible and the girls were a bit aggressive, so it put me off the idea.'

Martina enjoyed home economics at school. 'My mother was a wonderful person, but she was a terrible cook. As far as she was concerned, when it was black it was cooked. I loved bringing home buns that we made in class and I did some competitions too. I won a fish cookery competition at one stage. But home economics

wasn't just about cooking. I loved the sewing but I didn't have the stomach for the biology part.' She also did a gardening course at school and loved it. 'It's in the blood,' she says, 'and I thought about doing horticulture, but I was drawn to cooking. My older cousin is a chef and I thought it was really glamorous.' Martina enquired about training as a chef, but a waiter/service course was available sooner, so she enrolled with CERT in Cathal Brugha Street. Her work experience was at the Westbury Hotel.

The CERT course gave Martina certain basics, such as how to flambé at the table, menu French and silver service. But she always had an interest in wine. 'I wondered what made particular wines distinctive. In 1986 there wasn't a lot you could do, but I did learn a bit on my feet as I worked in Stoker's in Harcourt Street and in Dobbin's.'

At the age of 25, Martina headed for Australia and got work waitressing in Sydney. 'I was bowled over by the seafood. I loved barbecued squid and barramundi and the Balmain bugs. I experimented like mad. And I had the opportunity to taste a lot of wines and to see vineyards for the first time.'

It was very tempting to stay, but home was far away. Martina returned to Ireland when her mother became ill and got work as number three in the front-of-house team at the Old Dublin in Francis Street. It was here that she was spotted by Derry Clarke.

'Derry was there for an RAI dinner and we got chatting,' she recalls. 'He and Ray Hingston interviewed me for a job over a pint in Larry Murphy's and I came to L'Ecrivain as a waitress in 1994.' Martina fondly remembers the days in the basement in Fitzwilliam Square and is full of praise for Sallyanne and Derry, whose hard work and vision have built today's restaurant from those modest beginnings. The first thing Martina did when she joined L'Ecrivain was to sign up for a Wine and Spirit Education Trust course. 'After that, wine pretty well took over my life outside work.'

The structured approach and regular tastings in the WSET courses were very helpful. 'It told me what I wanted to know,' she says. 'Why wines are different from each other, what's behind the individuality. It made me understand the complex relations between producer, microclimate, *terroir*, aspect, sunshine, soils, maceration, ploughing . . . lots and lots of different elements that all go into making the wine unique, almost like a fingerprint or a DNA pattern.'

Her first trip abroad with the express purpose of exploring wine was to Jerez. 'I was worried because I just couldn't handle sherry,' she remembers. 'But I got converted very rapidly. At first I gagged at fino and manzanilla, but I loved the smell in the bodegas. Wow!'

She was thrilled when she found that she could tell the difference between fino and the slightly saltier manzanilla. 'And I couldn't get over the quality of the old olorosos,' she says. 'Such incredible length and concentration, just fabulous. And tapas. What a brilliant way to eat. Yes, that trip to Jerez was a real eye-opener and I've loved good sherry ever since.' Martina has also enjoyed her contact with the Champagne Academy, especially in relation to having the opportunity to taste widely and learn what makes each house unique. 'The first thing you notice,' she says, 'is

how a Pinot-dominated wine is different from a Chardonnay-dominated one, Bollinger versus Ruinart for example.'

If Martina has a desert island wine, it would have to be fine white burgundy. 'It's the complexity,' she says. 'How everything hangs together and balances. It's the contradiction in how a wine can be both rich and delicate at the same time. It's the same with many fine wines, but you are really acutely aware of it in great burgundy.'

Sallyanne and Derry have encouraged and supported Martina in building up the impressive wine list. There are over two hundred wines, with the emphasis on the Old World but with a good representation from the New, especially California. Martina sees her role as guiding customers through the list. 'Guests are very knowledgeable these days,' she says, 'but you know instinctively when people would like advice. Sometimes it's the real wine buffs who will ask for a steer in terms of vintage or maybe they just want to know if I've made any discoveries recently. Regulars know that I'm always looking and that I travel a lot in the wine regions.'

Martina feels privileged to work in L'Ecrivain. 'I get to taste incredible wines and Alain and the team are marvellous to work with. And I've met so many wonderful people and made many friends through the restaurant.'

Martina made a significant contribution to the chapter on matching wine and food.

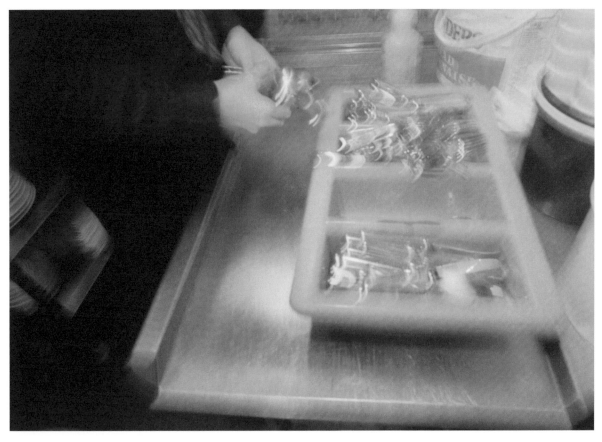

| Michael Cody

Ruth

Ruth Freeman, who started as a commis chef in L'Ecrivain in 1997, has a busy and complex role. Her title of larder chef is something of a misnomer. Although she takes responsibility for the larder and its stock, plus meat and fish, sauces and stocks, she also coordinates both the hygiene programme and the ordering system.

'I love the buzz and the responsibility,' she says. 'It seems to be my niche. This is my kind of thing: it's very focused, it's about getting it right, mixing art and science. And you have to be a bit of a disciplinarian without stressing people out, being friendly but still keeping a kind of professional distance.'

At first Ruth thought of doing Marine Science at UCG, but, when she was offered a place on the course, she turned it down in favour of doing professional cookery at Tallaght. She had done a post-Leaving Certificate course in catering in Crumlin and spent a summer working in the kitchens at Jury's. 'After that, I knew I wanted to go into the kitchen. Again, it was the buzz that attracted me.'

After Tallaght, Ruth worked for a while at Cooke's Café and then travelled for a year through south-east Asia and Australia. 'I travelled with an adventurous palate,' she says. 'I even ate snake in Vietnam and I liked the meaty, slightly waxy texture. I loved the quality of the produce and the seafood in Australia.'

Ruth has worked at the Park Hotel in Kenmare, Richard Corrigan's Lindsay House in London, Aqua in Howth and Bang Café in Dublin.

At home Ruth likes to cook simply. 'Something that takes ten or fifteen minutes. I cook a lot of fish. I love John Dory, but I avoid salmon and monkfish because I see so much at work. I don't cook meat very often and the one thing I can't eat is offal.'

Looking after hygiene in a restaurant context is challenging for many reasons, not least because the environment is constantly changing. 'It's not just about biology,' she says, 'it's about people. I have to monitor a team of fourteen. We have a visit from the hygiene consultant every six weeks. They do an audit for us. We even have an automated hand-washing system.'

Ruth is glad that she took time out earlier in her career to do an ECDL computer course, not just because of the technology involved in hygiene management but also because larder management, however artisan the produce, is highly computerised.

When she is not working, Ruth likes to go to the theatre and she is also involved in amateur dramatics, something that few people in the restaurant business can square with their schedule. 'That's the great thing about my job,' she says. 'It may be tough and it may be pressurised but at least I have my evenings off!'

Andrea

Andrea Hussey, restaurant manager, joined the team at L'Ecrivain after training in hotel management and working in various hotels and restaurants both at home and abroad. She is originally from Limerick, but thanks to having a father whose work as an accountant involved considerable mobility, she was brought up in London and in Youghal, Co. Cork.

'I started working in hotels during my school holidays when I was fifteen,' she says. 'So it was a logical choice to do a four-year degree course in hotel management. After that, in 1996, I spent two years at the Shelbourne as room service manager and doing front of house, then I spent a year going round the world, including a stint living in Australia.'

On her return she worked in Fitzer's and then went to the Pearl Brasserie as manager. She joined L'Ecrivain from there as assistant manager to Kevin Watson. 'The first thing I noticed about working here is the team spirit and the huge input that Sallyanne has,' she says. 'There's a very low level of staff turnover because the people are chosen carefully and we don't get bored. L'Ecrivain is busy, but it's very well structured. Our job satisfaction is all about quality and consistency. That's what gives us real pride in our work. Why would anyone want to leave?'

She found it easy to integrate. 'The systems are in place and they work, Sallyanne's management skills are superb and Derry is simply buzzing with creative energy. The whole thing just flows and everyone knows where they are, including the customers.'

Andrea loves the buzz. 'I enjoy that element of the unexpected in a structured environment where we have the coping mechanisms in place.' And the hours involved in the restaurant business don't bother her. 'It's better being off during the week,' she says. 'You're not out with the nine-to-fivers.'

Andrea believes that customers come to L'Ecrivain for the totality of the experience. 'It's not just the food, it's the service and the ambience and knowing they are going to be looked after,' she says. 'A lot of people come here for special occasions, but over 60 per cent of our customers are regulars, which is a great vote of confidence.'

She grew up with food as an important element in daily life. 'My mum was a great traditional cook, but she was creative too. We always had home-made bread and cakes at home and we always made a point of eating around the table. Family meals were not just about food – they were about chat and communication too.'

Andrea likes to cook at home. 'Maybe it's because I work front of house. I'm not in the kitchen all day. I cook to relax: lots of stir-fries, Asian dishes, really simple fish dishes. I have a French boyfriend, so food is important to him too.'

She ate her first oyster when she was sixteen and still remembers being bowled over by the taste. But her ultimate meal, she says, would have to be rare steak with béarnaise sauce, really fresh salad and lots of crusty bread.

'The philosophy at L'Ecrivain is all about excellent dining,' she says. 'But it's still relaxed, informal, not in any way stuffy. The staff help people to relax, but the customer dictates the feel of the experience. Most people enjoy being spoiled rotten by a great team. And the quality of that team makes my job a whole lot easier.'

| Alain Catheline

| Aiden Maloney

| Stephen Gibson

| Ruth Freeman

Aiden

Aiden Maloney joined the L'Ecrivain team as sous chef in June 2001. Brought up in rural Co. Galway, he had wanted to be a chef since he was fourteen, possibly because his mother worked in a small country restaurant where he got summer work as a 'general dogsbody'. 'I loved the buzz in the kitchen,' he says. 'From the word go I could handle the frenetic atmosphere of a busy kitchen. I've never wanted to work in a quiet kitchen, if such a thing exists.'

After school he joined the CERT course in Galway at the age of eighteen and, on graduating, moved to the Connemara Coast Hotel. 'It was a tough placement,' he recalls, 'but the food was good and I was exposed to lots of new cooking experiences. Then I went to the Malt House in Galway, off Quay Street, which at the time was the place for fine dining in the city. After a year there I went to the Lanesborough in London in 1998, which had just won Hotel of the Year. It was one hell of a culture shock.'

'I was up at 5.30 am to start work at 7 am with forty chefs in a really huge kitchen. I was right in at the deep end and, even though I learned an enormous amount, it wasn't a friendly environment. I got grabbed by the throat and thrown against the wall by one of the head chefs for throwing out a rotten banana. He was browned off because it could have gone into the banana bread!'

But the Lanesborough Hotel, near Hyde Park, was a good place to work. 'This was real-time food,' he says. 'The presentation was stunning and the whole place was run with complete precision. It had to be. The banqueting section ran four different function rooms. But eight months was as much as I could take.'

In the summer of 1999, Aiden worked at Pádraig Keane's celebrated pub in Furbo, Co. Galway, before moving to K C Blake's in Galway City, where he spent a year and a half 'doing bistro stuff'. His subsequent move to Dublin was to follow his fiancée, now his wife. He found work at Roly's Bistro as one of a team of 25 chefs, which 'was hectic but the menu didn't change a lot'. He came to L'Ecrivain in June 2001.

'The first thing that struck me was that it was like London – really busy, lots going on, the same kind of standard and level of presentation, but the atmosphere was great. It was really friendly, totally unlike the Lanesborough. The buzz is terrific and there's real team work, unlike other places where it's every man for himself,' he says. 'And there's lots of feedback.'

He believes that television programmes have helped to make the Irish palate much more adventurous. Back home in Galway, when he was growing up, the family ate well. 'My mother would stew wild venison,' he recalls. 'And her bacon and cabbage with brown bread was fantastic. There were really floury potatoes with a good bit of butter.'

Aiden looks for balance in cooking. 'You have to balance rich and light,' he says. He doesn't cook at home. 'My wife is a vegetarian and I'm a meat man. I don't feel I've eaten unless I've had a bit of meat. But I love fish too.' He believes that many Irish chefs are unwilling to move forward. 'There's too much conservatism,' he says. 'And down the

country it's all chicken, beef and lamb. There's a
real shortage of good raw materials and you have
to look hard because most of the good stuff is
going abroad where they appreciate it. You have to
work hard at sourcing and be prepared to order
well ahead.'

Aiden's advice to any fourteen-year-old who, like
himself at that age, wants to be a chef is to try life
in the kitchen and, if you can hack it at all, stick
with it. 'But travel,' he says. 'You won't learn
enough here in Ireland. The first two or three
years are the hardest, when you're learning to deal
with the heat and the stress. You have to take on
board that the hours are unsociable. It can be
hard to have a relationship when you're working
like that.'

Aiden's ultimate ambition is to have a restaurant
back home in Co. Galway. 'I would do good honest
food, and not chef it up. A good, fresh sole on the
bone is as good as sea bass or turbot any day. Just
seared in the pan and smeared with butter.'

Mary

Mary Weddick is front office manager. 'For as long as I can remember,' she says, 'I wanted to work in the restaurant industry. Both my mother and father had done so and I can honestly say that I never had any other career in mind. As soon as I realised that I was hopeless at cooking, I decided to work in front-of-house operations. My parents weren't too keen. They wanted to spare me the antisocial hours and hard work involved. My parents made a deal with me that, if I repeated my Leaving Certificate and worked part-time in L'Ecrivain and hadn't changed my mind by the end of the year, they would support my decision to go to Galway RTC to study hotel and catering management.'

Unknown to Mary, her dad had a word with Sallyanne and asked her to go out of her way to put Mary off the idea. 'I still don't know whether Sallyanne tried very hard or whether, despite her best efforts, I just loved working in L'Ecrivain, but by the end of the year I was addicted.'

Mary first began working in L'Ecrivain in 1993, when the restaurant was still located in a small basement with 36 covers. 'My first job was waiting tables, working mostly with Sallyanne and Ray Hingston, the restaurant manager. It was intimidating to be a novice waitress in such a fine restaurant. Gradually, as my confidence grew, so too did my love for the restaurant. Working so closely with the owners, witnessing on a daily basis their passion, commitment and exhausting hard work, you could not help but be inspired by them. I think it becomes a bit contagious in L'Ecrivain.'

All through Mary's time in college in Galway she continued to work weekends and holidays in L'Ecrivain as a waitress. Mary had two college placements. The first was in Rosslare Harbour, where she worked as an assistant to the banqueting manager. 'It was a real "wedding hotel" and I received great training there in function planning, organisation and service. My second college placement was in Le Grand Hotel de Cap Ferrat on the French Riviera. It was an absolutely beautiful hotel in a stunning location, highly professional. The only drawback about the placement was that we were living in the most beautiful and most expensive region of France on trainees' wages. It didn't take long to discover that we couldn't live the same lifestyles as our privileged guests.'

When she finished college, Mary moved back to Dublin from Galway. As a colleague was going on maternity leave, Mary took over reservations, dealing with enquiries, looking after the phones, dealing with correspondence, handling customer feedback (both positive and negative), billing, day-to-day accounts and working with the book-keepers. When Mary's colleague chose not to return, the job became permanent. 'As soon as it really became "my job",' she says, 'I felt I was a lot more comfortable with the responsibility involved.'

The period after the restaurant reopened in January 2000 was a very exciting time. 'We were delighted that, despite our long closure, all our regular customers and lots of new ones could not wait to sample the new and improved L'Ecrivain. The feedback we got was great. Along with the new furniture and fittings there was capacity for an extra forty customers, so staff numbers increased again.' During the renovations Mary met Lorcan Keating, now her husband, who was working on the site as an electrician. She has a son aged seven, a stepson aged five and a baby daughter, Ella, born in July 2004. 'I love my job at L'Ecrivain, but I love being a mammy too,' she says.

'Even with the increase in staff after the new restaurant opened, Sallyanne and Derry have maintained excellent relationships with their staff,' says Mary. 'That relationship is one of mutual respect. They are at all times approachable, and they ensure that any problems are nipped in the bud. They motivate their staff by sharing their thoughts, ideas and worries about the restaurant. They want to know our ideas, they care about our judgements, they are interested in our suggestions. We know we can voice our concerns to them, too, and they will listen to us.'

L'Ecrivain has a large number of regular customers, and Mary doesn't underestimate their importance in making L'Ecrivain the restaurant it is today. 'After all,' she says, 'it's our customers who contribute so much to the overall ambience of the place. I like to think that, although the food and wine in L'Ecrivain are superb, it's the overall "meal experience" that draws the customers back.' One of Mary's most important daily duties is the table plan, which has to maximise the number of diners without jeopardising comfort.

Because L'Ecrivain is often fully booked, reservations staff have the unenviable job of informing would-be customers that they can't be accommodated. Mary has worked in reservations for five years, and it still amazes her that some people, when told that the restaurant is fully booked, think a loud sigh or a prolonged silence will magically produce a table for them. Or a quiet voice will ask, 'Even for a party of four around 8 o'clock?' Many people who desperately need a table suddenly become very good friends of the owners 'Gerry and Suzy Anne'. 'Our tables are allocated on a first-come first-served basis. We don't hold tables and we don't turn people away just for the sake of it. If we can accommodate people we do, if we can't we tell them.'

A lot of people who dine in restaurants like L'Ecrivain have no concept of the behind-the-scenes work that goes into making each service run like clockwork. That's not to say that things always run smoothly. Mary recalls: 'On one occasion, when we had torrential rain, anyone arriving half an hour early would have found Sallyanne on a ladder in the middle of the reception area holding an ice bucket under a hole in the ceiling. On another occasion, 15 minutes before service, we somehow developed a beautiful water feature in the middle of the restaurant, which was helpfully spraying water all over the tables in the centre of the dining room. But we just deal with the situation, handle the crisis, and somehow everything is all right on the night!'

When Mary began working in the restaurant, there were so few staff that it felt more like a family. Even though staff numbers have increased, she feels that Derry and Sallyanne have managed to maintain that closeness. Among the staff themselves there is a very family-style relationship. Occasionally there are disagreements, but nobody holds a grudge. 'There is a great atmosphere amongst the staff,' says Mary. 'We have such pride in the restaurant.'

There is never a problem with recruitment in L'Ecrivain and staff turnover is very low for the industry. Mary loves working with such a strong team. 'My job is selling the product of L'Ecrivain and I have 100 per cent confidence in the product I am selling. I know that any guarantee I give to customers before they arrive in L'Ecrivain will be met and the customers will be happy with their experience in the restaurant. There are no weak links in the L'Ecrivain chain. I don't hope this, I know it!'

Stephen

Stephen Gibson joined the L'Ecrivain team in July 2004 as head chef. He is, in his own words, 'a Dubliner who emigrated to Donegal at the age of four'. This is because his father, who worked in the insurance business, was posted there. Stephen spent the first few years of his life in Malahide, but grew up just outside Letterkenny.

His first experience of cooking was when he spent holidays with his grandmother in Dublin. 'I suppose I must have been about six when I started helping her in the kitchen. That was my first experience of baking.' At the tender age of eleven he caught a glimpse of the workings of a local bakery and was intrigued. 'My dad knew the owner and I was able to get work in the bakery during my school holidays. It was brilliant, working on novelty birthday cakes and good old Black Forest gateaux. There was a French pastry chef and it was fascinating to watch him at work.'

After graduating from the professional chef's course at the highly respected Killybegs Regional Technical College, Stephen headed off to Paris with no job and a profound wish that he had worked on his French while at school. A friend introduced him to Fauchon, the fashionable food store with a brasserie and a Michelin-starred restaurant. 'It was a tough assignment,' he says. 'The language barrier was terrible, but I was determined to learn kitchen French and I did.'

A spell in Café Otto in Sydney in 1995 was quite a culture shock in some ways, but at least everyone spoke English. 'This was real Australian fusion cooking and it broadened my view of food.' Back in Dublin, Stephen worked for a short while with Paul Flynn, who was then heading the kitchen at La Stampa. After nine months he got itchy feet and a friend suggested that he join him on the *QE2*.

'This was hard work,' he says, 'but it was Old School food done really well, very seventies but very good. We did breakfast, lunch and dinner. It was murder. I came in for dinner service one evening and found one of the team making scrambled eggs. He had lost track of time.'

Stephen spent one year with the *QE2* and then headed for London, where he joined Nico Ladenis's team at 90 Park Lane. 'It was a bit overwhelming at first,' he says. He started as larder chef, looking after cold starters, and progressed to fish. 'We started at seven in the morning and got the last Tube home after midnight. I'd start the day shelling a hundred scallops – if you spoiled one of them you were in trouble.'

After a two year stint in Gothenburg in Sweden at Fiskekrogen, Stephen returned to Dublin in September 2001, where he worked as a sous chef here in L'Ecrivain. Stephen's travels then took him to New Zealand, but, when he got a call from a friend saying that the head chef's job at L'Ecrivain was coming up, he decided to go for it. 'It's a good place to be,' he says, 'because there's real team spirit. Arguments happen, but they're rare. There's real passion in what we do. When the crew get pleasure out of what they do, the customers get pleasure too. In a lot of Irish restaurants people are just working for a wage. At L'Ecrivain there's a whole lot more to it than that.'

Seamus

Seamus Commons, head chef at L'Ecrivain from 2001 until summer 2004, grew up in Co. Mayo, close to the River Moy, where his parents were farmers. 'We had our own chickens, eggs, lamb and vegetables,' he says. 'And I'll never forget the first of the new spuds with the first wild salmon of the season gently fried in bacon fat. My dad shoots, so we always had pheasant, duck and pigeon. In my innocence, I thought this was normal!'

The family also grew a lot of fruit – apples, pears, plums, rhubarb and gooseberries – and picking all this was quite a job. His school was co-ed and Seamus was one of four boys in his year to opt for domestic science, 'just to be closer to the girls. There was plenty of slagging but it was worth it,' he adds. His studies in this area stood him in good stead when he went to work as commis chef at a restaurant in Castlebar during the school holidays. 'The owner had brought in chefs from France, it was great, but the whole idea was ahead of its time for rural Ireland.'

'There were only two Irish lads in the kitchen and the other fellow didn't stay. I got the tough jobs – getting barnacles off the mussels, veg prep, putting stuff through the Mouli-Légumes to make purées. Everything was done by hand, but I learned loads,' he says, 'including how to flambé at the table without setting off the fire alarms!'

After school Seamus went to Sligo RTC to do catering, where he worked two days a week in a restaurant to pay his way. 'I started in a hotel,' he recalls, 'and we used lots of frozen stuff. It was all melon cocktail and mixed grills, pretty primitive. It felt like a life sentence, but it was a learning experience. I learned to manage costs, which is important.'

Afterwards he went to the newly opened Ferrycarrig Hotel near Wexford Town, where the head chef thought he was a chef de partie instead of a fourth-year commis. Pastry was a weak spot in the kitchen, so Seamus was sent to Cathal Brugha Street to do an advanced course in this area. Later he went to Adare Manor in Co. Limerick, where he worked on sauces for the better part of a year before moving back closer to home at the Glenlo Abbey Hotel in Galway. 'This was a good place to be,' he says. 'There was a huge effort to upgrade the food and set new standards. But it was all about cooking good food, not chasing awards.'

From Glenlo Abbey Seamus went to work for CERT in Dublin as a trainer for four months, but found the curriculum very old-fashioned. 'It wasn't for me, so I leaped at the opportunity to join the kitchen at Muscat in South William Street. It was small. We could do 55 covers at a push from six gas rings. And the kitchen was open, so you couldn't yell. But if looks could kill . . .' He stayed for two years, but increasingly wanted to work in a bigger kitchen.

After a short stint at Longfield's in Fitzwilliam Street he effectively swapped places with Kevin Arundel, who was then head chef at L'Ecrivain. Kevin took over at Longfield's as a franchisee and Seamus crossed the road to step into his role.

'I was offered the franchise,' says Seamus, 'but it was the wrong time for me and anyway I was forever eating at L'Ecrivain because I thought it was brilliant. I jumped at the opportunity to work here.'

During his time at L'Ecrivain Seamus built up a team. 'What we try to do here is to combine simplicity with perfection,' he says. 'Generally

Alain

speaking, people try to do too much. I mean, if you order salmon, it's the salmon that should take centre stage. And most customers come here because that's what we do. Derry is very good at sharing the credit. He has real passion, loads of it, and Sallyanne has a cool head. It's a fantastic combination.'

Seamus's passions include cooking game, but he also shoots, with a 12-bore Beretta. He is a keen fly fisherman too. 'It's magic,' he says. 'You're out for the whole day in the most wonderful landscapes: Lough Mask and the Corrib, for example.'

Unlike many chefs, Seamus likes cooking at home for his wife, Gail, and his two young daughters, Hannah and Andrea. 'For Mother's Day I did mozzarella salad, roast pork cutlet with red pepper sauce, with caramelised apples and mushroom fricassée,' he says. 'I like to cook fairly simply. I think my dream meal would be wild salmon followed by my mother's rhubarb pie.'

Alain Catheline, assistant manager, grew up in Brittany, south of Rennes. 'It's a bit like Kerry,' he says, 'lots of forests and lakes but maybe a little less wild.' His mother was a full-time homemaker and his father worked in the building industry, but several of his uncles had farms and a pig would be killed every year. 'The pork was great,' he says. 'I still love really good charcuterie served with cornichons and a glass of wine.'

At home the family had a garden full of vegetables, salad vegetables and tomatoes and, with the coast just over an hour away, there was always lots of fresh fish. Wine tended to be Muscadet or Côtes du Rhône, both bought in bulk and bottled at home for those days when the family wanted a change from the excellent local cider.

Growing up in such an environment, it was no surprise – and a source of considerable pride – when Alain's brother Philippe decided to become a chef. He eventually ended up working with Paul Bocuse. 'In France, being a chef is a very highly regarded thing,' says Alain. 'Anything to do with food is respected.'

Alain himself briefly toyed with the idea of training as a chef, but decided that he would prefer to go to college in Rennes to study English. 'I had no idea what to do next. I thought about teaching but, in the end, it didn't appeal. When I got the opportunity to go abroad for a year under the Erasmus programme, I did drama studies at the Samuel Beckett Centre at Trinity College.'

It was hard going back to college in France. 'Trinity was so beautiful and I was going back to this concrete place in Rennes and then on to do my army service. After that, in October 1995, I headed back to Ireland. The army taught me the need to have a job, so I sent out my c.v. to lots of places. Then one day Sallyanne called me and asked me to come in for a chat.'

'I was petrified,' he says. 'This was my first real job and they wanted me to start right away. But it was so friendly and positive that I felt at home very soon. At first I did "set-up" – the bread, the butter, the water, desserts, coffee. I knew very little about wine but Martina is a great teacher. She has passion about wine and she values other people's opinions.'

Being from cider country and having been exposed to a very limited range of wines at home, Alain made many new discoveries as he learned the ropes. 'The first time I got really excited about a wine was when I tasted some big red Californians. The wine that stood out was Ridge Santa Cruz; I loved the way it was so powerful yet so subtle. Unusually for a Frenchman, I like oaked New World Chardonnay, especially the more delicate ones from New Zealand. I love Craiglee Shiraz from Victoria. Maybe it's because it has a kind of European style instead of the full-on style you expect from Australia.'

Alain finds that customers are increasingly likely to ask for advice in selecting wines. 'In fact,' he says, 'when people order the tasting menu most of them ask me to choose for them. I always find it hard to describe wine, but I do have the English vocabulary to do it rather than the French one, which I suppose may be very different.'

Alain enjoys living in Ireland. He lives in Ringsend within walking distance of the restaurant. 'Maybe Dublin is getting a bit too busy,' he says.

'Everybody complains about their country here in Ireland, so I feel at home because the French do that all the time. But Dublin is looking good these days, it's a good city to be in. There's still a kind of laid-back thing that I like.'

As for his work at L'Ecrivain, he says, 'It's a family thing. The team really feels like a family. Ireland for me is Dublin and L'Ecrivain. If I ever leave L'Ecrivain, I would be leaving Ireland.'

Aidan

Before Aidan Meyler joined L'Ecrivain as assistant manager, he worked on board the *QE2*, the world's largest cruise ship, with 1,500 crew and 2,000 passengers. He grew up in Raheny in north Dublin and considered training as a chef when he left school.

'I've always like cooking,' he says. 'But I'm more of a people person, so when I left school in 1986 I did the City & Guilds food and beverage management course in Cathal Brugha Street and had a couple of placements in Waterford. Then I headed off to California, working in restaurants during the day and in bars at night in places like Sausalito and Marin County. I came back via New York, where I did a stint as assistant restaurant manager in Fitzpatrick's.'

Back home in Ireland, Aidan was working at Slane Castle when it burned down. 'Nothing to do with me, honestly, it was my night off!' he laughs. Suddenly finding himself out of work, he joined the crew of the *QE2* as a waiter. 'It was amazing,' he says. 'I saw the whole world – every continent – but the workload was phenomenal. I did every service, literally every one, for five months solid. The money was good, but the work was just too much.'

He was on board the *QE2* in mid-Atlantic when Hurricane Louis struck, knocking the vast vessel on to its side. It righted itself after a 130-foot wave slammed into it and lifted it upright again. 'It was incredible,' he recalls. 'We had to wedge the cabin doors open in case the ship capsized. The buzz was beyond belief.' Aidan returned to Dublin in 1991 and joined L'Ecrivain shortly afterwards, but he was invited to go on the maiden voyage of the new *Queen Mary 2*. 'It's a fabulous ship,' he says, 'very bling bling. It's so utterly tacky I adore it!'

The biggest change in Aidan's life came in 1997, when he was diagnosed with Hodgkinson's lymphoma. He was forced to take two years off work and is now in remission. Back at work, he has regular CAT scans to ensure that the disease is beaten.

'What I love about L'Ecrivain,' he says, 'is that it's not stuffy. Here you have this ace restaurant where it can still be informal. You judge your customers and work out whether they want to chat, have a bit of banter. They dictate how we react. Generally, you get to know your customers well because so many of them are regulars. The other great thing about L'Ecrivain is the way that the restaurant is the sum of everybody's experience and professionalism. Ideas are shared, credit is shared, even the odd drama is shared.'

Margaret

Margaret Parker-Grimes, Sallyanne's younger sister, has been involved with L'Ecrivain for over ten years and now oversees the accounts for the restaurant from her home in Westport, Co. Mayo. 'It's great to be able to do it like this,' she says. 'The technology is very simple really. All I need is a fax machine – I get several faxes a day from the restaurant – e-mail and a way of plugging in online to the system at L'Ecrivain and I could be working in the same building.'

Margaret married Frank Grimes, a Westport man, in 2003 and moved to Westport from Dublin. They now have a baby boy and Margaret insists that she doesn't miss the Dublin traffic. She has had a long association with L'Ecrivain.

'I remember when Sallyanne and Derry got married. At the wedding reception Derry made a very important point in his speech. He said that they were not just a married couple, but a team. And that's as true now as it ever was. They both know that team work is what makes L'Ecrivain tick.'

Margaret was fifteen when Sallyanne and Derry got married. After school she worked in England and in the telecommunications business in the US before coming home to Dublin. 'I worked in the first restaurant, in the basement, and in all the subsequent ones,' she says. 'I was meeting and greeting and looking after the floor. I loved it. So many customers are regulars it's like meeting all these friends every day.'

Gradually, Margaret moved from reception to dealing with invoices, payments and all the other minutiae of the day-to-day accounts of a busy restaurant. And when the time came to move to Co. Mayo, it seemed a straightforward matter to take this area of responsibility with her. And so it has proved. 'I get a big bundle of stuff in the post each week,' she says, 'and we can supplement by fax or e-mail. And, of course, I can log into the system at the restaurant at any time of the day or night and get a real-time picture of what's going on.'

Margaret also manages the L'Ecrivain web site. 'I love to be still involved in the restaurant. Even at this distance it seems much closer than it really is. The only thing I miss is the buzz, the atmosphere, the can-do spirit when things are really hotting up. But at least I don't have to deal with the hours and the traffic!'

Denise

Denise McBrien, reception manager, joined the L'Ecrivain team in 2003 after a career that included time spent working for Marco Pierre White at both the Oak Room and the Criterion in London. She works in reception from Monday to Friday and also ensures that the menus are prepared for each service.

Denise was born in Enniskillen, her father being a Fermanagh man, her mother from Dublin. Her first experience of working in the hospitality industry was as a schoolgirl, when she had a part-time job in the Green Isle Hotel, close to her family's home in Dublin.

'I think I was destined to work in the business,' she says. 'I tried secretarial and office work but I just couldn't get excited about it. When I was offered an apprenticeship at the Clarence, I leaped at the opportunity. It was great. I went into the Tea Room and trained as a sommelier when Michael Martin was there. After that I worked in Dante's in Rathmines and then, when I was on maternity leave, I got part-time work with Conrad Gallagher before eventually heading off to London for a few years.'

Denise admits that she was somewhat daunted at the prospect of working at L'Ecrivain, a restaurant about which she had heard a great deal. 'I was terrified,' she says. 'I loved working with Marco Pierre White and with Conrad, but the atmosphere was always pretty frenetic. I thought that it would be the same here, really having to keep on your toes the whole time. In fact, it turned out to be very different. Just because L'Ecrivain is relaxed, it doesn't mean that a whole lot of work doesn't go into it behind the scenes. It looks relaxed because it's a well-oiled machine and it knows how to work. The team is fantastic. I reckon Derry and Sallyanne have a real instinct for staff; they just keep picking people who fit in, get on with the rest, and have a common sense of purpose.'

Maurice

Maurice Supple returned to L'Ecrivain to take over as bar manager in 2003. Having worked as a lounge boy in Dublin during his school holidays, he was offered an apprenticeship with Guinness Pubs, but turned down the opportunity in favour of the hotel business. His first job was with the late Mahon O'Brien at the Vale View Hotel in Co. Wicklow when he left school. This enabled him to do the block-release four-year course in hotel management in Galway, after which, in 1990, he went to work at Longfield's, just across the road from L'Ecrivain.

In the meantime he worked briefly at L'Ecrivain, did a stint in the film business and as general manager of the Mercer Hotel in Dublin city centre, before coming back to Baggot Street. 'I took over from Paul McLoughlin,' says Maurice, 'and we overlapped for a while, which was useful.'

Maurice's background was quite peripatetic in that his father was in the entertainment business (with a showband) and his parents travelled where work was to be found. He grew up in Youghal, Co. Cork, and Donegal, with four years in Germany, of which he says he remembers very little.

'But I remember the German legacy,' he says. 'We would always have stuff like pumpernickel bread and all sorts of mustards and chutneys and cured sausages. Our friends thought we were mad in those days.' His mother was an excellent cook and his father was not averse to getting stuck in in the kitchen. 'His food was farming food,' says Maurice. 'You know, lots of red meat, that sort of thing. My mother made the most fabulous stews and her boxty was famous.' His own interest in cooking is enjoying a renaissance. 'I cook a lot at home now. And when we eat out we tend to go somewhere really good; we prefer to eat at home rather than in average restaurants.'

He has noticed a big increase in interest in cocktails recently, although, he admits, the most common order is gin and tonic or vodka and tonic. 'But a proper dry martini is more of a ritual; it makes you feel better about yourself because you're being given this special service: the best spirits – Grey Goose vodka or Hendrick's gin from Scotland – and the faintest whisper of Noilly Prat, perfect olives . . . it's a kind of work of art.'

Cosmopolitans and Sex in the City are probably the most popular cocktails, but there is constant experimentation. 'For example, we have the Luke Rhineheart, which involves fresh orange and passion fruit juice, which is let stand with basil and mint to infuse the flavour right through, then it's served with a touch of white rum. It was invented by Eoin and John, two of our waiters.'

With the smoking ban in place, Maurice has to work harder in the bar area. 'In the past, people would come down for a cigarette and it was the obvious thing to do to have a drink. Now we need to make more suggestions, have a brilliant range of drinks and be imaginative. People are very receptive, but it's up to us to create the interest and the demand.'

One thing Maurice likes about L'Ecrivain is how many regulars there are. 'I don't just mean the people who are in and out every second day. You can be a regular who eats here four times a year, even once a year, but the point is that you keep coming back. It's no wonder that so many of them feel like friends rather than customers.'

SUPPLIERS

of

QUALITY GOODS

NULLIFYING THE NEED TO CREATE
SILK PURSES FROM SOWS' EARS

I hope it doesn't sound pious when I say that a restaurant like L'Ecrivain needs a group of suppliers who share the same kind of vision. After all, cooking isn't alchemy. Without quality in the raw materials, there is no way that a kitchen can put quality on the plate.

Over the years, suppliers have come and gone. Now, fifteen years after we started, we have a strong core of people who supply us with what we need to ensure that the food at L'Ecrivain is what it is.

It wasn't always like this, I have to admit. In the very early days we dealt with anyone who was prepared to give us credit! And in those days, of course, I was still at the stage when I wanted to show off as a chef. I never tried to turn a sow's ear (now there's an interesting raw material) into the gastronomic equivalent of a silk purse, but I suppose I had yet to learn the lesson – fully – that

raw materials are what it's all about. These days, I like to let them do the talking, with minimal interference from me.

I learned about the importance of seasonality and about the sheer quality of small artisan producers through listening to food writers like John and Sally McKenna in the early 1990s and through direct contact with great produce. There were several sources of inspiration. Visiting the vegetable garden at Ballymaloe, for example, and going with Euro-Toques to Assolas, also in Co. Cork, where the salad grows right outside the dining-room window. Myrtle Allen, who started Euro-Toques in Ireland, has always been a champion of what you might call real food.

Seasonality is a key element in what we do at L'Ecrivain and suppliers are critical to this. In fresh produce it's vital that suppliers understand the nature of the seasons and it's sometimes shocking to realise how few do. Our suppliers are the exception rather than the rule.

I like to visit our suppliers. There's no substitute for it: not just in putting a face to a name but also in establishing a real relationship. And in this way I've come to realise that all our suppliers are real characters. They are dogged, stubborn, striving for a goal. They aren't in it for the money. If they were, they would have realised that there are easier ways to make a fortune.

You only have to think of Bill Hogan, whose cheeses taste of the passion that he has for proper food. But, when you meet him on his own turf, you get the whole picture and hear his trenchant views on the industrialisation of food and his loathing of government policy. Most of all, you realise how happy and fulfilled and contented he is in doing what he does. That goes a long way to explaining the flavour of Desmond and Gabriel.

Penny Lange, too, whom I first met way back in my Kinsale days, is someone who has that kind of dedication and integrity. She isn't just selling organic vegetables, she is educating people. Great producers don't just do the obvious job, I reckon they want to change the world.

None of these people are bland. They are not go-getting entrepreneurs (if you're looking for something, they either have it or they don't; there's no tap that can be turned on and off, depending on the market). These are the kind of people whose produce we like at L'Ecrivain. And I really like the idea of dealing with people who want to change the world!

Some of our suppliers are featured in the following pages. A full list of L'Ecrivain suppliers appears at the end of the chapter.

Cheese

Croghan Cheese

When Ann and Luc Van Kampen got married in 1976, Luc missed the good cheeses of his native Holland. They were living in Co. Clare at the time and Luc decided to try making cheese for home consumption. Using books sent from Holland and fresh cows' milk from his neighbour, he produced his first cheese. Then the neighbour asked him to milk a few goats; in no time he had produced his first goats' cheese.

Eventually the Van Kampens ended up on eleven acres in Co. Wexford with a herd of goats. By 1984 they had gone into small-scale cheese production and thus was born Croghan, a semi-hard goats' cheese that does not have a label. 'It's not in the supermarkets,' Ann says, 'but you can buy it in good cheesemongers. It doesn't need a label. A name is enough!'

Then, in 1994, came Mine Gabhar, a soft-rinded goats' cheese that has taken the world by storm. The name is unusual in that it is old Irish dialect meaning 'the cry of a snipe', which can sound uncannily like a baby goat.

The Van Kampens produce about four tons of cheese a year, much of it going for export. Half the production goes to one very appreciative customer, Neal's Yard Dairy in London. Croghan was Champion Cheese at the World Cheese Awards in 2003 and the Van Kampens regularly win awards at the British Cheese Awards. Indeed, in 1996 they received more awards at this event than any other cheese producer.

Their son, Matthew, has recently joined the business and will be carrying it on into a second generation.

Sheridan's Cheesemongers

Delia Smith, no less, has referred to Sheridan's being run 'with messianic zeal' by brothers Seamus and Kevin Sheridan, who founded the business in 1995, and their business partner Fiona Corbett. Sheridan's started life as a stall at St Nicholas Market in Galway City and then became a shop, which still operates there. A Dublin shop was opened in 2000 and the company acquired an old creamery in Co. Meath in 2001 to mature cheese in optimum conditions. Cheese maturation, taken for granted on the Continent, is still rare in Ireland. A visit to Sheridan's retail shops will confirm that they like to sell cheese at the peak of perfection. They also like to stress the seasonality of certain cheeses.

Although they deal in cheeses from the whole of Europe – their Portuguese selection is a real eye-opener – the Sheridans are hugely proud of our native produce. 'Irish farmhouse cheeses are amazing,' according to Seamus. 'We have the best pasture in the world and you can taste that in the cheese. That's why the French love our cheeses. They don't have anything like the grass we have here in Ireland.'

Ballynadrishogue
Blackwater
Enniscorthy
Co. Wexford

Tel 053 27331
www.croghan.netfirms.com

Athboy Creamery
Athboy
Co. Meath

Tel 046 943 0373
www.sheridanscheesemongers.com

Irish farmhouse cheeses

L'Ecrivain sources much of its cheese through Sheridan's. Here we give a brief outline of the best-known Irish farmhouse cheeses.

Abbey Organic: Award-winning cheeses made with cows', goats' and sheep's milk by the Hylands in Co. Laois.

Ardrahan: Mary Burns' washed-rind cows' milk cheese from Co. Cork. Ardrahan has an earthy, smoky flavour that grows more robust and tangy with age. The rind of the cheese is golden brown. A smoked version is also available.

Bandon Vale: Three cheeses are produced by the Mahons in West Cork: Glandor, Murragh and Vintage. Glandor is based on Red Leicester, Murragh on Gloucester and Vintage resembles Cheddar.

Bay Lough: A hard-pressed waxed cheese, made by the Keatings of Tipperary, that develops a robust flavour after a few months' ageing.

Boilíe: Soft, fresh cream cheese packed in jars with sunflower oil and herbs. The cheese, made in Co. Cavan by Mark Brodie, has a delicious sweet flavour. Delicious in salads.

Cahills Farm Cheese: Marion Cahill produces a range of flavoured Cheddar cheeses in Co. Limerick. Ballintubber is made with chives, Ballyporeen with mixed Irish herbs, Ardagh with wine and Cahills with porter, whiskey, ham or hazelnuts.

Carrigaline: Milk from Friesian cows is used by Ann and Pat O'Farrell in this semi-firm, delicate cheese with a light, sweet flavour that becomes fuller with age.

Cashel Blue: Louis and Jane Grubb produce this blue cheese in Co. Tipperary from pedigree Friesian cows. The buttery, rich flavours of Cashel Blue are best enjoyed when the cheese is about four months old. The Grubbs also produce Crozier Blue, an excellent ewes' milk blue.

Coolea: A cheese with its origins in Dutch Gouda. Cheeses are matured for up to two years. The flavours are complex – sweet and sour with grassy, herby hints. Made by Dick Willems of Co. Cork.

Cooleeney: Made in Co. Tipperary by the Mahers in the style of Camembert but with its own personality. Smooth, robust flavours reminiscent of oak and mushrooms. Lovely thick, velvety texture when ripe.

Corbetstown: Goats' milk cheese from Co. Westmeath made by Anne Holton. The cheese has a natural rind and a semi-hard texture. Flavours, sweet while young, develop tanginess after about six months but still retain sweetness.

Corleggy: Silke Crop makes this natural-rind hard goats' milk cheese in Co. Cavan. Corleggy has a smooth texture and richly layered flavours. Silke also makes Drumlin, a cows' milk cheese with a natural rind.

Cratloe Hills Gold: The first Irish ewes' milk cheese of modern times. Sean and Deirdre Fitzgerald make this lightly waxed cheese from March until October in Co. Clare. The cheeses are matured for two to six months and have a semi-firm texture and a light caramel tinge.

Durrus: This washed-rind cheese has a complex, earthy flavour and a herbal dimension. The texture is velvety and moist. Jeffa Gill makes this cheese in Co. Cork.

Gubbeen: Washed-rind cheese from Co. Cork with a unique scented mushroom flavour, intensifying to an oakiness with age. Tom and Giana Ferguson also produce a smoked version.

Kerry: A firm-pressed Co. Kerry cheese with a waxed rind and a distinct, long flavour. Sheila Broderick also makes a range of flavoured cheeses.

Killorglin: Made to a Gouda recipe in Co. Kerry by Wilma O'Connor. Cheese can be aged from two months to a year, when flavours develop from soft and light to firm, tangy and spicy.

Knockalara: The Schliebitzes have been producing this fresh cheese from their own herd of sheep in Co. Waterford since 1980. It comes in compact rounds, has a firm texture and flavours of citrus and light herbs. The version packed in jars with olive oil is delicious.

Knockanore: This Cheddar-like cheese from Co. Waterford is waxed and hard-pressed but not as dry as Cheddar. Flavours are deep and tangy, especially after ageing for a few months. Flavoured versions are also made by the Lonergans.

Knocknashee: Produced only since 1999, Knocknashee is a fresh curd cheese developed specifically for cooking. It won't become stringy or run and the mild flavour intensifies during cooking. Made with cows' milk by Julie Walker and Noelle Mekitarian.

Lavistown: Lavistown has a natural brushed rind and moist, fresh texture. It's a low-fat cheese with a clean taste and a buttermilk tang. Flavours vary according to the season – fresh and lively in the spring and richer and firmer in the winter.

Milleens: Veronica Steele began making Milleens from cows' milk in 1976 in Co. Cork. A washed-rind cheese with a soft texture, flavours are herby, spicy and tangy.

Mont Bellair: Large, waxed rounds of semi-hard cheese with a silky, moist texture and a full flavour. Pat Stones has been making this cheese since 1983 in Co. Offaly. A sister cheese, Cáis na Rí, is younger and milder.

Oisin: The van der Vaards make a range of cheese from both goats' and cows' milk – a fresh goats' cheese log, a cows' milk washed-rind cheese, a blue goats' cheese and a Cheddar type.

Old McDonnell's Farm: A light, fresh goats' cheese made in Co. Wicklow. The cheese, which is sold fresh, is smooth with a light floral flavour.

Poulcoin: After the goats kid in the summer months, this cheese is produced by Annelies Bartelink. It has smooth, gentle flavours with herbs, reflecting the summer pastures in Co. Clare. Annelies also produces a cows' milk cheese.

Riverville: A Gouda-style cheese from cows' milk that is best young, when the cheese is still creamy and flavours are light and subtle. Made in Co. Galway by Anne and Robbie Gannon.

St Killian: The best-known Carrigbyrne cheese, which resembles Camembert but is lighter, though still rich, with a lovely grassy aroma.

St Tola: John McDonald uses organic goats' milk to make this delicate fresh cheese, which comes as a log or a crottin. From Co. Clare, it's sweet, fresh and floral and can be eaten fresh or mature.

West Cork Natural Cheese Company

Bill Hogan and Sean Ferry produce two of Ireland's most celebrated farmhouse cheeses, Desmond and Gabriel, in West Cork. As Bill says, his cheeses are produced 'on the Mizen peninsula, the southernmost tip of Ireland, from the milk of small herds that graze between Mount Gabriel and the sea'. The mixture of wild and cultivated grasses, heather and other plants helps to make these cheeses unique, underlining the point that Seamus Sheridan makes about Irish pasture.

Desmond and Gabriel, naturally, rely for much of their character on the local grasslands in the same way as wine depends on its *terroir*, but the starter culture and method of cheesemaking are crucial too. These are thermophilic cheeses and the starter culture requires a much higher temperature in order to operate than that of other cheeses.

According to Bill, thermophilic cheese was made in Ireland until the Famine in the 1840s. He reintroduced the technique to the country in the late 1980s, having trained in cheesemaking in Switzerland.

Desmond and Gabriel are unusual in many ways, not least in being equally good on the cheeseboard and in cooking, especially in sauces and fondues. Desmond has a hard yet friable texture and what Bill describes as a brisk taste. Gabriel is harder, with a compact texture, a suggestion of hazelnuts and a citrus-like tang. It is a highly complex cheese in terms of flavour and becomes more intense with age. Uncut wheels of both Desmond and Gabriel will last almost indefinitely, acquiring further layers of complex flavour over time.

Bill's passion burns fiercely. He is not just a cheesemaker but someone with a holistic view of the world and he is sceptical of many government initiatives. 'Quality producers enjoy no representation on the relevant government bodies like Bord Bia,' he says. 'Today's alert consumer deserves integrity and purity. The trend towards real food opens new horizons of opportunities for human viability and healing the earth.' He also likes to quote from his hero, Dr Martin Luther King, who said in 1964 that 'before the turn of this century there will be a worldwide non-violent movement for environmental vindication'.

Schull
Co. Cork

Tel 028 28593
www.wcnc.ie

Fish & shellfish

Belvelly Smokehouse

Frank Hederman's smokehouse overlooks the beautiful eighteenth-century bridge at Belvelly, where Great Island is linked to Fota Island in Co. Cork. He uses beech chips for his smoked salmon because, he says, they impart a more delicate flavour than the more common oak. 'The quality of the wood is very important,' he says. 'I've seen old crisp packets and off-cuts of chipboard in some cheap smoking material.'

He is also, in a perverse way, grateful for the mass-produced product of which there is so much these days. 'When I started,' he says, 'customers had nothing to judge my quality against. Now the best smoked salmon can be seen to be just that.'

How can you judge smoked salmon by appearance? 'The best smoked salmon is known by its physical imperfections,' he says. 'If one side looks exactly the same as all the others, as if it came out of some kind of injection mould, you know it's been intensively farmed and that it spent its life swimming, in so far as it could, around in circles.'

Frank is excited by the quality of the new organically farmed salmon that is now becoming available. 'This is very non-intensive,' he says. 'The fish have space and natural food. They are almost indistinguishable from the wild version.'

The salmon are salted for about six hours, rinsed, dried and then hung in the smokehouse, the position of each side being determined by size and thickness. Depending on the fish and the time of year, the actual smoking process takes between 7 and 24 hours.

Salmon is not his only product. Frank also smokes mussels, haddock, mackerel and eels. The latter two are smoked over mesquite chips, which impart a very subtle flavour. The secret in smoking, according to Frank, is subtlety. 'You have to be able to taste the fish, the smoke, everything,' he says.

Belvelly　　　　　　　　　*Tel 021 481 1089*
Cobh
Co. Cork

Beshoff's of Howth

Beshoff is a name well known in Dublin because of its association, in the past, with the fish-and-chip business. Alan Beshoff's grandfather, who hailed from Odessa and who served on board the battleship *Potemkin*, came to Dublin in 1914 and opened his first shop in Parkgate Street near the Phoenix Park. The surviving chain of fish-and-chip restaurants that trades under the Beshoff name is no longer owned by the family.

But fish is in the blood and Alan, who had worked in the family business, started Beshoff's of Howth in 1994, operating as a fishmonger and wholesaler. The retail shop in Howth has such a loyal following that it now opens on Sundays, reflecting the fact, as Alan says, that fish now competes with the weekly roast in Irish homes.

Beshoff's sources fish from Kilmore Quay, Kilkeel, Killybegs, Dunmore East, Connemara and from Howth itself. Prawns come mainly from the east coast, crab from Donegal, but cod is sourced specifically from Kilkeel. This is because the fishermen there use a special technique of fishing whereby trawling is carried out over shorter periods and the fish are in better shape when they are landed.

'L'Ecrivain is very stringent about quality and freshness,' according to Alan. 'And so are we.' Restaurants in general have become much more adventurous and demanding in recent years, he says. 'Organically produced salmon is a big seller these days. The quality is amazing.'

East Coast Fish

Thomas O'Callaghan took over the business that is now East Coast Fish some forty years ago. The company is a wholesaler but also acts as an agent for a group of thirty fishermen who operate out of ports such as Greencastle, Clogher Head, Arklow and Dunmore East. In this way they can guarantee quality and freshness, as they bypass the markets. The company, which deals mainly in cod, ray, plaice and haddock, also buys at auctions at the Foyle Co-op and Clogher Head.

East Coast Fish supplies restaurants in the Dublin area and a number of small, independent fishmongers such as Caviston's in Glasthule.

17–18 West Pier
Howth
Co. Dublin

Tel 01 839 0766
www.beshoffs.com

Corporation Fish Market
Dublin 7

Tel 01 873 3277

Sally Barnes's Woodcock Smokery

In 1981 Sally Barnes's husband Colin was a salmon fisherman in West Cork. A large bad debt left him in financial difficulties and the debtor, a fish processor, offered him a smoking kiln as part payment. Sally had been experimenting with smoking fish using improvised equipment involving an old tea chest. Colin initially wanted to sell the kiln, but Sally decided to put it to good use. 'One Christmas we had very little money and that was always a problem with two small children. I discovered that I could produce something that people really wanted at that time of year – smoked salmon,' she says.

At first the smokery dealt solely with friends and neighbours, but word soon spread and Sally's smoked salmon became amongst the most highly prized in the world. Jancis Robinson, the doyenne of international wine writers, wrote recently that she would be starting her Christmas dinner with wild salmon from the Woodcock Smokery.

Sally has managed to find time to complete two Open University degrees, one in food production, the other in oceanography. 'It's all very well to do things by instinct,' she says, 'but it's great when you understand the science and the biology.'

The Woodcock Smokery uses only wild fish and never uses dyes. The process is a traditional one. 'Smoking evolved as a preservation technique in order to spread the enjoyment of harvest beyond the glut at the height of the season,' says Sally. 'The salting and the esters in the smoke kill the bacteria and keep the proteins fresh. These days, smoking is not so important in terms of preservation, so, in a sense, it can be used more as a seasoning. I prefer the robust flavours you get with really traditional smoking.'

Woodcock's haddock, kippers, sprats, mackerel, tuna and wild salmon all have a robustly smoky flavour, but still retain the innate character of the fish. Haddock is Sally's favourite and she supplies it to L'Ecrivain. She adds a proportion of fruit wood to the usual blend of beech and oak chips, since haddock reacts well to the subtle nuances it imparts.

As to smoking time, a question she is often asked, she says there are no convenient rules. 'It all depends on the fish and the atmospheric humidity,' she says. 'It varies with the day and the position of the fish in the kiln.' The very antithesis of mass production.

Gortbrack
Skibbereen
Co. Cork

Tel 028 36232
sallybarnes@iolfree.ie

Shellfish de la Mer

Peter O'Sullivan and Richard Murphy were inshore fishermen until they formed Shellfish de la Mer in 1987. They had been fishing mainly for lobster and, naturally, they caught a lot of crab as a by-catch. They realised that it made more sense to cook and process crab meat than simply sell live crabs to the industry.

At this stage the company has six purpose-built 40-foot boats in Castletownbere, catching lobster, crab, prawns and white fish. Much of the company's trade is in European exports. 'We have a great resource here on the west coast,' says Peter. 'We have excellent seafood of the sort that the French and Spanish want. But we will have to be careful to preserve that resource and ensure that it's not over-fished.'

The big seller for Shellfish de la Mer is crab. 'The brown meat doesn't sell in Ireland,' according to Peter, 'but the Europeans love it and it sells well even in England.'

Peter believes that restaurants are leading the revolution in seafood consumption in Ireland. 'People might still be a little wary of cooking fish at home, but in restaurants the menu might be half seafood or even more. That tells you something,' he says.

Wrights of Marino

The shop that gives its name to this company was opened in 1934 and has been trading there ever since. The Wrights have been involved in the fish trade since 1916, when they acquired the old RIC barracks in Malahide, which had been burned out by the IRA, and turned it into a successful fishmonger's.

Wrights' business history is complex and another branch of the family is known as Wrights of Howth. In 1995 Wrights of Marino opened a processing plant in Howth, something that can lead to confusion.

Wrights of Marino is run by John Wright, grandson of the founder, and by his sons Jonathan, James and Jeffrey (all the Js, as they say). The retail business, based in Marino, continues to thrive, but the company is now well established as a leading supplier of seafood to restaurants, 'from Michelin-starred establishments to family pubs', Jonathan says.

'Derry is very choosy about his fish,' he adds. 'Virtually all the fish he uses is Irish and all of it is wild.' Wrights of Marino sources fish from all the major Irish ports and the company also buys exotics, such as yellowfin tuna, twice a week at the great Paris market of Rungis. This underlines the truth behind the company's now famous slogan: 'If it swims – we have it!'

'We have six vans on the road because restaurateurs demand instant service to ensure freshness,' says Jonathan. 'That means that we might be in the same restaurant two or three times on the same day. We have 300 restaurant customers in Dublin and we typically make 110 deliveries every day.'

Dinish Island
Castletownbere
Co. Cork

Tel 027 70461
www.shellfishireland.com

21 Marino Mart
Dublin 3

Tel 01 833 3636
www.wrightsofmarino.com

Game

Wild Irish Game

Mick Healy originally worked for a small company dealing in wild game, but the operation folded in the 1990s. Mick felt that there was still a market for this most free-range of meats. With his late wife Jane he started the current business in 1998, supplying a handful of restaurants in and around Dublin. However, interest in and appreciation of wild game have grown enormously in recent years and the business has grown at a tremendous rate.

The company deals in a huge range of products: venison, pheasant, mallard, widgeon, teal, rabbit, woodcock and snipe, all from Ireland, and grouse, partridge and hare, which come from Britain. The venison is supplied by licensed hunters and by Coillte and Dúchas as part of their wildlife management programme.

Wild Irish Game has the only EU-approved facility in Ireland for handling and processing all forms of game. The company supplies restaurants and wholesalers with specific cuts of venison and oven-ready game birds that require a minimum of preparation.

Mick is enormously proud of where the business has got to. 'I couldn't have done it without Jane,' he says. 'It's such a shame she can't see it now.'

Glenmalure
Co. Wicklow

Tel 0404 46773
E-mail: wigltd@eircom.net

Meat & meat products

Clonakilty black pudding

The recipe that makes Clonakilty black pudding unique dates back to 1880 and originated in the butcher's shop in Clonakilty, where you can still buy this remarkable Irish delicacy. Clonakilty black pudding was invented by Philip Harrington and his recipe remains a closely guarded secret. The precise blend of spices and herbs gives a highly distinctive flavour, but what makes Clonakilty a unique black pudding is the fact that it is made from beef blood and beef fat, while others use pigs' blood and pork fat. The high proportion of barley explains the characteristic crumbly texture.

Edward Twomey, who bought the shop in 1976, recognised that he had a national treasure on his hands and spent many years spreading the good news. Clonakilty black pudding found a very appreciative audience amongst chefs, who respond to this unique version of a traditional Irish food.

Such has been the success of Clonakilty black pudding that a new facility was built in 1983 to cope with demand. However, despite the high-tech production plant, the pudding remains exactly the same as the one first made by Philip Harrington well over a century ago.

M & B Butchers

Michael Ladrigan and his wife Barbara started M & B Butchers when they took over an established shop on the South Circular Road in Kilmainham in 1982. They have always prided themselves on service and quality. As time went by, M & B found that they were doing more and more wholesale business with restaurants. Eventually, they decided to specialise in this area and in 1999 they opened a factory at Valleymount, which is now run by a team of ten. There are three vans on the road.

'Some of our customers put price first,' says Michael, 'but Derry's first concern is quality – and service, naturally. I'm not saying that he doesn't mind about price, of course!' M & B provide beef and lamb to L'Ecrivain. 'The quality is essential,' says Michael, 'but absolute consistency is vital too. Everything here is done by hand, judged by the eye and based on experience. In big meat facilities you just set the parameters and the machines do the lot. That's a huge difference and our customers appreciate it.'

Although at L'Ecrivain a lot of meat preparation (trimming, boning and so forth) is done in the kitchen, many of M & B's restaurant customers expect a product that is ready to cook. 'A lot of these skills have vanished from restaurant kitchens,' says Michael. 'There's a generation of chefs who don't want to know about cutting up large pieces of meat, so we do all that here.'

Michael and Barbara have a roast every Sunday, either rack of lamb or a sirloin. 'It's a ceremony,' says Michael, 'part of what we are. All of our meat is Irish and we're very proud of it.'

Edward Twomey
16 Pearse Street
Clonakilty
Co. Cork

Tel 023 33365
www.clonakiltyblackpudding.ie

Unit 53
Western Parkway
Ballymount Business Park
Dublin 12

Tel 01 460 1433

M & K Butchers

M & K is the business of two master butchers, Michael Bermingham and Karl Freeman, who first met when they were training in the craft in the early 1980s. At the age of 21 the two friends decided to go into business together and rented a small shop in Drimnagh. Two years later they bought a butcher's shop in Tallaght from Paddy Reilly, which still bears his name in recognition of the fine tradition that he established there over fifty years ago.

The business has grown and the two partners recently opened a state-of-the-art facility at Greenogue Industrial Park in Newcastle, Co. Dublin. Michael and Karl pride themselves on providing proper personal service for their customers, both wholesale and retail. 'We offer nothing but the best of Irish meat, straight from the farm with full traceability. We always know the origin of everything we sell,' says Michael. 'We make it our business to pick our meat to ensure that customers are getting the best there is.'

Main Street   *Tel 01 451 0697*
Tallaght
Dublin 24

Herbs

Cottage Garden Herbs

When Michelle Power moved to Co. Carlow from Dublin in the mid-1990s, one of the first things she did was to plant a small herb garden. She was so pleased with the quality of her fresh produce that she started to plant more and, as she worked in a restaurant in Dublin and commuted in those days, she soon found that she had customers. 'Derry was, I think, my second customer. He loved the freshness and the range of plants I could offer,' she recalls.

Although it is still a cottage industry, Michelle has given up commuting and now tends her acre of herbs, complete with polytunnels to extend the growing season, on a full-time basis.

The herbs are grown organically, but Michelle has not applied for certification on the basis that the business is too small. 'I grow on demand,' she says, 'which is good for me, the producer, and for the customer. We both know where we stand.' Flowering chives and flowering oregano are enormously popular with her customers and she has noticed a recent upsurge of interest in thyme. Her own favourite herb is coriander. 'I'd eat it for breakfast,' she says.

Ballyconnell Lodge
Ballyconnell
Tullow
Co. Carlow

Tel 059 915 6312
www.cottagegardenherbs.ie

Vegetables

Penny & Udo Lange

Penny and Udo Lange met when they were working on an organic farm in Norway over twenty years ago. Udo is German and Penny is originally from Kinsale, where she knew the young Derry Clarke.

In 1988 they moved to the sixty-acre Ballinroan Farm, six hundred feet above sea level, in Co. Wicklow and started to grow vegetables organically. 'We knew how to grow,' recalls Penny, 'but we had no idea how to sell the stuff.'

Their first outlet was the Dublin Food Co-op in Pearse Street and then, in 1994, they started doing weekly bag deliveries of organic vegetables to customers in and around Dublin. In the early days the farm was managed not just organically but biodynamically too, according to principles laid down by Rudolf Steiner. Penny spent a number of years on the standards committee of Demeter, the international biodynamics organisation. While they still use many biodynamic methods, they no longer apply the full range of BD preparations. 'Now that the children are older there are not quite so many willing hands and, of course, a fully biodynamic system is very, very demanding.'

Nevertheless, Penny and Udo's organic farm is a closed unit – something that Steiner insisted upon – in that it produces all its own fertility. At Ballinroan this is provided by cattle who are overwintered inside, by grazing sheep and by large amounts of compost.

Their crops are mainly carrots, leeks and potatoes, the great staples of the Irish vegetable diet, and salads. Their first restaurant customer was David Keane of Juice, the vegetarian cafe in George's Street. Penny was left with a large bag of carrots after a customer failed to turn up at the Food Co-op. 'I couldn't lug it all over town and we were going to the theatre that night, so I walked into this restaurant and said that these carrots were brilliant. They bought them, and they still do,' she says.

Another early customer was Danette O'Connell, who was then running a restaurant in Co. Carlow. 'Danette asked me if I'd ever heard of Derry Clarke and I said that the name rang a bell. Then I remembered this chubby teenager years ago down in Kinsale. Danette said he was now one of the best chefs in the country and I said, "You're kidding . . ."'

Soon afterwards, she went into L'Ecrivain and asked to see the chef. After reminiscing about the old days in Kinsale and the fact that Penny, too, had worked in Man Friday's, Derry placed an order. 'We've been supplying them ever since,' says Penny. 'We're very small, really. Out of the sixty acres we have, only about ten are used for vegetables. But we are passionate about what we do. Organic growing is getting quite mainstream these days. We want to hang on to the really holistic approach.'

Ballinroan Farm   *Tel 059 647 3278*
Kiltegan   *E-mail: pennyveg@eircom.net*
Co. Wicklow

Beer, wines & spirits

Dublin Brewing Company

In a world where beer is dominated by huge brewing conglomerates, it is always refreshing to come across something different. And, in terms of beer, it doesn't get more different than micro-breweries. Ireland's first was established in the 1970s in Co. Clare (Biddy Early's, which continues to go from strength to strength), then came the Porterhouse brewpub in Temple Bar. The Dublin Brewing Company opened in 1996. Kieran Finnerty is the managing director and their brewer is a Canadian, Liam McKenna.

The first beer was Beckett's Gold, named in honour of Sam, a light, crisp, refreshing lager with an aromatic nose. The following year, the company launched D'Arcy's Dublin Stout and promoted it in pubs south of the Liffey with the proud legend 'Imported from the Northside', a reference to the brewery's location just beside Smithfield in the north inner city, close to the old Jameson Distillery in Bow Street.

D'Arcy's immediately wowed the cognoscenti of the beer world and in 1998 it was voted Best Stout in the Irish Independent Brewers' Awards. These two champion beers have since been joined by Maeve's Crystal Wheat Beer, a spicy, aromatic ale, and by Revolution Ale, a rich, red beer with a smoky character, launched in time to celebrate the bicentenary of the 1798 uprising.

North King Street
Dublin 7

Tel 01 872 8622
www.dublinbrewing.com

Morgan's Wine Merchants

Tom Keaveney established Morgan's, in conjunction with Baron Patrick de Ladoucette, when he retired as managing director of Gilbeys of Ireland in 1996. Patrick de Ladoucette's celebrated Loire wines from Sancerre and Pouilly-Fumé have long been represented in Ireland by Gilbeys (which has now become Diageo), but the Baron's portfolio of wine interests has been steadily expanding over the past twenty years. Wines from Burgundy, Champagne and Vouvray are now part of the de Ladoucette operation and Morgan's was set up to represent them in Ireland. The company's offices are located in what was John Howard's Le Coq Hardi restaurant.

In 1787 the Comte Lafond, ancestor of the present Baron Patrick de Ladoucette, travelled down the Loire Valley towards the Atlantic to sell his harvest of burgundy and Beaujolais wines. Once there, he made a timely stop in Pouilly-sur-Loire, where he tasted the wines of the region. As a connoisseur and *négociant*, he made enquiries about properties for sale.

He learned that the largest wine-growing estate in the region, the Château du Nozet, which belonged to an illegitimate daughter of Louis XV, was for sale. Comte Lafond bought the property in 1788 and the family of de Ladoucette took over wine production at the château, where wine has been made for over six hundred years.

Winemaking continued at the château through the difficult time of the Revolution. Napoleon finally took the Imperial Crown and a period of some stability followed, albeit short-lived. Comte Lafond set about reorganising the cellars at

Nozet and was soon producing a Pouilly-Fumé far superior to any previously seen. Such was its success that it found favour at the Imperial Court as Napoleon's favourite white wine. In letters from Russia Napoleon complains bitterly to his secretary that his barrels of Pouilly-Fumé have not arrived.

The château made steady progress during the next century. Then, as for all other vineyards in France, a deadly menace appeared: the insect known as *Phylloxera vastatrix*. This organism virtually destroyed the vineyard in the closing years of the nineteenth century. Baron Patrick de Ladoucette's grandfather began a programme of replanting using different strains and grafting techniques, but his efforts were hampered by two world wars; it was virtually an impossible task to restore the vineyard to its former size.

Baron Patrick's father finally completed the work at Nozet in the 1950s and restored its vineyards to their former glory. It now stands at 165 hectares, the largest and most famous vineyard in the region.

The Pouilly-Fumé vineyards have been in the hands of the Lafond and Ladoucette families for over two centuries, but, like many families with famous vineyards, winemaking was not their principal activity. Their main occupation was banking. Several members of the family have served as governors of the Banque de France.

Baron Patrick de Ladoucette took over the vineyard in 1972. He was the first member of the family to concentrate exclusively on wine producing and began a series of investments to increase the importance and diversity of his vineyards. In 1975 he created a private reserve of Pouilly-Fumé, the Baron de L, the first such *cuvée*, in a special, heavy bottle made in an eighteenth-century style. This wine is considered to be one of the best Sauvignon Blancs in the world.

Baron Patrick then extended his activities to Sancerre, where he owns the vineyards of Comte Lafond and the house of La Poussie. In 1980 he acquired Marc Brédif, the famous house in Vouvray. In 1985 he first entered the burgundy market when he acquired the houses of Albert Pic and Régnard. Further acquisitions were made in 1998, when he bought land holdings and a château in the town of Beaune. Baron Patrick's latest venture is the purchase of Château d'Epernay, which he acquired from the LVMH group, on the Avenue de Champagne in Epernay. His first champagne *cuvée* was released in 2003 under the Brut de Canteneur label.

The philosophy behind Baron Patrick's policy has been to bring out the quintessence of wines from very specific vineyards, many of which have enjoyed international recognition for hundreds of years.

35 Pembroke Road
Dublin 4

Tel 01 660 3374
E-mail: morgans@iol.ie

Irish Distillers Group

Irish Distillers was formed when the five remaining distilleries producing whiskey on the island of Ireland came together to form one company in 1968. Many famous names converged under one umbrella: Jameson, Power's, Paddy, Bushmills and Tullamore Dew. Jameson's distillery, in the heart of north inner-city Dublin, ceased production in 1971 and has since become the company's corporate headquarters and a museum known as the Whiskey Corner. Production of all but one of the brands was transferred to a new plant built beside the Midleton Distillery in the east of Co. Cork. The Bushmills Distillery in Co. Antrim remains the source of the one remaining whiskey and, indeed, it has some claim to the title of oldest distillery in the world, dating as it does from the seventeenth century.

The remarkable thing about Irish Distillers is that the core identity and the true, traditional character of each whiskey in the brand portfolio have remained completely intact and distinct. There is no danger of a Power's being mistaken for a Jameson or a Paddy for a Tullamore Dew. Even the premium versions, such as the Jameson 15 Year Old or the Power's 12 Year Old, are true to their origins, the Jameson with its ripe, round character and sweet vanilla nose, the Power's with its deep, long flavour and distinctive pure pot-still nature, which comes across as a whiff of ripe peach.

There are, of course, other Irish whiskeys on the market these days and some of them are excellent (such as the Tyrconnell Malt and The Connemara), but they have all been invented within the last two decades. Irish Distillers' whiskeys are a direct link to an ancient distilling tradition and an embodiment of what the Irish version of the spirit is all about.

The company, now part of Pernod-Ricard, also distributes a range of wines from all over the world.

Bow Street Distillery   *Tel 01 872 5566*
Dublin 7

Wines Direct

Wines Direct started in a very small way in 1991, when army officer Paddy Keogh decided to import some of the interesting wines he had encountered on his regular trips to the Languedoc. In this he was ahead of his time. Back then, very few wine merchants had recognised that this part of France, traditionally a source of cheap and undistinguished wines, had vast potential for quality. Paddy's unerring nose for good wine meant that he was way ahead of the posse when he started the company.

In time, of course, the wine won out over Paddy's military career and he was soon a full-time wine merchant specialising in direct-mail sales to individuals and supplying restaurants that recognised the remarkable value-to-quality ratio represented by the Wines Direct portfolio.

In the meantime, Paddy has trawled other parts of the wine world for examples of excellence combined with keen prices. Wines Direct now has wines from the Rhône, Burgundy, Italy, Australia and New Zealand, all sourced from small, quality-conscious producers with whom Paddy has a direct relationship. He buys only from wineries he has visited personally and where, as he likes to put it, he has tasted *sur place*. Very few wine merchants can say that.

Ashe Road
Mullingar
Co. Westmeath

Tel 1890 579579
www.winesdirect.ie

Other suppliers

L'Ecrivain also uses the following suppliers.

Suppliers

Allied Drinks
Allied Fine Fare
Artisan Foods
Atlantis Seafood Wexford
Bacchus
Banim Wine Merchants
Barry & Fitzwilliam
Barry Kavanagh
Berry Bros & Rudd
Best Cellars
Brodericks
Browns Eggs
Burgundy Direct
Cassidy Wines
Creme de la Creme
Creot Wine
Didier Fiat
Ecolab
Edward Dillon & Co.
Eircom plc
Environment Ireland
Erik Beving Wines
ESB
Euroveg Distribution
Evelyn & Klaus Filsinger
Febvre & Co.
Fields Wine Merchants
Findlater Wine Merchants
Finnebrogue Venison Company
Fitzwilliam Post
Frank McManus
G Duke & Co.
Gilbeys of Ireland
Gold River Farm
Grace Campbell
Guinness Ireland
Guinness UDV
Hazell Hyman Kosher Caterer
IMRO
Independent Newspapers
International Cheese Company

Ipodec Ireland
Java Republic
La Rousse Foods
M & J Gleeson
McGeough's Butchers
McGrath Refrigeration & AC
Mitchell & Son
Moore's Wines
Moyallon Foods
Musgraves
National Linen
Norton Group
O'Briens Wine Off-Licence
Odaios Foods
Pallas Foods
Papillon Wines
Paramount Hyclene
PHS Group plc
PPI
Raheny Wine Cellars
Redmonds of Ranelagh
Rentokil Hygiene Systems
Robert Roberts
S K J Moyles
Select Wines from Italy
Servequip
Statoil
Strathroy Ireland
Sullivan Fish
Sweeney O'Rourke
Table View Wines
Tankersley Wine Brokers
Taserra Wine Merchants
TDL Distributors
Tyrrell & Co.
United Beverages
Wineknows

Trade associations

Blue Book
Euro-Toques
Restaurants Association of Ireland

How to use this book

Making the recipes

All the recipes in this book have been adapted for domestic kitchens by independent recipe testers. Cooking techniques used should be well within the grasp of a keen amateur cook; however, it is important to plan ahead. Some of the ingredients we use may need to be ordered in advance, but they are all available from good grocers, delis, greengrocers, butchers or fishmongers. If you don't want to make all of a recipe, just make one or two parts and choose your own accompaniments or garnishes. The photographs show how the restaurant presents the dishes. Some 'To serve' sections have been simplified and may not be an exact match of the photograph.

Basic recipes

Basic recipes, such as chicken stock, are in a separate section. Page references to basic recipes are given in the main recipes when they are required.

Conversion charts

We use metric measurements in the restaurant, but we include a ready reckoner here for readers who use a non-metric system. Most recipes should adapt without any problem, but do remember that the recipes have been tested using metric measurements only.

Weights

Grams/kilograms	Ounces/pounds
25 g	1 oz
50 g	2 oz
100 g	4 oz
225 g	8 oz
350 g	12 oz
450 g	1 lb
1 kg	2¼ lb

Volume

Millilitres/litres	Fluid ounces (imperial)	American cups
150 ml	5	⅔
300 ml	10	1¼
450 ml	15	2
600 ml	20	2½
1 litre	35	4¼

Measurements

Centimetres	Inches
½	¼
1	½
5	2
10	4
20	8

Bon Appétit

A COLLECTION OF L'ECRIVAIN'S MOST ENJOYED RECIPES

Cream of spiced parsnip & coriander, curry oil

{serves 4}

**Cream of spiced parsnip &
coriander**
*3 medium-sized parsnips,
  peeled & sliced in half lengthways*
1 teaspoon ground coriander
3 tablespoons sunflower oil
1 clove of garlic, peeled & sliced
1 large onion, peeled & diced
1 leek, sliced
2 sprigs of thyme
1 litre chicken stock (see page 210)
salt & freshly ground white pepper

Curry oil
*100 ml sunflower oil plus 1
  tablespoon*
1 shallot, peeled & diced
1 pinch of ground coriander
1 pinch of turmeric
1 pinch of ground cumin

Cream of spiced parsnip & coriander
Preheat the oven to 160°C/325°F/gas mark 3.
Sprinkle the ground coriander over the parsnips,
place them in a roasting tin and drizzle with 2
tablespoons of sunflower oil. Roast for 35 minutes
until tender.

In a separate medium-sized saucepan heat 1
tablespoon of sunflower oil and gently cook the
garlic, onion, leek and thyme for 5 minutes until
tender. Cut the roasted parsnips into large chunks
and add them to the onion mixture. Next add the
chicken stock, bring to the boil and simmer for
15–20 minutes. Blend the soup with a hand blender,
then sieve and season with salt and pepper.

Curry oil
Heat 1 tablespoon of oil in a small saucepan and
gently cook the shallot and spices until tender. Add
100 ml sunflower oil and warm through. Transfer to
another container to cool and infuse overnight. Pass
through a sieve, retaining the oil.

To serve
Divide the cream of spiced parsnip and coriander
between four warm bowls and drizzle the curry oil
over the soup.

Cream of sweet potato scented with lemongrass & coconut milk

Cream of sweet potato scented with lemongrass & coconut milk

*4 sweet potatoes, peeled &
  each cut into 5*
1 tablespoon sunflower oil
25 g butter

1 medium onion, peeled & diced
*½ lemongrass stalk,
  broken up to release the flavour*
*½ red chilli, chopped, seeds
  retained*
*1 cm piece of root ginger,
  peeled & diced*

1 teaspoon curry powder
1 clove of garlic, peeled & sliced
3 coriander seeds
1 litre chicken stock (see page 210)
1 large tin of coconut milk
1 tablespoon honey
salt & freshly ground white pepper

Cream of sweet potato scented with lemongrass & coconut milk

Preheat the oven to 190°C/375°F/gas mark 5. Place the sweet potato chunks in a roasting tin, drizzle them with the sunflower oil and roast for 30 minutes until tender.

In a large, heavy-based saucepan melt the butter and gently cook the onion, lemongrass, chilli, ginger, curry powder, garlic and coriander seeds until soft. Add the cooked sweet potatoes and chicken stock, bring to the boil and simmer for 15 minutes. Next add three-quarters of the tin of coconut milk and the honey.

Blend with a hand blender until the mixture is smooth and pass it through a sieve. Season to taste. Reduce the remaining quarter-tin of coconut milk over gentle heat for 3–4 minutes.

To serve
Ladle the soup into four warm bowls and drizzle each one with the reduced coconut milk.

Dublin coddle soup with buttermilk cream

{serves 4}

Dublin coddle soup
Leek & potato soup
50 g butter
*1 medium onion, peeled &
  roughly chopped*
*2 leeks, white part only,
  roughly chopped*
2 sticks of celery, roughly chopped
salt & freshly ground white pepper
275 ml milk
*275 ml cream plus extra to
  adjust consistency*
4 potatoes, peeled & sliced

Coddle mix
8 cocktail sausages
4 slices of bacon, diced
2 potatoes, peeled & evenly diced
1 carrot, peeled & cut in batons
¼ turnip, peeled & evenly diced
salt

Buttermilk cream
150 ml cream
3 dessertspoons buttermilk
salt & freshly ground white pepper

Garnish
2 tablespoons parsley, chopped

Dublin coddle soup
Leek & potato soup: Melt the butter in a heavy-based saucepan and add the onion, leeks and celery. Season and cook gently until soft (about 20 minutes). Add the milk and cream and bring to the boil. Add the potatoes and simmer for about 10 minutes. Liquidise the soup and pass it through a strainer. Taste for seasoning and add cream if necessary to adjust the consistency.

Coddle mix: Poach the sausages and bacon in a medium-sized saucepan of simmering water until cooked. In a separate pan blanch the potatoes, carrot and turnip in boiling salted water until tender but still with some bite.

Buttermilk cream
Semi-whip the cream and add the buttermilk. Season. Whisk until firm.

To serve
Heat the soup, add the coddle mix and simmer until heated through. Place in four warm soup bowls. Garnish with a spoonful of buttermilk cream and some parsley.

Roasted celeriac & smoked bacon soup, truffle slices

{serves 4}

Roasted celeriac & smoked bacon soup
1 celeriac, peeled & cut into chunks
50 g butter
1 onion, peeled & diced
1 leek, sliced
2 cloves of garlic, peeled & sliced
1 sprig of thyme
160 g smoked bacon, diced

1 potato, peeled & roughly chopped
1¼ litres chicken stock
  (see page 210)
200 ml cream
salt & freshly ground white pepper

Truffle slices
2 slices of black truffle, finely diced

Roasted celeriac & smoked bacon soup
Melt the butter in a large saucepan and gently cook
the celeriac, onion, leek, garlic and thyme with the
saucepan lid on. Add the smoked bacon and potato,
stir and continue cooking for another 5–7 minutes
until all the ingredients begin to soften. Next add the
chicken stock and simmer for 30–35 minutes. Add
the cream and blend in a food processor until the
soup is smooth. Pass through a fine sieve and season
to taste.

To serve
Ladle the soup into warm bowls and sprinkle with
the diced truffle.

Roasted plum tomato & red pepper soup with vodka crème fraîche

Roasted plum tomato & red pepper soup
6 plum tomatoes, halved
2 red peppers,
*   halved & deseeded*
2 tablespoons olive oil
25 g butter
1 onion, peeled & diced
1 leek, diced

1 clove of garlic, peeled & crushed
1 carrot, peeled & diced
1 large potato, peeled & diced
1 tablespoon white wine vinegar
1 tablespoon tomato paste
1 litre hot chicken stock
*   (see page 210)*
salt & freshly ground white pepper

Vodka crème fraîche
25 ml vodka
2 tablespoons crème fraîche

Garnish
snipped chives

Roasted plum tomato & red pepper soup
Preheat the oven to 180°C/350°F/gas mark 4. Place the tomatoes and the peppers in a roasting tin, drizzle with the olive oil and roast for 25 minutes. When they are cool enough, remove the skins.

Melt the butter in a large saucepan and cook the onion, leek and garlic until soft. Add the roasted tomatoes and peppers, diced carrot, potato, wine vinegar and tomato paste. Gradually add the hot stock. Bring the soup to boiling point, stirring all the time, and allow it to simmer for 30 minutes. Season. Liquidise the soup and pass it through a sieve.

Vodka crème fraîche
Mix the vodka and crème fraîche together in a bowl.

To serve
Ladle the hot soup into warm bowls and drizzle with some vodka crème fraîche. Garnish with a few snipped chives.

Chicken & wild mushroom consommé, blue cheese & tarragon dumpling

{serves 4}

Chicken & wild mushroom consommé
Chicken consommé
1 onion, unpeeled & halved
2 litres chicken stock (see page 210)
2 egg whites
300 g lean minced beef
1 chicken carcase, lightly roasted
1 leek
1 medium carrot, trimmed & diced
2 celery stalks, trimmed & diced
1 bay leaf
1 sprig of thyme
7 white peppercorns
1 teaspoon salt

Wild mushrooms
1 tablespoon sunflower oil
100 g wild mushrooms,
  cleaned & chopped
salt & freshly ground white pepper

Blue cheese & tarragon dumpling
1 tablespoon sunflower oil
1 teaspoon tarragon, chopped
1 shallot, peeled & diced
½ clove of garlic, peeled & sliced
25 g self-raising flour
12 g suet
1 egg yolk
10 g blue cheese, grated
salt & freshly ground white pepper
300 ml chicken stock (see page 210)

Chicken & wild mushroom consommé
Chicken consommé: Brown the cut side of the onion in a dry hot pan for 5 minutes and cool. Place the cold chicken stock and egg whites in a large heavy-based saucepan and whisk briskly before adding all the other ingredients except the salt. Allow to stand for 30 minutes before cooking. Bring to the boil quickly, reduce the heat and simmer gently for 2 hours, leaving the consommé uncovered. Don't stir it. During cooking, the protein from the egg white and minced beef coagulates and rises to the surface of the consommé, leaving a clarified liquid below.

Remove the consommé from the heat, place a sheet of muslin inside a sieve and pass the consommé through it. Repeat with a fresh piece of muslin. Season with salt only. Degrease with a sheet of kitchen paper on the surface of the consommé.

Wild mushrooms: In a separate saucepan heat the oil and cook the wild mushrooms gently. Season lightly and drain on a sheet of kitchen paper.

Blue cheese & tarragon dumpling
Heat the oil in a medium-sized saucepan and gently cook the tarragon, shallot and garlic. Allow to cool. Sieve the flour into a bowl and combine with the suet and egg yolk. Add the blue cheese and the cooled tarragon, shallot and garlic mixture. Season with salt and pepper, then, with floured hands, roll the dumplings into small balls about 5 g each. Bring the chicken stock to simmering point in a medium-sized saucepan and drop in the dumplings. Simmer for 5 minutes or until they are cooked. Remove with a perforated spoon.

To serve
Add the wild mushrooms to the consommé to heat through just before serving. Ladle the consommé into four warm bowls and pop the blue cheese dumplings into them.

Spider crab & tomato consommé, cheese & onion sticks

{serves 8}

Spider crab & tomato consommé
3 egg whites
3 litres fish stock (see page 211)
500 g spider crab meat
1 teaspoon salt
1 stick of celery, washed & roughly chopped

1 small leek, white part only, washed & roughly chopped
3 shallots, peeled & roughly chopped
1 bunch of parsley stalks, roughly chopped
8 white peppercorns
3 tomatoes, skinned, deseeded & chopped into ½ cm dice

Cheese & onion sticks
250 g puff pastry (see page 214 or use frozen)
1 egg yolk, beaten
100 g Parmesan cheese, finely grated
1 shallot, peeled & finely chopped

Spider crab & tomato consommé
Place the egg whites in a large saucepan with 500 ml cold fish stock and whisk briskly together. Add the crab meat and salt, mix thoroughly and leave for 30 minutes. Add the celery, leeks, shallots, parsley stalks and peppercorns, then add the remaining stock and mix well. Bring to the boil quickly and reduce the heat immediately. Simmer very gently for 2 hours, then strain the consommé through a double layer of muslin. Season with salt only, cool and refrigerate.

Cheese & onion sticks
This quantity makes 16 sticks. Preheat the oven to 180°C/350°F/gas mark 4. Roll out the puff pastry to ½ cm thickness. Cut into strips about 15 cm long and ½ cm wide and twist them twice. Brush the sticks with beaten egg yolk and sprinkle with the Parmesan cheese and shallot. Bake for 5 minutes or until golden. Cool on a wire rack.

To serve
Add the diced tomato to the consommé and ladle it into chilled bowls. Serve two cheese and onion sticks with each portion.

Prawn bisque with tortellini of cheese & prawn, scented with brandy

Prawn bisque with tortellini of cheese & prawn, scented with brandy
Prawn bisque
150 g butter (50 g diced)
1 medium onion, peeled &
  roughly chopped
1 medium carrot, peeled &
  roughly chopped
1 medium leek, roughly chopped
1 bay leaf
10 fennel seeds, cracked

50 ml brandy
2 litres (1 recipe) langoustine stock
  (see page 211)
1½ tablespoons tomato paste
200 ml dry white wine
100 ml cream
salt & freshly ground white pepper

Tortellini of cheese & prawn
½ recipe pasta (see page 214)
8 prawns, shelled & deveined
200 g smoked Applewood cheese,
  grated
1 egg, beaten
salt

Prawn bisque with tortellini of cheese & prawn, scented with brandy

Prawn bisque: Melt 100 g butter in a large saucepan and cook the onion, carrot, leek, bay leaf and fennel seeds until light brown. Pour over the brandy and flambé, taking care to stand well clear. Add the langoustine stock, tomato paste and wine, and simmer for 20 minutes or until the stock has reduced by half. Strain the stock through a fine sieve into a clean saucepan and reduce a little until it reaches the consistency of thin soup. Finish the bisque by adding 50 g diced butter and the cream. Season. Bring to simmering point (don't let it boil) and serve.

Tortellini of cheese & prawn: Make half the basic pasta recipe and allow it to rest in the fridge overnight. Take the dough out the next day and roll it through a pasta machine set to the thinnest setting. Boil some salted water in a medium-sized saucepan and poach the prawns for 2–3 minutes, then plunge them into ice-cold water and drain. Remove and leave in a bowl until needed.

Cut out 12 circles of pasta about 8 cm in diameter. Place some cheese and a prawn in the centre of each pasta circle, brush around the edges of the disk with beaten egg and fold in half. Press the edges well to seal, ensuring that there are no air pockets or tears. Take each semicircle in your hand and curl the two tips of the straight edge around your index finger, pressing well to seal. Then turn up the edges to form the 'brim of a hat'. Repeat with the remaining dough and filling. Cook the tortellini in boiling salted water for 2 minutes. Drain and serve.

To serve
Serve hot in warm bowls, with two tortellini in each bowl.

Baked rock oysters with bacon & cabbage, Guinness sabayon

{serves 4}

Baked rock oysters with bacon & cabbage
2 dozen rock oysters,
  opened & checked (see below)
4 green leaves of York cabbage,
  finely shredded
pinch of salt
4 slices cured bacon, finely sliced
1 tablespoon olive oil

Guinness sabayon
2 egg yolks
150 ml Guinness
dash of lemon juice
salt & freshly ground white pepper
150 g butter, clarified

Guinness sabayon
Clarified butter: Melt the butter in a small saucepan over low heat until it's completely liquid. Skim the foam from the surface and discard it. Let the butter settle for 1–2 minutes, then slowly pour the clarified butter into a small bowl, leaving the milky layer behind.

Sabayon: Whisk the egg yolks in a heatproof bowl over a saucepan of simmering water. Add the Guinness very gradually, whisking all the time. Add the lemon juice and seasoning. Whisk until the mixture holds the mark of the whisk. Remove from the heat and add the clarified butter gradually in a fine stream, whisking all the time.

Baked rock oysters with bacon & cabbage
Oyster opening requires practice and can be dangerous, as the knife can slip. To prevent injury, hold the oyster with a thick cloth to protect your hand. Insert a knife with a rigid, sharp, short blade (preferably an oyster knife) into the hinge of the shell and twist the knife to prise open the shell.

Remove the oysters from their shells and wash the shells, but don't wash the oysters. Plunge the cabbage into a large saucepan of boiling salted water for 1 minute, then strain it and run it under cold water. Fry the bacon in the olive oil until it's crisp. Place a little cabbage in the shell, place the oyster on the cabbage and top with the bacon.

Preheat the oven to 180°C/350°F/gas mark 4 and preheat the grill to high. Put the oysters on a baking tray in the oven for 3–4 minutes to warm through. Cover the oysters with the Guinness sabayon and brown under the grill.

To serve
Place the oyster shells on rock salt to keep them level. Serve the oysters hot from the grill.

Marinated native oysters, teriyaki & soy dressing with crisp greens

{serves 4}

**Marinated native oysters, teriyaki &
soy dressing**
*24 oysters in shells (must be fresh),
  juice retained*
2 tablespoons teriyaki sauce
1 tablespoon honey
1 tablespoon soy sauce

Crisp greens
225 g green vegetables:
  French beans (topped & tailed),
  sugar snap peas (trimmed),
  leeks (cut into thin strips)

*½ pak choi cabbage
  (outer leaves),
  torn into pieces*
*4 leaves of Savoy cabbage,
  torn into pieces*
salt & freshly ground black pepper

Marinated native oysters, teriyaki & soy dressing
Oyster opening requires practice and can be
dangerous, as the knife can slip. To prevent injury,
hold the oyster with a thick cloth to protect your
hand. Insert a knife with a rigid, sharp, short blade
(preferably an oyster knife) into the hinge of the
shell and, holding the oyster over a bowl to catch any
juice, twist the knife to prise open the shell. Remove
the oysters from the shells.

Combine the oyster juice, teriyaki sauce, honey and
soy sauce in a bowl. Add the oysters, cover and
marinate overnight in the fridge.

Crisp greens
Bring a saucepan of salted water to the boil, add the
French beans and remove after 2 minutes and refresh
in ice-cold water. Repeat the process with the sugar
snap peas, boiling them for 1 minute only. Repeat
with the leeks, pak choi and Savoy cabbage for 30
seconds only. Strain all the vegetables and season
with a little salt and pepper. Drain well, removing any
excess water. Serve cold.

To serve
Place a mound of crisp greens in the centre of each
plate and top with six marinated oysters.

Deep-fried Dublin Bay prawns in ketaifi pastry, lemon mayonnaise & chilli jam, cucumber relish

{serves 4}

Deep-fried Dublin Bay prawns in ketaifi pastry
*20 Dublin Bay prawns,
  shelled & deveined
100 g plain flour, sifted
2 eggs, beaten
1 packet of ketaifi pastry*

Lemon mayonnaise
*4 tablespoons mayonnaise
  (see page 212)
zest & juice of ½ lemon*

Chilli jam
*150 ml red wine vinegar
150 ml red wine
100 g sugar
1 cm piece of root ginger,
  peeled & grated
8 red chillies, deseeded &
  finely diced*

Cucumber relish
*50 g sugar
1 teaspoon fennel seeds
150 ml white wine vinegar
1 cm piece of root ginger,
  peeled & grated
½ cucumber, deseeded &
  cut into fine strips
2 tablespoons dill, chopped*

Lemon mayonnaise
Combine the ingredients together in a bowl. Chill.

Chilli jam
Place all the ingredients except the chillies in a saucepan. Cook over gentle heat for 20 minutes. Remove from the heat, add the chillies and allow to cool.

Cucumber relish
Simmer the sugar, fennel seeds, vinegar and ginger in a saucepan for 20 minutes. When the liquid is cool, add the cucumber and dill.

Deep-fried Dublin Bay prawns in ketaifi pastry
Preheat a deep-fat fryer to 160°C/325°F. Dip the prawns in the flour and then the beaten egg. Tear the ketaifi pastry into short lengths, about 10 cm. Roll the prawns in the pastry and deep fry until crisp and golden, about 3–4 minutes.

To serve
Place five prawns in ketaifi pastry on each plate and place a spoonful of lemon mayonnaise, chilli jam and cucumber relish around the prawns.

Dublin Bay prawn plate: sautéed with lemongrass, light tempura & chilled wrapped in Parma ham

{serves 4}

Prawns sautéed with lemongrass
8 Dublin Bay prawns, shelled &
  deveined
4 lemongrass stalks, trimmed,
  outer layers removed
zest of 1 lime
1 cm piece of root ginger,
  peeled & finely chopped
1 chilli, deseeded & finely chopped
3–4 tablespoons olive oil

Light tempura prawns
12 prawns, shelled & deveined
100–150 ml water
100 g cornflour, sifted
salt & freshly ground black pepper
2 tablespoons flour

Chilled prawns wrapped in Parma ham
4 prawns in their shells
2 slices of Parma ham, halved

Garnish
4 sprigs of coriander

Chilled prawns wrapped in Parma ham
Bring a small saucepan of water to simmering point and poach the prawns for 2–3 minutes. When cool, peel off the shells and wrap each prawn in half a slice of Parma ham. Chill.

Light tempura prawns
Preheat a deep-fat fryer to 180°C/350°F. Add the cold water to the cornflour, whisking continuously until it reaches batter consistency. Season with salt and pepper. Toss the prawns in flour, just enough to dust. Dip in tempura batter to coat. Deep fry the prawns for 3–4 minutes or until golden brown.

Prawns sautéed with lemongrass
Skewer two prawns on to each lemongrass skewer. Marinate the prawns for 30 minutes with the lime zest, ginger, chilli and olive oil. Heat a frying pan to hot and fry the prawns for 2 minutes each side.

To serve
Place two prawns sautéed with lemongrass, three tempura prawns and one prawn wrapped in Parma ham on each of four plates. Garnish with a sprig of coriander.

Dublin Bay prawn risotto with saffron, orange & dill crème fraîche, Parmesan crisp tuile

{serves 6}

Dublin Bay prawn risotto with saffron, orange & dill crème fraîche
100 g Dublin Bay prawns, cooked
  & shelled
½ teaspoon saffron
800 ml warm fish stock
  (see page 211)
50 g butter
2 shallots, peeled & diced
1 clove of garlic, peeled & crushed
200 g Arborio rice
1 tablespoon dill, chopped
juice of 2 oranges, reduced by half
zest of 1 orange
2 tablespoons crème fraîche
salt & freshly ground
  white pepper

Parmesan crisp tuile
100 g Parmesan cheese,
  finely grated
1 teaspoon olive oil plus oil for
  greasing baking tray

Dublin Bay prawn risotto with saffron, orange & dill crème fraîche
Set aside the saffron in 1 tablespoon of fish stock to infuse the colour and flavour. Melt the butter in a heavy-based saucepan. Add the shallots and garlic and cook on a low heat for a few minutes. Add the Arborio rice, stirring until it is coated with the butter. Add the rest of the fish stock, ladle by ladle, allowing each to be absorbed before adding the next. Add the saffron-infused fish stock. Continue to cook until all the liquid is absorbed, but with the rice still retaining a bite. (This should take about 15–18 minutes.) Stir in the prawns, dill, orange juice and zest and, finally, the crème fraîche. Season to taste.

Parmesan crisp tuile
Preheat the oven to 140°C/275°F/gas mark 1. Grease a baking tray with olive oil and arrange four 8 cm round pastry cutters on the tray. Mix the teaspoon of olive oil with the grated Parmesan cheese to form a paste and divide the mixture between the four cutters. Remove the cutters before placing the tray in the oven. Bake for 18–20 minutes until the tuiles are golden. Remove the tuiles with a palette knife and set aside to cool.

To serve
Divide the risotto between six warm bowls. Insert the Parmesan tuiles to stand proud of each dish.

Carpaccio of scallop & Woodcock smoked salmon with whiskey yoghurt & sweet mustard dressing

{serves 4}

Carpaccio of scallop & Woodcock smoked salmon
4 large scallops
2 slices of Woodcock smoked salmon
115 g mixed salad leaves

Whiskey yoghurt
85 ml Greek yoghurt
2 tablespoons whiskey

Sweet mustard dressing
2 tablespoons runny honey
4 tablespoons wholegrain mustard
salt & freshly ground black pepper

Carpaccio of scallop & Woodcock smoked salmon
Prepare the scallops by pulling away the frilly membrane and black intestine and discarding the orange coral. Wrap the scallops tightly in clingfilm and freeze. Remove the scallops from the freezer and cut them into wafer-thin slices, using a sharp, long-bladed knife.

Whiskey yoghurt
Combine the yoghurt and whiskey in a small bowl and season to taste.

Sweet mustard dressing
Place the honey and mustard in a small bowl and stir until well combined. Season to taste.

To serve
Place the salad leaves in a bowl and drizzle over the sweet mustard dressing, tossing to combine. Arrange the scallops in a fan shape, slightly overlapping, on chilled plates. Arrange a small mound of salad with sweet mustard dressing beside the scallop slices and decorate them with strips of smoked salmon. Drizzle the whiskey yoghurt over the smoked salmon.

Crisp roll of crab, goats' cheese & pine nuts, beetroot preserve, vegetable salad, spicy oil

{serves 4}

Crisp roll of crab, goats' cheese & pine nuts
150 g firm goats' cheese
150 g white crab meat
1 tablespoon pine nuts,
  toasted & cooled
1 teaspoon honey
1 teaspoon basil, chopped
1 teaspoon tarragon, chopped
salt & freshly ground white pepper
4 sheets of spring roll pastry

Beetroot preserve
200 g beetroot
2 tablespoons sunflower oil
½ red onion, peeled & sliced

½ clove of garlic, peeled &
  crushed
1 bay leaf
pinch of ground coriander
pinch of five spice powder
40 g caster sugar
1 tablespoon white wine vinegar
salt & freshly ground white pepper

Vegetable salad
4 baby carrots, peeled
salt
50 g cauliflower florets,
  divided into four
2 baby courgettes,
  halved lengthways
1 tablespoon olive oil
1 teaspoon balsamic vinegar

Spicy oil
100 ml good-quality vegetable oil
  plus 1 tablespoon
½ clove of garlic, peeled
  & crushed
1 cm piece of root ginger,
  peeled & finely sliced
¼ red chilli (including seeds), diced
¼ lemongrass stalk, sliced
1 teaspoon cumin seeds, crushed
1 teaspoon coriander seeds,
  crushed
pinch of turmeric
pinch of five spice powder
salt & freshly ground white pepper

Spicy oil
Heat 1 tablespoon of vegetable oil in a saucepan and gently cook the garlic, ginger, chilli and lemongrass. Add the spices and cook them lightly. Next add 100 ml vegetable oil and allow it to heat through. Season to taste and allow the oil to rest overnight. Strain through muslin the next day.

Beetroot preserve
Preheat the oven to 180°C/350°F/gas mark 4. Place the beetroot on a roasting tin and drizzle 1 tablespoon of sunflower oil over it. Cook for 1 hour until tender, depending on the size of the beetroot. When it's cooked, allow it to cool and then peel and grate it, using the largest size of the grater. In a medium-sized saucepan, heat the other tablespoon of sunflower oil and gently cook the onion and garlic for 5 minutes until soft. Add the bay leaf and spices and cook for another 2 minutes. Add the sugar and vinegar and caramelise. Stir in the grated beetroot and heat. Remove the bay leaf and season to taste. Refrigerate.

Vegetable salad
Plunge the baby carrots into a medium-sized saucepan of boiling salted water. After 1 minute add the cauliflower florets and cook for 1 minute before adding the baby courgettes. Cook all the vegetables for 1 more minute. Remove the vegetables with a slotted spoon and refresh them in a bowl of ice-cold water. Drain the vegetables and dry them on kitchen paper. Mix the olive oil and balsamic vinegar together in a bowl and stir in the cooked vegetables. Refrigerate.

Crisp roll of crab, goats' cheese & pine nuts
Crumble the goats' cheese into a bowl and add the crab meat. Next add all the other ingredients except the spring roll pastry and mix thoroughly. Divide the mixture into four cylinders of about 80 g each. Wrap the cylinders in spring roll pastry, tucking in the ends and sealing them with water. Refrigerate.

Preheat the deep-fat fryer to 180°C/350°F. Deep fry the rolls for 3–4 minutes until they are crisp and golden on the outside and soft in the middle. Drain the rolls on kitchen paper.

To serve
Divide the vegetable salad between four plates. Spoon a tablespoon of the beetroot preserve at the side. Place the crisp roll on top and drizzle it with the spicy oil.

Crispy beignets of crab with spinach, cheese & tofu, herb mayonnaise

{serves 4}

Crispy beignets of crab with spinach, cheese & tofu
110 g white crab meat
50 g white Cheddar cheese, grated
110 g tofu
50 g spinach, cooked & chopped
juice of 1 lemon
50–70 g plain flour, sifted
1 egg, beaten
salt & freshly ground white pepper
1 small bunch of coriander,
chopped
½ small onion, peeled & finely diced

Coating
100 ml milk
1 egg, beaten
100 g soft white breadcrumbs
1 tablespoon sesame seeds
flour for coating

Herb mayonnaise
½ recipe mayonnaise
(see page 212)
1 bunch of mixed herbs, chopped

Herb mayonnaise
Mix the mayonnaise with the chopped herbs. Chill.

Crispy beignets of crab with spinach, cheese & tofu
Put the crab, cheese, tofu and spinach in a large bowl and mix well. Add the lemon juice, 50 g of the flour, the egg, seasoning, coriander and onion. Mix well. If the mixture is too wet, add a little more flour. Check for seasoning. On a floured board roll the mixture into small balls about 2 cm in diameter. Refrigerate for 1 hour.

Preheat a deep-fat fryer to 160°C/325°F. Combine the milk and egg in a small bowl. Mix the breadcrumbs and sesame seeds together in a separate bowl. Roll the beignets in flour and coat with the combined milk and egg before rolling in the breadcrumb and sesame seed mixture. Deep fry for 2–3 minutes until golden.

To serve
Divide the crab beignets between four warm plates and place a spoonful of herb mayonnaise at the side.

Roasted farmyard quail with leg ballotine & peppered quail egg, truffled Savoy cabbage, red wine glaze

{serves 4}

Roasted farmyard quail with leg ballotine
4 quail
salt & freshly ground black pepper
1 tablespoon olive oil

Marinade
1 sprig of thyme
1 small orange, peeled &
  sliced into small pieces
4–5 juniper berries, crushed
1 clove of garlic, peeled & crushed
salt & freshly ground white pepper

Farce for the leg ballotine
40 g foie gras

20 g duck leg confit, finely
  shredded (see page 128)
20 g butter
½ red onion, peeled & finely sliced
1 teaspoon caster sugar
1 sprig of thyme, leaves picked
salt & freshly ground white pepper
100 g pig's caul, washed & dried
  (available from good butchers)

Peppered quail egg
1 tablespoon vegetable oil
4 quail eggs
Maldon sea salt & freshly
  crushed black peppercorns

Truffled Savoy cabbage
4 leaves of Savoy cabbage,
  finely shredded
100 ml cream
salt & freshly ground white pepper
2 slices of black truffle,
  cut into thin strips

Red wine glaze
200 ml red wine
200 ml ruby port
400 ml chicken stock
salt & freshly ground white pepper

Roasted farmyard quail with leg ballotine

Marinade: Combine all the marinade ingredients together in a bowl and cover the quail. Marinate the quail for a couple of hours or overnight.

Leg ballotine: Remove the legs from the quails by cutting them off at the joint with a heavy, sharp knife. Remove the base bone from the quail's leg. Using a heavy knife, take the lower half of the leg bone and push it up until it's almost out of the leg, then cut it out, leaving the upper leg bone in place and retaining the skin. Season with salt and pepper.

Melt 20 g butter in a small saucepan and fry the red onion gently until soft. Add a teaspoon of sugar and cook until the onion is caramelised. Season and allow to cool before adding to the farce.

Make the farce by mixing all the ingredients except the pig's caul in a bowl until smooth. Insert the farce into the cavity and roll the leg back into shape. Lay out the pig's caul on a work surface, cut it into eight pieces with a sharp knife, and wrap each ballotine very tightly in it. Secure the ballotine with clingfilm, tying the ends to ensure that the farce does not escape. Bring a medium-sized saucepan of water to simmering point and poach the quail ballotines for 4 minutes. Remove the ballotines from the water with a perforated spoon and allow them to cool. When they are cool, remove the clingfilm and pan fry the ballotines in a dry frying pan over a moderate heat for 2–3 minutes each side until they are golden brown.

Roasted farmyard quail: Preheat the oven to 180°C/350°F/gas mark 4. Season the quail crowns, drizzle a little olive oil over them and roast them for 8–10 minutes. Remove the crowns and allow them to rest.

Truffled Savoy cabbage

Plunge the shredded Savoy cabbage into a saucepan of boiling salted water. Cook the cabbage for 2–3 minutes, then drain it and plunge it into ice-cold water. Reduce the cream by half in a heavy-based saucepan and season the mixture with salt and pepper. Heat the cabbage in this sauce for serving. Add the sliced truffle.

Red wine glaze

Heat the red wine and port in a heavy-based saucepan until it has reduced by two-thirds. Add the chicken stock and continue reducing until the glaze has a coating consistency. Season.

Peppered quail egg

Heat the oil in a small frying pan. Carefully break the eggs into the pan one at a time and fry them for 30 seconds, then turn off the heat and allow the eggs to set for 2 minutes. Remove the eggs from the pan with a palette knife and trim them with a small knife if necessary for presentation. Sprinkle with Maldon sea salt and freshly crushed black peppercorns.

To serve

Take the quail breasts off the bone. Spoon the cabbage on to the centre of four warm plates. Lay two breasts and two leg ballotines on either side. Drizzle the red wine glaze about the plates. Finally, place a peppered quail egg on top of each quail.

Roasted wood pigeon on a tart of caramelised red onion, madeira jus

{serves 4}

Roasted wood pigeon
4 x 120 g prepared wood
* pigeon crowns*
2 tablespoons sunflower oil
salt & freshly ground white pepper

Marinade
8 tablespoons red wine
15 juniper berries, crushed
1 clove of garlic, peeled & crushed
2 sprigs of rosemary

Tart of caramelised red onion
Tart
250 g plain flour
pinch of salt
100 g butter, diced
30 g lard, diced
100 ml cold water

Filling
50 g butter
2 medium red onions, peeled &
* finely sliced*
1 clove of garlic, peeled & crushed
1 sprig of thyme, leaves picked
salt & freshly ground white pepper

Madeira jus
200 ml jus (see page 212)
50 ml madeira
salt & freshly ground white pepper

Roasted wood pigeon
Mix the marinade ingredients together and marinate the wood pigeon crowns in a covered, shallow earthenware dish overnight in the fridge. Remove from the marinade the next day and pat dry with kitchen paper. Preheat the oven to 190°C/375°F/gas mark 5. Heat the oil in an ovenproof frying pan. Season the wood pigeon crowns and sear for 1 minute each side. Transfer to the oven and roast for 12–15 minutes. Remove the pigeon crowns from the oven and allow to rest for a few minutes before serving. Using a sharp boning knife, carefully remove the fillets from the crown and slice them.

Tart of caramelised red onion
Tart: Sift the flour with the salt into a large bowl. Add the diced butter and lard and rub lightly with your fingertips until the mixture has the texture of fine breadcrumbs. Slowly add the cold water and work the dough until it comes together. Wrap the pastry in clingfilm and refrigerate for 1 hour.

Preheat the oven to 180°C/350°F/gas mark 4. Roll out the dough on a lightly floured work surface until it is ½ cm thick. Grease four 10 cm tartlet tins and line with the pastry. Press the pastry well into the sides and make sure that there are no tears. Lay a square of greaseproof paper on top of each pastry and fill with ceramic baking beans or dried beans and bake blind for 10 minutes. Remove the greaseproof paper and bake for a further 10–12 minutes until golden brown.

Filling: Melt the butter in a large, heavy-based saucepan and cook the sliced onions, garlic and thyme very gently for about 10 minutes until soft and brown. Season. Divide the mixture between the four tarts.

Madeira jus
Warm the basic jus in a medium-sized saucepan, add the madeira and season. Keep warm.

To serve
Place a hot caramelised red onion tart on each warm plate. Arrange slices of pigeon breast on each tart and drizzle the madeira jus over them.

Crisp organic salad Landaise, selection of farmyard fowl with pommes sautées, sherry & walnut dressing

{serves 4}

Crisp organic salad Landaise
8 leaves lamb's lettuce (organic)
8 leaves frisée lettuce (organic)
4 sprigs of chervil
4 sprigs of tarragon
150 g smoked duck, thinly sliced
salt & freshly ground black pepper

Selection of farmyard fowl
Duck ballotine
½ recipe duck ballotine,
* (see page 128)*

Poussin
4 poussin breasts
1 tablespoon sunflower oil
salt & freshly ground white pepper
12 slivers of black truffle

Pommes sautées
400 g potatoes
2 rashers of streaky bacon
30 g butter
salt & freshly ground white pepper

Marinade
3 tablespoons sea salt
1 clove of garlic, peeled & chopped
1 sprig of thyme
1 sprig of rosemary

Duck breast confit
2 duck breasts
250 g duck fat

Sherry & walnut dressing
300 ml chicken stock (see page 210)
4 morels, cleaned & sliced
1 tablespoon sherry
1 tablespoon sherry vinegar
40 g walnuts, blanched for
* 1 minute in boiling water,*
* roughly chopped*
3 tablespoons grapeseed oil
salt & freshly ground black pepper

Pommes sautées
Marinade: Scatter half the sea salt into a small earthenware dish. Lay the duck breasts on top and scatter the remaining dry ingredients over them. Cover and refrigerate overnight. Remove from the marinade the next day, rinse the duck breasts under cold water and pat dry with kitchen paper.

Duck breast confit: Preheat the oven to 130°C/250°F/gas mark ½. Heat the duck fat gently in a flameproof casserole on the hob. Place the duck breasts in the casserole and bring to a gentle simmer. Transfer to the oven and cook for 1½ hours until tender. Remove the duck breasts with a slotted spoon. When it's cool enough, remove the fat from the duck confit and dice the meat.

Pommes sautées: Boil the potatoes in salted water until just cooked, then peel and dice them. Cut the streaky rashers into thin strips and blanch in boiling water for 1–2 minutes, then remove them with a slotted spoon. Melt the butter in a frying pan and lightly cook the diced potatoes for 2–3 minutes, then add the bacon pieces and cook for 2–3 minutes. Finally, add the diced duck and warm through. Season and keep warm.

Selection of farmyard fowl
Duck ballotine: Make the duck ballotine from the Assiette of duck recipe on page 128, using half quantities.

Poussin: Preheat the oven to 190°C/375°F/gas mark 5. Heat 1 tablespoon of sunflower oil in a frying pan and seal the poussin breasts for 1 minute each side. Season. Make three diagonal slits with a sharp knife on the top of each breast and insert three slivers of truffle into each. Transfer to a roasting tin and roast for 4–5 minutes. Keep warm.

Sherry & walnut dressing
Pour the chicken stock, sliced morels and sherry into a medium-sized saucepan and reduce by two-thirds. Cool. Using a whisk, add the sherry vinegar and walnuts, then add the oil slowly. Season.

Crisp organic salad Landaise
Wash and dry the salad leaves and herbs, then tear them into small pieces. Toss the lettuce, herbs and smoked duck together gently in the sherry and walnut dressing. Add a little salt and pepper to taste.

To serve
Divide the smoked duck salad between four chilled plates. Place a cold ballotine of duck and a hot poussin breast on each plate and spoon some hot pommes sautées at the side.

Assiette of duck: Jerusalem artichoke & smoked duck terrine, duck ballotine, confit duck & black truffle Pithiviers

{serves 8–10}

Jerusalem artichoke & smoked duck terrine
4 smoked duck breasts,
  fat removed, sliced
2 Cox's apples, peeled,
  cored & cut into large chunks
1 tablespoon water
1 litre chicken stock (see page 210)
6 leaves of gelatine
4 Jerusalem artichokes,
  peeled & sliced 1 cm thick
1 litre vegetable oil
1 bulb of garlic, outer layers peeled,
  cut in half
pinch of salt
2 large leeks, whites only,
  sliced in half lengthways

Duck ballotine
1 duck foie gras
1 teaspoon salt
1 teaspoon freshly ground
  black pepper
1½ litres duck stock (see page 210)

Confit duck & black truffle Pithiviers
2 duck legs
250 g duck fat, melted
3 shallots, peeled & finely chopped
4 tablespoons madeira
250 ml chicken stock (see page 210)
2 black truffles, finely diced

4 ceps, cleaned & finely chopped
200 g puff pastry
  (see page 214 or use frozen)
1 egg, beaten
Marinade
4 tablespoons sea salt
1 sprig of thyme, chopped
1 sprig of rosemary, chopped
1 bay leaf
1 clove of garlic, peeled & chopped

Garnish
50 g redcurrants

Jerusalem artichoke & smoked duck terrine

Place the chopped apples in a large, heavy-based saucepan with a tablespoon of water. With the lid on, cook gently until the apple is soft. Remove from the heat and pass through a sieve to form a purée. Spoon the apple purée into a double layer of muslin and hang it up over a bowl for a day until dry.

Boil the stock in a medium-sized saucepan until it has reduced to 500 ml. Put the gelatine leaves in a bowl of ice-cold water for 3–4 minutes, remove them, shake off the excess liquid and place in a bowl. Remove the stock from the heat and pour on to the gelatine leaves, stirring until they have dissolved.

Preheat the oven to 180°C/350°F/gas mark 4. Place the sliced artichokes in a roasting tin with the oil and garlic and cook until tender. Bring some salted water to the boil and plunge in the leeks for 1 minute, then plunge them into ice-cold water.

Coat a 22 cm x 8 cm terrine mould with layers of overlapping clingfilm. Dip the leek pieces into the gelatine/stock mixture to coat them and use these to line the terrine mould, making sure they overlap, leaving extra length hanging over the edges of the mould. These will be folded over at the end, sealing the whole terrine. Layer the terrine as follows: duck, apple purée, artichoke. Repeat this process, pouring a little of the gelatine/stock mixture between each layer. Once the terrine is full, pour in enough gelatine/stock to submerge the ingredients.

Fold over the leeks and wrap the terrine in clingfilm. Place a weight on top of the terrine and refrigerate overnight.

Run a knife around the edges of the terrine and turn it out. Using a serrated knife, cut the terrine into thick slices.

Duck ballotine

Take the foie gras from the fridge and leave covered until it reaches room temperature and becomes soft and pliable. Carefully part the lobes so that the artery and veins become visible. Using a long, thin, pointed knife, pull the veins away from the liver, taking care not to break the lobes in two. Season the open lobes with salt and pepper, then close them and wrap tightly in clingfilm. Refrigerate overnight.

Remove the foie gras from the clingfilm, wiping away any excess seasoning. Weigh the foie gras and calculate cooking time at 4 minutes per 110 g. (You must weigh the foie gras before poaching it, as it is essential to cook it accurately. Overcooked foie gras simply melts away, leaving a soggy texture, while undercooked foie gras will taste raw. The foie gras must be cooked at a constant temperature until the centre reaches 60°C/140°F. A thermometer to guarantee temperature control during cooking would be useful.)

Place the duck stock in a large saucepan and bring it to 72°C/160°F. Add the foie gras and bring the temperature up to 72°C/160°F again and poach for 4 minutes per 110 g, regulating the temperature throughout the process. To check whether the liver is cooked, part the lobes. The centre should be warm and slightly pinkish and should have the consistency of lightly set egg white. Lift the foie gras out of the stock, using two large slotted spoons. Wrap the liver in muslin and roll it into a cylindrical shape, cool it on a wire rack and refrigerate overnight.

Confit duck & black truffle Pithiviers

Marinade: Scatter half the salt in a small earthenware dish. Lay the duck legs in the dish and sprinkle the remaining marinade ingredients over them. Cover the dish and refrigerate overnight. The next day, rinse the duck legs under cold running water and pat dry.

Confit duck: Preheat the oven to 130°C/250°F/gas mark ½. Heat the duck fat gently in a flameproof casserole on the hob. Place the duck legs in the casserole and bring to a gentle simmer. Transfer to the oven and cook for 1½ hours or until the meat is tender and falling off the bone. Remove from the oven and leave the legs to cool in the fat. Once cool, remove the confit legs from the fat, strip the meat from the bones and shred it.

Black truffle Pithiviers: Place the shallots and madeira in a small saucepan and boil until the madeira has reduced to 2 tablespoons. Add the stock and reduce again by half. Add the truffles and shredded duck and reduce the liquid to a glaze consistency. Finally, add the ceps. Cool.

Roll out the pastry to ½ cm thickness and cut it into 30 cm squares, allowing one square per portion. Put a heaped teaspoon of mixture in the middle of each pastry square, brush the edges with beaten egg and pull in the four corners towards the centre to form a parcel, sealing the edges by pinching the pastry together. Brush the top with the remaining egg and bake at 180°C/350°F/gas mark 4 for 15 minutes or until golden brown. Serve the Pithiviers warm.

To serve

Place a slice of terrine on each plate. Remove the ballotine from the muslin and slice it with a hot, thin-bladed knife, cleaning and reheating the knife in hot water between each slice. Place one slice on each plate. Place one confit duck and black truffle Pithiviers on each plate and garnish with some redcurrants.

Seared duck foie gras with banana dressing, spiced brûléed banana, walnut & raisin brioche

{serves 4}

Seared duck foie gras
300 g foie gras
salt & freshly ground white pepper

Banana dressing
1 banana
1 tablespoon crème de banane
1 tablespoon white wine vinegar
2 tablespoons olive oil
1 shallot, peeled & diced
salt & freshly ground white pepper

Spiced brûléed banana
1 banana
pinch of curry powder
1 tablespoon caster sugar

Walnut & raisin brioche
15 g fresh yeast or 8 g dried yeast
25 g caster sugar
2 tablespoons water
500 g strong white flour, sifted
pinch of salt
1 tablespoon walnuts,
* roughly chopped*
25 g golden raisins
4 eggs, beaten
150 g unsalted butter,
* diced*
flour for sprinkling

Walnut & raisin brioche
This quantity makes two 500 g loaves. Place the yeast, sugar and water in a bowl. Set aside in a warm place for about 10 minutes until the mixture is foamy. Put the flour in another bowl with the salt and the walnuts. Add the raisins. Add the eggs to the yeast mixture before stirring it into the bowl of flour. Mix well until the dough comes together.

Turn the dough out on to a flat, lightly floured surface and knead well. Incorporate the butter into the dough a few pieces at a time, kneading well all the time. Sprinkle a large bowl with flour, put in the dough and cover with clingfilm. Leave the dough in a warm place for 2 hours or until it has doubled in size.

Knock back the dough by punching it a couple of times. Transfer to two greased 16 cm x 10 cm loaf tins. Set aside to prove for another hour in a warm place. Preheat the oven to 200°C/400°F/gas mark 6. Bake the loaves for 30 minutes, remove them from the tins and turn them out to cool on a wire tray.

Banana dressing
Peel the banana and halve it lengthways. Purée one half of the banana and dice the other half. Put the puréed banana, crème de banane, vinegar and olive oil in a food processor and blend until smooth. Remove and place in a bowl. Add the diced banana and the shallot, mix and season to taste. Refrigerate.

Spiced brûléed banana
Peel, halve lengthways and quarter the banana. Sprinkle it with the curry powder and then sprinkle it evenly with the caster sugar. Brûlée the coated banana with a blowtorch until the sugar caramelises to golden brown.

Seared duck foie gras
Take the foie gras from the fridge and leave covered until it reaches room temperature and becomes soft and pliable. Carefully part the lobes so that the artery and veins become visible. Using a long, thin, pointed knife, pull the veins away from the liver, taking care not to break the lobes in two. Cut the foie gras into slices 1½–2 cm thick. Season with salt and pepper. Place a non-stick frying pan over high heat. When the pan is very hot, add the foie gras and cook for 30–40 seconds each side. Serve immediately.

To serve
Toast four slices of walnut and raisin brioche. Place a brûléed banana at the top of each warm plate. Put a slice of toasted brioche on one side of the plate and top with a slice of foie gras. Pipe a line of banana dressing on the other side of the plate.

Pressed ham hock with chicken confit & roasted shiitake mushrooms, fig compote

{serves 8}

Pressed ham hock with chicken confit & roasted shiitake mushrooms
Pressed ham hock
2 ham hocks
1 medium carrot, peeled & diced
1 medium onion, peeled & diced
1 leek, sliced
1 tablespoon Dijon mustard
1 tablespoon flat leaf parsley
salt & freshly ground white pepper

Chicken confit
5 chicken legs
1 tablespoon sea salt
1 bay leaf
1 sprig of thyme
500 ml duck fat

Foie gras
150 g foie gras
50 ml madeira
salt & freshly ground white pepper

Roasted shiitake mushrooms
1 tablespoon olive oil
200 g shiitake mushrooms, sliced

Terrine
9 slices of Parma ham

Fig compote
500 g fresh figs
100 ml ruby port
100 ml water
100 ml maple syrup

Pressed ham hock with chicken confit & roasted shiitake mushrooms

Pressed ham hock: Soak the ham hocks in a bowl of water overnight. Drain the water and transfer the hocks to a large saucepan. Cover with fresh water and bring to the boil. Drain, cover with fresh water, add the carrot, onion and leek and bring to the boil again. Simmer the hock for 2 hours. Cool, remove the fat and cut the meat from the bone, then cut it into 2 cm pieces. While it is still slightly warm, mix in the Dijon mustard and parsley. Season to taste. Cool and refrigerate.

Chicken confit: Marinate the chicken legs in a bowl with the sea salt, bay leaf and thyme. Refrigerate overnight. Preheat the oven to 160°C/325°F/gas mark 3. Wash the salt off the chicken legs and dry them. Place the chicken legs in a roasting tin, heat the duck fat until just warm in a saucepan and pour it over the chicken legs. Cover with tinfoil and roast the legs until the meat falls off the bone (1 hour). Remove from the oven and transfer the chicken legs to a plate to cool. Remove the skin and bones from the legs and cut the meat into small pieces. Refrigerate.

Foie gras: Cut the foie gras into 1 cm cubes and marinate overnight in a bowl with the madeira and a pinch of salt. In the morning, remove the foie gras cubes from the madeira. Heat a frying pan until very hot and sear the foie gras in the dry pan for 30 seconds each side. Cool the foie gras, season it and transfer it to a plate, retaining the pan juices. Refrigerate. Add the chicken confit to the foie gras and pan juices.

Roasted shiitake mushrooms: In a separate pan heat 1 tablespoon of olive oil and sauté the sliced shiitake mushrooms for 2 minutes and cool them. Mix the cooled shiitake mushrooms with the diced ham hock.

Terrine: Line a 23 cm x 9 cm terrine mould in a criss-cross fashion with clingfilm. Cover the bottom and sides of the terrine mould with the Parma ham, leaving some Parma ham hanging over the sides to cover the top. Layer the terrine with a layer of ham hock and shiitake mushrooms, then a layer of confit chicken and foie gras. Repeat. Fold the Parma ham hanging over the top over the last layer. Place a weight on top and refrigerate for 2 days to allow the flavour to mature.

Fig compote
Cut the figs into quarters and remove the stems. Marinate in the port and water overnight. Transfer to a saucepan, add the maple syrup and bring to the boil. Remove from the heat. Cool and refrigerate.

To serve
Remove the terrine from the mould. Slice it into eight pieces with a long-bladed, sharp knife and arrange the slices on cooled plates. Place a spoonful of fig compote on each slice of terrine.

Carpaccio of aged Angus beef with wild asparagus & horseradish oil

{serves 4}

Carpaccio of aged Angus beef
Method 1
400 g fillet of beef, preferably aged Angus, trimmed of any fat or sinew
1 tablespoon Dijon mustard
1 tablespoon black peppercorns, crushed
1 tablespoon sea salt
1 tablespoon flat leaf parsley, chopped

Method 2
as above, plus olive oil for coating

Wild asparagus
12 spears of wild asparagus, trimmed
1 tablespoon vegetable oil
4 quail eggs

Horseradish oil
50 g horseradish, peeled & grated
100 ml sunflower oil

Garnish
12 shavings of Parmesan cheese

Carpaccio of aged Angus beef
Method 1: Rub the beef fillet on all sides with the Dijon mustard. Mix the peppercorns, salt and parsley together and roll the beef in the mixture. Roll up tightly in clingfilm and freeze for 4–5 hours. Slice the carpaccio very thinly with a meat slicer. As most domestic kitchens don't have meat slicers, we have included a second method for making the carpaccio.

Method 2: As an alternative to the freezer method, brush the prepared fillet all over with a little olive oil. Heat a pan until very hot and quickly sear the fillet for 60 seconds each side, turning with a tongs. Leave the beef to cool and refrigerate for 3–4 hours before serving. Use a long, straight-edged knife to carve the fillet into 24 thin slices.

Wild asparagus
Plunge the wild asparagus into a medium-sized saucepan of simmering salted water and cook for 1 minute. Drain the asparagus and plunge it into ice-cold water. Drain again.

Heat the oil in a small frying pan. Carefully break the eggs into the pan one at a time and fry them for 30 seconds, then turn off the heat and allow the eggs to set for 2 minutes. Remove the eggs from the pan with a palette knife and trim them with a small knife if necessary for presentation.

Horseradish oil
Place the horseradish in a bowl. Warm the sunflower oil and pour it over the horseradish. Strain, retaining the oil, and allow to cool.

To serve
Lay the beef carpaccio on four chilled plates. Arrange the wild asparagus at the side topped with the quail egg. Garnish each carpaccio with three Parmesan shavings and drizzle the horseradish oil around the plate.

Boudin of Clonakilty black pudding with Cashel Blue cheese & cider sorbet, crisp cured bacon, stout jus

{serves 6}

Boudin of Clonakilty
black pudding
300 g Clonakilty black pudding
1 boneless chicken
breast, skinned
25 g butter
1 shallot, peeled & diced
1 sprig of thyme, chopped
salt & freshly ground
black pepper
1 tablespoon olive oil

Cashel Blue cheese &
cider sorbet
300 ml stock syrup (see page 215)
juice of ½ lemon
90 g Cashel Blue cheese, crumbled
100 ml cider

Crisp cured bacon
1 teaspoon vegetable oil
6 rashers of streaky bacon

Stout jus
200 ml Guinness
200 ml jus (see page 212)

Boudin of Clonakilty black pudding
Remove the skin from the black pudding and crumble the pudding into a bowl. Blend the chicken breast in a food processor until it is puréed. Heat the butter in a saucepan and gently cook the shallot with the thyme for 3–4 minutes. Allow to cool. Combine the black pudding, puréed chicken and cooked shallot mixture in a bowl and season with salt and pepper. Form the mixture into a sausage shape 5 cm in diameter and roll the sausage in clingfilm and then in tinfoil. Place in a pot of simmering water and poach for 45 minutes. Allow to cool.

Cashel Blue cheese & cider sorbet
Bring the stock syrup to the boil. Remove from the heat, add the lemon juice and allow to cool. Transfer the syrup to an ice-cream maker and churn. Just as the sorbet is at the soft stage, add the blue cheese and cider. Continue churning until the mixture is firm. Transfer it to a bowl and place in the freezer. Alternatively, pour the mixture into a shallow container and freeze to a slush. Whisk well so that the sorbet becomes very light and fine grained. Add the cheese and cider just before it becomes firm.

Crisp cured bacon
Preheat the oven to 180°C/350°F/gas mark 4. Grease an oven tray with the vegetable oil and lay the rashers flat on the tray without overlapping. Grease the underside of another tray and place it on top. Bake for 15–18 minutes until crisp.

Stout jus
In a heavy-based saucepan simmer the Guinness until it has reduced by half. Add the jus and warm through.

To serve
Slice the boudin in 1 cm pieces and pan fry in the olive oil for 1 minute each side, ensuring that it is heated through. Place on six warm plates. Top each one with a scoop of Cashel Blue cheese and cider sorbet. Arrange the crisp cured bacon on the sorbet. Finally, drizzle the stout jus around the plate.

Roasted veal kidney with a nage of garden peas, beans & asparagus, parsnip mash, black truffle jus

{serves 4}

Roasted veal kidney
4 x 160 g portions of veal kidney
50 g butter

Nage of garden peas, beans & asparagus
100 g garden peas
100 g French beans, topped
 & tailed
100 g asparagus tips
salt
1 tablespoon sunflower oil
1 leek, roughly chopped
1 carrot, peeled & roughly chopped
1 stick of celery, roughly chopped
100 ml chicken stock, clarified
 (see page 210)
1 bay leaf

Parsnip mash
2 parsnips, peeled &
 roughly chopped
salt & freshly ground white pepper
400 g mashed potato

Black truffle jus
1 recipe jus (see page 212)
50 g black truffle shavings, made
 using a vegetable peeler

Black truffle jus
Make the basic jus recipe and add the truffle shavings before reducing.

Nage of garden peas, beans & asparagus
Clarified chicken stock: Boil the chicken stock and remove scum from the surface with a ladle. Cool. Pass the stock through a muslin-lined sieve.

Nage: Plunge the peas, beans and asparagus tips into a medium-sized saucepan of boiling salted water and cook for 2 minutes. Remove the vegetables with a slotted spoon and refresh them in a bowl of ice-cold water. When the vegetables are cool, drain them and dry on kitchen paper. Heat the sunflower oil in a medium-sized saucepan, add the leek, carrot and celery and cook gently for a few minutes without browning. Add the chicken stock and bay leaf, bring the mixture to a simmer and reduce it by a third. Strain. Reheat the vegetables in the flavoured stock when the kidney is cooked.

Parsnip mash
Preheat the oven to 180°C/350°F/gas mark 4. Season the parsnips and roast them for about 30 minutes or until soft. Purée in a food processor. Transfer to a bowl, add the mashed potato and mix well. Keep the mash warm.

Roasted veal kidney
Remove the skin, membrane, core and bloody vessels from the kidney, using a kitchen scissors. Heat the butter in a frying pan, add the kidneys and cook over a medium heat for about 5 minutes, turning occasionally, until the kidney is brown on the outside but still pink on the inside.

To serve
Spoon some hot parsnip mash into the centre of each warm bowl and top with a veal kidney. Divide the peas, beans and asparagus tips, with the flavoured stock, between each plate and drizzle the hot black truffle jus over each kidney.

Ravioli of goats' cheese with char-grilled aubergine, red pepper & courgette dressing, Jerusalem artichoke froth

{serves 6}

Ravioli of goats' cheese
½ recipe pasta (see page 214)
150 g goats' cheese
30 g pine nuts, toasted & cooled
1 tablespoon honey
4 sprigs of basil
salt & freshly ground white pepper
1 egg
1 tablespoon milk

Char-grilled aubergine
1 aubergine, cut lengthways into
   slices 1 cm thick & scored
2 cloves of garlic, peeled & crushed
pinch of sea salt
1 sprig of thyme
3 tablespoons olive oil

Red pepper & courgette dressing
1 red pepper
100 ml olive oil
½ courgette, trimmed &
   finely diced
4 basil leaves
35 ml raspberry vinegar
salt & freshly ground white pepper

Jerusalem artichoke froth
1 recipe froth (see page 213)
1 Jerusalem artichoke,
   peeled & diced

Ravioli of goats' cheese
Place goats' cheese, pine nuts, honey and basil into a food processor and blend until smooth. Season. Roll out the pasta to the thinnest setting on the pasta machine and cut into twelve 10 cm circles. Beat the egg and milk lightly together to make an egg wash. Using two teaspoons, divide the goats' cheese mixture between the twelve discs. Brush the edges of the pasta with egg wash and fold over to form a half circle. Seal the ravioli with your fingertips. Bring a saucepan of salted water to the boil and cook the pasta for 3 minutes. Drain and immerse in ice-cold water until cold. Drain. Reheat in a little boiling salted water for serving.

Char-grilled aubergine
Rub the aubergine slices with the garlic, sea salt and thyme. Leave to marinate for 2 hours. Heat a griddle pan, oil the aubergine slices and lightly char-grill the aubergines for 2 minutes each side.

Red pepper & courgette dressing
Preheat the oven to 150°C/300°F/gas mark 2. Put the red pepper in a roasting tin, drizzle it with 1 tablespoon of the olive oil and roast it for 35 minutes. Remove the pepper from the oven, peel and deseed it while it is still warm, then dice it finely. Meanwhile bring a saucepan of salted water to the boil and cook the courgette for 2 minutes. Drain and refresh the courgette in a bowl of iced water, then drain it again. Chop the basil into fine strands. Mix the courgette, red pepper, basil and vinegar together in a bowl. Pour in the remaining oil, whisking to make a dressing. Season.

Jerusalem artichoke froth
Make the basic froth recipe, boiling the Jerusalem artichoke with the stock and cream for 15–20 minutes. Blend the mixture, then froth it, using a hand blender or a whisk.

To serve
Slice the aubergine slices in two and arrange them on six plates. Top with two ravioli on each plate. Place a spoonful of red pepper and courgette dressing on the ravioli and drizzle the artichoke froth around the plate.

Chilled goats' cheese parfait, pickled pear & brioche crouton

{serves 6}

Chilled goats' cheese parfait
300 g goats' cheese
6 large spinach leaves, washed
50 g pine nuts, toasted & cooled
5 g tarragon, finely chopped
5 g flat leaf parsley, finely chopped
10 g basil, finely chopped
1 clove of garlic, peeled & crushed
2 tablespoons honey
180 ml cream, semi-whipped
salt & freshly ground white pepper

Pickled pear
200 g sugar
200 ml water
2 ripe Conference pears, peeled, cored & diced
100 ml white wine vinegar
100 ml caster sugar
1 whole star anise
½ teaspoon fennel seeds
salt & freshly ground white pepper

Brioche crouton
15 g fresh yeast or 8 g dried yeast
25 g caster sugar
2 tablespoons water
500 g strong white flour
pinch of salt
4 eggs, beaten
150 g unsalted butter, diced
flour for sprinkling

Garnish
1 tablespoon olive oil
4 cherry tomatoes
30 g pine nuts, toasted & cooled

Chilled goats' cheese parfait
Plunge the spinach into a saucepan of boiling water and blanch for 15 seconds before removing and plunging into a bowl of iced water. Drain and set aside. In a food processor, blend the goats' cheese, then add the pine nuts, herbs, garlic and honey. Gently fold in the cream and season. Line a small 18 cm x 8 cm terrine with clingfilm in a criss-cross fashion, then add a layer of blanched spinach leaves, making sure the sides are covered but leaving a little overhang to cover the top later. Fill the terrine with the goats' cheese mixture and cover lightly with the overlapping spinach leaves and clingfilm. Refrigerate overnight to set.

Pickled pear
In a medium-sized saucepan, dissolve 200 g sugar in 200 ml water, bring to the boil, then reduce the heat until the syrup is gently simmering. Poach the diced pear in the sugar syrup for 5 minutes, then remove it with a perforated spoon and discard the syrup. In a separate saucepan bring the vinegar, caster sugar, star anise, fennel seeds, salt and pepper to the boil. Pour over the poached pears and allow to pickle overnight in the fridge. Drain the next day.

Brioche crouton
This amount makes 2 x 500 g loaves. Put the yeast, sugar and water into a bowl and set aside in a warm place for about 10 minutes until it is quite foamy. In a separate bowl sift the flour with the salt. Add the eggs to the yeast mixture, then add the yeast/egg mixture to the bowl of flour. Mix until the dough comes together.

Turn the dough out on to a lightly floured surface and knead well. Incorporate the butter into the dough a few pieces at a time, kneading well all the time. Sprinkle a large bowl with flour and put the dough in it. Cover the bowl with clingfilm and leave in a warm place for 2 hours or until it has doubled in size.

Knock back the dough by kneading it for a few seconds. Transfer to two greased 16 cm x 10 cm loaf tins. Set aside to prove for another hour in a warm place. Preheat the oven to 200°C/400°F/gas mark 6. Bake for 30 minutes, remove the loaves from the tins and turn them out on to a wire tray.

Garnish
Preheat the oven to 170°C/325°F/gas mark 3. Place the cherry tomatoes in a roasting tin, drizzle with the olive oil and cook for 20 minutes.

To serve
Cut and toast six slices of brioche and cool. Slice the parfait with a sharp knife and place a slice on each cooled plate. Place a pickled pear on top of each parfait and arrange a toasted brioche, a roasted cherry tomato and some pine nuts around each plate.

Roasted white asparagus wrapped in Parma ham with garden peas, tomato & Parmesan butter, poached duck egg, black olive tapenade

{serves 4}

**Roasted white asparagus wrapped
in Parma ham with garden peas**
*16 white asparagus spears, peeled
  & trimmed to about 14 cm*
4 slices of Parma ham
2 tablespoons olive oil
salt & freshly ground white pepper
120 g garden peas

Tomato & Parmesan butter
100 g unsalted butter, softened
25 g Parmesan cheese, finely grated
*1 plum tomato, skinned, deseeded,
  diced & dried on kitchen paper*

Poached duck egg
4 duck eggs
2 teaspoons white wine vinegar
salt

Black olive tapenade
*1 recipe black olive tapenade
  (see page 152)*

**Roasted white asparagus wrapped in Parma ham
with garden peas**
Preheat the oven to 180°C/350°F/gas mark 4. Bundle
four spears of asparagus together and wrap with a
slice of Parma ham. Repeat with the remaining
asparagus spears. Transfer all the bundles to a
roasting tin, drizzle them with the olive oil and
season with salt and pepper. Cover the tin with tinfoil
and roast for 15–20 minutes until tender. The exact
time will depend on the thickness of the asparagus
spears. Remove the asparagus bundles from the oven
and keep them warm.

Boil the peas in simmering salted water in a medium-
sized saucepan for 1–2 minutes or until they float to
the top. Drain the peas, refresh them in ice-cold
water, then drain them again.

Tomato & Parmesan butter
Soften the butter nearly to melting point and fold in
the grated Parmesan and diced tomato.

Poached duck egg
Pour boiling water into a shallow pan, add salt and
vinegar, and carefully break in the duck eggs, one at
a time. Simmer for 1 minute. Remove the pan from
the heat and leave the eggs in the hot water for 5–6
minutes. This gives a translucent white and a soft,
creamy yolk. Remove the poached eggs carefully with
a draining spoon.

Black olive tapenade
Make the black olive tapenade from the Pan-seared
John Dory recipe on page 152.

To serve
Divide the peas between four warm plates. Place the
asparagus spears on top and spoon the tomato and
Parmesan butter over them. Place a small mound of
tapenade at one side of the plate and the poached
duck egg on the other.

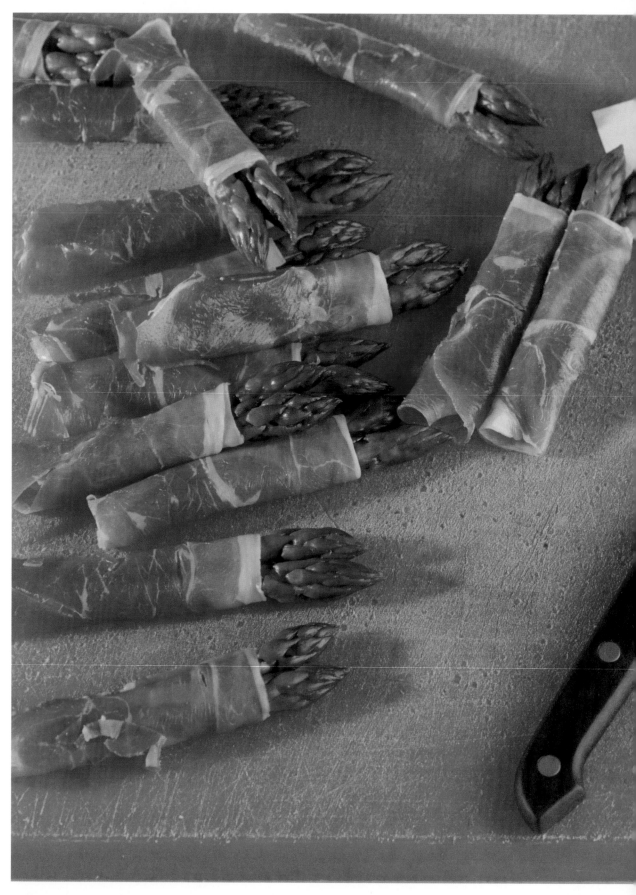

Caesar salad with aged Parmesan shavings, crispy croutons & fresh anchovies, topped with Parma ham

{serves 4}

Caesar salad with aged Parmesan shavings, crispy croutons & fresh anchovies, topped with Parma ham
24 leaves of Cos lettuce
250 g Grana Padano or Parmesan cheese, shaved
12 fresh anchovy fillets or anchovies in brine
4 slices of Parma ham

Crispy croutons
50 g crustless white bread
½ clove of garlic, peeled & crushed
1 sprig of thyme, chopped
pinch of sea salt
1 tablespoon olive oil

Caesar dressing
4 cloves of garlic, peeled & crushed
125 g anchovies
juice of 1 lemon
salt & freshly ground white pepper
1 recipe mayonnaise (see page 212)

Caesar salad with aged Parmesan shavings, crispy croutons & fresh anchovies, topped with Parma ham

Crispy croutons: Preheat the oven to 180°C/350°F/ gas mark 4. Cut the bread into 1½ cm cubes. Place the cubes on a baking tray and sprinkle the garlic, thyme and sea salt over them. Drizzle with the olive oil and bake for 3–5 minutes until golden.

Caesar dressing: Blend all the Caesar dressing ingredients except the mayonnaise in a food processor. Mix into the mayonnaise. Combine the lettuce leaves with the dressing in a large bowl, ensuring that the leaves are completely coated.

Parma ham: Preheat a deep-fat fryer to 180°C/350°F. Deep fry the Parma ham slices for about 2 minutes until they are crisp.

To serve
Place the coated lettuce leaves in a shallow bowl with the croutons and shaved Parmesan cheese and arrange three anchovies and the crisp Parma ham on top of the salad.

Ballotine of wild Irish salmon with lobster salad & tomato fondue

{serves 4}

Ballotine of wild Irish salmon
*1 large side of wild salmon,
  trimmed*
*1 bunch of flat leaf parsley,
  chopped*
½ bunch of mint, chopped
salt & freshly ground white pepper
*1 teaspoon lemon oil
  (available from good delis)*

Lobster salad
200 g cooked lobster meat
1 teaspoon creamed horseradish
1 bunch of chives, chopped
1 shallot, peeled & chopped
1 teaspoon lemon juice
4 teaspoons crème fraîche

Tomato fondue
2 tablespoons grapeseed oil
1 onion, peeled & chopped
1 clove of garlic, peeled & chopped
*3 beef tomatoes, skinned,
  deseeded & roughly chopped*
salt & freshly ground white pepper
2 tablespoons tomato paste
2 tablespoons sugar
pinch of saffron
6 basil leaves
2 tablespoons powdered aspic
*250 ml double cream,
  whipped to full peak*

Garnish
4 sprigs of dill

Ballotine of wild Irish salmon
Skin and trim the salmon to approx 4 cm wide.
Sprinkle the herbs over both sides of the salmon and
season. Wrap the salmon in clingfilm, rolling tightly.
Let the salmon meat roll into a cylinder shape. Tie at
both ends with string. Poach in simmering water for
7 minutes. If you have a temperature probe, bring
the salmon to 35°C/95°F.

Once cooked, remove the salmon and place in iced
water, then hang it in the fridge for 8 hours (pierce
the end of the clingfilm, allowing the excess water to
run from the salmon).

Lobster salad
Dice the lobster meat. Mix all the other ingredients in
a large bowl. Add the lobster meat and mix again.

Tomato fondue
Heat the oil in a medium-sized frying pan and cook
the onion and garlic gently until soft. Add the
chopped tomatoes, salt and pepper to taste and cook
slowly over a low heat, stirring frequently, until most
of the liquid has evaporated. Press through a fine-
mesh sieve into a heavy-based saucepan. Add the
tomato paste, sugar, saffron and basil. Cover and
cook over a low heat, stirring occasionally, until it
reaches the consistency of tomato paste. Remove the
basil leaves, adjust the seasoning and allow to cool.
Add the aspic powder and mix well. Fold 125–175 ml
of the tomato reduction into the cream, using more
or less depending on the desired density. Refrigerate.

To serve
Slice the salmon 3 cm thick or to your preferred
thickness. Rub the surface with lemon oil and place a
slice of salmon in the centre of each cooled plate.
With two dessertspoons shape the tomato fondue
mixture into four quenelles. Place a quenelle and a
spoon of the lobster salad beside the salmon. Garnish
each plate with dill.

Smoked fish & wild salmon fish cake, stir-fried vegetables, herb & garlic aïoli

{serves 6}

Smoked fish & wild salmon fish cake
100 g smoked cod, deboned, skinned & sliced into small strips
100 g smoked haddock, deboned, skinned & sliced into small strips
100 g smoked eel, deboned, skinned & sliced into small strips
100 g raw wild salmon, deboned, skinned & sliced into small strips
1 tablespoon Thai fish sauce
1 tablespoon dill, chopped
1 tablespoon coriander, chopped
1 tablespoon parsley, chopped
200 g mashed potato
½ red chilli, deseeded & finely diced
salt & freshly ground black pepper
2 tablespoons sunflower oil

Breadcrumb coating
1 egg, beaten
50 ml milk
120 g seasoned plain flour
100 g fresh white breadcrumbs

Stir-fried vegetables
2 tablespoons sunflower oil
1 red pepper, deseeded & cut into 5 cm strips
2 carrots, peeled & cut into 5 cm strips
100 g green beans, topped & tailed
100 g sugar snap peas, trimmed
50 g bean sprouts
1 head pak choi, roughly chopped
salt & freshly ground black pepper
2 tablespoons soy sauce

Herb & garlic aïoli
1 recipe aïoli (see page 212)
1 teaspoon chervil, finely chopped
1 teaspoon parsley, finely chopped
1 teaspoon chives, finely chopped

Smoked fish & wild salmon fish cake
Preheat the oven to 180°C/350°F/gas mark 4. Mix all the fish cake ingredients except the sunflower oil in a bowl, binding well and seasoning. Shape into six round cakes about 5 cm in diameter.

Beat the egg and milk together. Arrange three shallow dishes: the first with the seasoned flour, the second with the egg wash, the third with the breadcrumbs. Use one hand to dip each fish cake in flour before using the other to immerse the fish cake in the egg wash. Shake off the excess. Finally, with the dry hand, dip the fish cake into the breadcrumbs and cover well. Repeat the process.

Heat the sunflower oil in an ovenproof frying pan and cook the fish cakes for 1 minute each side, carefully turning with a fish slice. Transfer to the oven and continue cooking for a further 10–12 minutes.

Herb & garlic aïoli
Make the basic aïoli recipe, adding the chopped herbs with the seasoning.

Stir-fried vegetables
Heat the oil and stir-fry the vegetables in a hot wok for 2–3 minutes so that they are still crunchy. Season with salt and pepper and add the soy sauce.

To serve
Arrange the stir-fried vegetables in the centre of six warm plates. Place a fish cake on top and serve with a little dish of the herb and garlic aïoli at the side of the plate.

Frank Hederman's beech smoked salmon with quenelle of crab & cauliflower tempura

{serves 4}

Frank Hederman's beech smoked salmon
100 g Frank Hederman's beech smoked salmon

Quenelle of crab
200 g white crab meat, picked over to remove any pieces of shell
½ red chilli, deseeded & very finely chopped
zest of 1 lime
1 pink grapefruit, segmented, chopped, sieved to remove excess juice

1 orange, segmented, chopped, sieved to remove excess juice
8 mint leaves, finely shredded
2 tablespoons mayonnaise (see page 212)
salt & freshly ground white pepper

Avocado purée
1 avocado, peeled & stoned
1 tablespoon crème fraîche
pinch of cayenne pepper
juice of ½ lime
salt & freshly ground white pepper

Cauliflower tempura
4 x 35 g cauliflower pieces
½ recipe tempura batter (see page 180)

Frank Hederman's beech smoked salmon
Using a long, straight-edged knife, slice thin horizontal slices from the smoked salmon. Cut these layers into even squares 4 cm x 4 cm.

Quenelle of crab
Quenelle mixture: Mix together the crab meat, chilli, lime, grapefruit, orange and mint in a bowl. Fold in the mayonnaise and season to taste. Pack the crab mixture into four 8 cm cylindrical moulds. Lift off the mould.

Avocado purée: Blend the avocado, crème fraîche, cayenne pepper and lime juice together in a food processor. Season to taste.

Cauliflower tempura
Make the tempura according to the recipe on page 180.

To serve
Arrange the smoked salmon on four chilled plates and top with a quenelle of crab, a cauliflower tempura and a teaspoon of avocado purée.

Wholegrain mustard & whiskey cured wild Irish salmon, pink grapefruit couscous, avocado cream

{serves 4}

Wholegrain mustard & whiskey cured wild Irish salmon
2 x 150 g fillets of wild Irish salmon, trimmed & pin bones removed
15 g sea salt
15 g caster sugar
5 white peppercorns, finely crushed
15 g dill, coarsely chopped
1 teaspoon Irish whiskey
2 teaspoons wholegrain mustard

Pink grapefruit couscous
130 g presoaked couscous
1 pink grapefruit, skinned, segmented, juice retained
15 g coriander, chopped
salt & freshly ground white pepper

Avocado cream
1 ripe Hass avocado, skinned, halved & stone retained
2 tablespoons crème fraîche
juice of ½ lemon
salt & freshly ground white pepper

Wholegrain mustard & whiskey cured wild Irish salmon
Mix the salt, sugar, peppercorns and dill together. In a separate bowl mix the whiskey and mustard together. Smear the salmon fillets with the mustard mixture. Spoon the salt, sugar, peppercorns and dill over it, using the mustard mixture to help it stick. Lay one salmon fillet on top of the other to form a sandwich. Wrap clingfilm around them, place a weight on top and refrigerate for 2–3 days. The salmon will exude a salty, sugary syrup. When you are ready to serve the salmon, unwrap it and rinse it gently under cold water. Using a long, straight-edged knife, slice off horizontal slices.

Pink grapefruit couscous
Cook the couscous in a saucepan of boiling salted water according to the instructions on the packet, as each brand varies. Cool the couscous and add the grapefruit segments and juice. Next add the chopped coriander and season with salt and pepper.

Avocado cream
Blend the avocado, crème fraîche and lemon juice together in a food processor. Season to taste, then transfer to a bowl and pop the avocado stone into the middle. (This prevents the avocado from going brown.) Seal with clingfilm and refrigerate.

To serve
Arrange three slices of cured salmon on each of four chilled plates. Serve with a spoonful of pink grapefruit couscous and a dollop of avocado cream.

Terrine of wild Irish smoked salmon with crab, Mascarpone cheese & horseradish, crisp capers & onion ice cream

{serves 8}

Terrine of wild Irish smoked salmon with crab, Mascarpone cheese & horseradish

750 g/1 side of wild Irish
  smoked salmon
5 gelatine leaves
juice of 1 lemon
350 g Mascarpone cheese
1 teaspoon creamed horseradish
1 tablespoon dill, chopped
350 g white crab meat
salt & freshly ground white pepper

Crisp capers

200 ml sunflower oil
4 teaspoons capers,
  non pareil (baby)
4 teaspoons seasoned plain flour

Onion ice cream

1 tablespoon sunflower oil
2 onions, peeled & sliced
175 ml semi-skimmed milk
125 ml cream
2 teaspoons caster sugar
1 teaspoon salt
pinch of freshly ground
  white pepper

Garnish

8 sprigs of dill

Terrine of wild Irish smoked salmon with crab, Mascarpone cheese & horseradish

Remove bones from the salmon with a tweezers. Using a long, thin knife, slice off thin, horizontal slices from the side of the salmon.

Soak the gelatine leaves in a bowl of ice-cold water for 3–4 minutes. Remove the gelatine from the water and squeeze out the excess liquid. Warm the lemon juice and pour over the gelatine, stirring and allowing to melt before cooling. Mix together the Mascarpone cheese, horseradish, dill, chopped smoked salmon trimmings and crab meat in a large bowl until the mixture is smooth. Stir in the cooled gelatine and lemon juice mixture, ensuring that it is well distributed. Season.

Line a 23 cm x 12 cm terrine mould with clingfilm in a criss-cross fashion, with a little excess on each of the sides. Line the mould with a layer of smoked salmon, ensuring that the smoked salmon covers the sides of the mould. Spoon half the crab mixture on top of the salmon and place a layer of smoked salmon on top. Next spoon in the remaining crab mixture. Finally, finish with a layer of smoked salmon. Seal with the excess clingfilm and refrigerate for 6 hours. Once refrigerated, turn the terrine mould upside down and remove the clingfilm. Slice the terrine with a very sharp knife.

Crisp capers

Preheat a small saucepan of sunflower oil. Remove the capers from the jar and drain them on kitchen paper. Toss the capers in seasoned flour and sieve to remove the excess flour. Hold the capers in a tea strainer and carefully fry in the oil for 1 minute until crisp. Drain on kitchen paper.

Onion ice cream

Heat the oil in a large saucepan. Cook the onions gently over low heat until they are soft, then transfer them to a food processor and blend until smooth. Return to the saucepan, add the milk, salt and pepper, and bring to the boil. Boil the cream and sugar in a separate saucepan. Add to the puréed onion mixture and allow to cool. Transfer to an ice-cream maker and churn until frozen. Alternatively, transfer the mixture to a shallow dish, place in the freezer and stir every hour until it has set.

To serve

Place a slice of terrine on each plate. Scoop a ball of onion ice cream and place it on top of the terrine. Scatter the crisp capers around the plate. Finally, garnish with a sprig of dill.

Terrine of smoked mackerel, mussels & salmon with leek & potato, pickled cucumber

{serves 8–10}

Terrine of smoked mackerel, mussels & salmon with leek & potato
500 g smoked mackerel, crumbled, bones & tough edges removed
40 g smoked mussels
1 side of presliced smoked salmon
500 g smoked eel, skinned & sliced
300 ml fish stock (see page 211)
6 leaves of gelatine
2 large leeks, whites only, sliced in half lengthways

1 litre duck fat
3 medium Rooster potatoes, peeled & cut into wafer-thin slices
zest & juice of 1 lemon
salt & freshly ground black pepper

Pickled cucumber
500 ml tarragon vinegar
300 g brown sugar
1 teaspoon turmeric
1 tablespoon coriander seeds

2 tablespoons fennel seeds
1 shallot, peeled & finely diced
1 kg cucumber, deseeded & diced
1 red pepper, deseeded & cut into thin strips
1 chilli, deseeded & cut into thin strips
10 g salt

Garnish
lemon wedges

Terrine of smoked mackerel, mussels & salmon with leek & potato
Bring the fish stock to the boil. Soak the gelatine in a bowl of ice-cold water for 3–4 minutes until it becomes soft and pliable. Remove the gelatine from the water and shake off the excess liquid. Pour the boiling stock over the gelatine and stir until it has melted. Bring some salted water to the boil and plunge in the leeks for 1 minute, then plunge them into ice-cold water. Put the duck fat into a heavy-based saucepan and heat gently. Add the potato slices and cook gently until tender, then allow them to cool. Place the mackerel in a food processor and blend until it has the consistency of pâté. Season with lemon zest and juice and pepper. Separate the smoked salmon slices.

Coat a 22 cm x 8 cm terrine mould with layers of overlapping clingfilm. Dip the leek pieces into the gelatine and stock to coat them and use these to line the terrine mould, making sure they overlap, leaving extra length hanging over the edges of the mould. These will be folded over at the end, sealing the whole terrine. Layer the terrine as follows: smoked salmon, smoked mackerel, potato, smoked mussels, smoked eel. Repeat this process, pouring a little of the fish stock/gelatine mixture in between each layer and tapping the mould gently to make sure there are no air holes. When you have filled the terrine, pour in enough fish stock/gelatine to submerge the ingredients. Fold over the leeks and wrap the terrine

in clingfilm. Place a weight on top of the terrine, wrap it tightly with clingfilm and leave for 2 days in the fridge to allow the flavours to develop.

Run a knife around the edges of the terrine and turn it out on to a cutting board. Using a serrated knife, cut it into thick slices.

Pickled cucumber
Put the vinegar, sugar, turmeric, coriander, fennel and shallot in a heavy-based saucepan and simmer for about 45 minutes. Pass through a fine sieve. Put the cucumber, red pepper and chilli into a bowl, sprinkle with the salt, cover with clingfilm and marinate in the fridge for 2 hours. Rinse the cucumber in water and pat dry. Add the cucumber to the pickle and cook for 30–40 minutes until it's almost dry and has the consistency of jam (it will run off a spoon in a syrupy stream). Be careful, as, once the liquid starts to reach a syrupy consistency, it will turn into hard caramel very quickly.

To serve
Arrange the slices of terrine on chilled plates with a spoonful of cucumber pickle. Garnish with lemon wedges.

Terrine of red mullet & Mediterranean vegetables scented with saffron & yellow pepper, opal basil dressing

{serves 8–10}

Terrine of red mullet & Mediterranean vegetables
4 x 160 g portions of red mullet
1 teaspoon saffron strands
2 tablespoons sunflower oil
1 courgette, trimmed & cut into
  1 cm slices lengthways
2 yellow peppers, deseeded & cut
  into 3 cm strips
2 red peppers, deseeded & cut
  into 3 cm strips
2 green peppers, deseeded & cut
  into 3 cm strips
1 aubergine, trimmed & cut into
  1 cm slices lengthways
3 leaves of gelatine
5 leaves of York cabbage

Saffron & yellow pepper scent
1 tablespoon olive oil
2 yellow peppers, peeled with a
  vegetable peeler, deseeded &
  finely diced
1 teaspoon saffron strands
15 g basil stalks
1 shallot, peeled & finely chopped
1 clove of garlic, peeled &
  finely chopped

Opal basil dressing
6 tablespoons olive oil
2 tablespoons red wine vinegar
20 g opal basil leaves
1 clove of garlic, peeled &
  finely chopped
2 shallots, peeled & finely chopped
salt & freshly ground black pepper

Terrine of red mullet & Mediterranean vegetables
Sprinkle the red mullet fillets with the saffron strands. Heat a griddle pan until hot, add a little oil and sear the fillets for about 4 minutes each side until cooked to medium. Leave to cool. Wipe the pan, add more oil and char-grill the vegetables in batches on the griddle pan until they are blackened and soft.

Soak the gelatine leaves in a bowl of ice-cold water for 3–4 minutes. Remove the gelatine leaves from the water and shake off the excess liquid. Line a 22 cm x 8 cm terrine mould with clingfilm and York cabbage leaves (see the recipe for Terrine of teal and swede on page 124). Brush the red mullet fillets with the melted gelatine. Layer the terrine with alternate layers of fish and vegetables. Fold the cabbage leaves over the terrine when it is full. Wrap tightly in clingfilm, place a weight on top of the terrine and refrigerate overnight.

Run a knife around the edges of the terrine and turn it on to a chopping board. Using a serrated knife, cut the terrine into thick slices, cleaning the knife in hot water between each slice.

Saffron & yellow pepper scent
Heat the olive oil in a medium-sized saucepan and cook the peppers with the saffron, basil stalks, shallot and garlic over a low heat without browning. Remove the basil stalks after 2 minutes. Blend half the mixture in a food processor, then mix the puréed half with the other half. Cool.

Opal basil dressing
Blend all the ingredients except the salt and pepper in a food processor for 30 seconds. Season to taste.

To serve
Place a slice of terrine on each chilled plate. Spoon some saffron and yellow pepper scent on top of each slice and serve with a spoonful of opal basil dressing at the side.

Sally Barnes's natural smoked haddock risotto with Parmesan & spinach, poached hen's egg & curry froth

{serves 4}

Sally Barnes's natural smoked haddock risotto with Parmesan & spinach

½ recipe risotto
  (see page 214)
300 g Sally Barnes's smoked
  haddock, skinned & diced
100 g spinach, washed,
  dried & chopped
50 g Parmesan cheese, grated

Poached hen's egg

4 hens' eggs
salt

Curry froth

1 recipe froth, substituting
  40 ml coconut milk &
  50 ml double cream for
  90 ml double cream (see page 213)
½ teaspoon turmeric
½ teaspoon ground cumin
½ teaspoon Thai green
  curry paste
2 cm stalk of lemongrass,
  broken up to release the flavour
1 cm piece of root ginger,
  peeled & sliced
½ red chilli, deseeded & chopped

Sally Barnes's natural smoked haddock risotto with Parmesan & spinach

Make the basic risotto, adding the smoked haddock just before the stock and adding the spinach and Parmesan when all the stock has been absorbed. Keep warm on the stove over a very gentle heat.

Poached hen's egg

Bring a large saucepan of salted water to simmering point. Break the eggs into the saucepan gently, one at a time. Cook for 1 minute before taking the saucepan off the heat and allowing the eggs to sit in the water for 6 minutes. This gives a translucent egg with a soft, creamy yolk. Remove the eggs with a slotted spoon.

Curry froth

Follow the basic froth recipe, boiling all the ingredients with the stock, cream and coconut milk. Pass through a fine sieve and froth the mixture, using a hand blender or whisk.

To serve

Divide the smoked haddock risotto between four warm plates and drizzle the curry froth around the plates. Finally, place a poached egg on top of each mound of risotto.

Seared peppered rare tuna loin, soy & honey glaze, red pepper escabèche, avocado & lime purée

{serves 4}

Seared peppered rare tuna loin
400 g fillet of bluefin tuna
2 tablespoons black peppercorns,
  crushed & roasted
2 tablespoons fresh coriander,
  chopped
1 tablespoon olive oil
salt

Soy & honey glaze
200 ml soy sauce
3 tablespoons honey

Red pepper escabèche
4 shallots, peeled & cut into
  fine strips
2 cloves of garlic, peeled & chopped
1 tablespoon olive oil
3 whole star anise
4 bay leaves
small pinch of saffron
2 cinnamon sticks
2 red peppers, deseeded & cut into
  fine strips
100 g brown sugar
zest & juice of 1 lemon
salt & freshly ground white pepper
250 ml chicken stock (see page 210)
1 tablespoon coriander, chopped

Avocado & lime purée
2 avocados, peeled & finely diced,
  stone retained
juice of 1 lime
1 tablespoon coriander, chopped
salt & freshly ground white pepper

Seared peppered rare tuna loin
Mix the peppercorns and coriander together and coat the tuna. In a hot frying pan sear the tuna fillet in the olive oil and season with salt. Set aside and chill.

Soy & honey glaze
Bring the soy sauce to the boil in a heavy-based saucepan, then reduce the heat until it's lightly simmering. Skim any impurities that rise to the surface as you are reducing the soy. When the soy is thick enough to coat the back of a spoon heavily, strain it through a fine sieve. Add the honey and stir well over a low heat until it comes together. Taste and add more honey if required.

Red pepper escabèche
Fry the shallot and garlic gently in the olive oil in a large saucepan. Stir in the star anise, bay leaves, saffron and cinnamon sticks. Add the peppers, sugar and lemon zest and cook for a few minutes. Season. Cover with stock and lemon juice and simmer until the peppers are cooked but not mushy. Strain the liquid, retaining the pepper mix in a separate bowl, then reduce the liquid until it has a syrupy consistency. Mix the peppers and liquid when cooled and stir in the coriander.

Avocado & lime purée
Combine the avocado and lime purée ingredients in a bowl and pop the avocado stone into the middle. (This prevents the avocado from going brown.) Seal tightly with clingfilm and refrigerate.

To serve
Slice the seared tuna loin and arrange it between four chilled plates. Spoon the red pepper escabèche and avocado and lime purée at the side. Drizzle with the soy and honey glaze.

Terrine of teal & swede with confit citrus fruits, bitter raisin preserve

{serves 8–10}

Terrine of teal & swede
4 teal crowns, prepared in the
* same way as the Roast crown of*
* wild mallard recipe on page 164*
30 g Maldon sea salt
1 sprig of thyme
3 cloves of garlic, peeled &
* finely chopped*
675 g duck fat
3 swedes, peeled & sliced into
* 6 mm slices*
1 lobe of foie gras, prepared in the
* same way as the Assiette of duck*
* recipe on page 128*
5 Savoy cabbage leaves

Confit citrus fruits
1 orange, peeled & sliced in
* narrow strips*
1 lemon, peeled & sliced in
* narrow strips*
50 g sugar
4 tablespoons water

Bitter raisin preserve
450 ml water
225 g granulated sugar
350 g raisins

Terrine of teal & swede
Marinate the teal crowns in sea salt, thyme and garlic overnight. Wash off the marinade and pat dry. Melt the duck fat in a large saucepan and cook the teal crowns on a low heat for about 30–40 minutes until tender. Remove the meat from the duck fat (keep the duck fat) and cool, then take the meat off the bone and cut it into 3 cm squares. Preheat the oven to 180°C/350°F/gas mark 4. Place the reserved duck fat and the swede in a roasting tin and roast for 30–40 minutes or until tender.

Slice the prepared foie gras into slices about the same size as the swede and sear them for about 30 seconds each side in a preheated frying pan on high heat until golden.

Plunge the cabbage leaves into a saucepan of boiling water for 2 minutes, then plunge them into ice-cold water. When they are cold, drain the leaves and pat dry.

Coat a 22 cm x 8 cm terrine mould with layers of overlapping clingfilm. Line the terrine with cabbage leaves, leaving some leaves hanging over the edges. These will be folded over once the terrine is full. Layer the terrine as follows: teal confit, foie gras, swede. Repeat until all the ingredients are used. Fold over the cabbage leaves and wrap the terrine tightly in clingfilm. Place a weight on top and refrigerate overnight.

Confit citrus fruits
Place the orange and lemon strips in a medium-sized saucepan of boiling water for about 1 minute and plunge them immediately into ice-cold water. Drain them when they are cold. Place the sugar in a medium-sized saucepan, add the water and dissolve the sugar over a low heat. Add the orange and lemon strips and cook for 3–4 minutes until soft. Cool. Use the confit citrus fruits to decorate the terrine.

Bitter raisin preserve
Place the water and sugar in a heavy-based saucepan and heat gently, allowing the sugar to dissolve, then bring to the boil and simmer until it is a thick stock syrup. Add the raisins and boil until thick. Test a little on a plate to check the set. Using your finger, push the cooled jam along the plate. If it wrinkles, setting point has been reached. If it doesn't, continue to simmer and check again.

To serve
Run a knife around the edges of the terrine and turn it out. Using a serrated knife, cut the terrine into thick slices, cleaning the knife with hot water between each slice. Place a slice of terrine on each cooled plate. Spoon some bitter raisin preserve at the side of the plate.

Bere Island scallops with mussel & clam orzo, sweetcorn & chervil sabayon

{serves 4}

Bere Island scallops
16 large Bere Island scallops
1 tablespoon sunflower oil
salt & freshly ground white pepper

Mussel & clam orzo
150 g orzo pasta
8 mussels, washed & debearded
8 clams, washed
1 shallot, peeled & diced
1 clove of garlic, peeled & crushed
juice of 1 lemon
3 white peppercorns, crushed
1 bay leaf
2 tablespoons white wine
salt & freshly ground white pepper

Sweetcorn & chervil sabayon
100 g frozen sweetcorn
4 egg yolks
60 ml water
10 g chervil, finely chopped
salt & freshly ground white pepper

Mussel & clam orzo
Bring a saucepan of salted water to the boil and cook the orzo for 10 minutes, then drain it. Heat a heavy-based saucepan until very hot. Add the mussels, clams and all the other ingredients except the wine and the seasoning. Cook for 1 minute before adding the wine and covering with a lid. Check after 2 minutes to see whether all the shellfish have opened and discard any unopened ones. Transfer the mussels and clams to a bowl and add the cooked orzo, then add the seasoning.

Sweetcorn & chervil sabayon
Cook the sweetcorn in boiling salted water for 1–1½ minutes, drain it and refresh in cold water. Drain. Place the egg yolks and water in a heatproof bowl and set it over a saucepan of simmering water. Whisk with a balloon whisk for a couple of minutes until the mixture has doubled in size and is pale and creamy. Add the chopped chervil and gently fold through the cooked sweetcorn. Season with salt and pepper.

Bere Island scallops
Prepare the scallops by pulling away the frilly membrane and black intestine and discarding the orange coral. Heat a frying pan until hot, heat the sunflower oil and sear the scallops for 1–1½ minutes each side, turning with a tongs. Season and serve.

To serve
Spoon the mussel and clam orzo on to the centre of each of four warm plates. Arrange the seared scallops about the orzo and drizzle with the sweetcorn and chervil sabayon.

Seared Bere Island scallops, caramelised red onion & pink grapefruit, cauliflower purée & spiced caper berries

{serves 4}

Seared Bere Island scallops
16 large Bere Island scallops
1 tablespoon sunflower oil
salt & freshly ground white pepper

Caramelised red onion & pink grapefruit
1 tablespoon sunflower oil
1 red onion, peeled & sliced finely
1 sprig of thyme
1 tablespoon caster sugar
1 teaspoon balsamic vinegar
1 tablespoon red wine
1 pink grapefruit, skinned & segmented
salt & freshly ground black pepper

Cauliflower purée
500 ml milk
1 head of cauliflower, cut into small florets
50 g butter
juice of ½ lemon
1 tablespoon extra-virgin olive oil
30 g butter, melted
salt & freshly ground white pepper

Spiced caper berries
150 ml sunflower oil plus 1 tablespoon
½ teaspoon turmeric
½ teaspoon ground cumin
1 teaspoon Thai green curry paste
½ lemongrass stalk, broken up
1 cm piece of root ginger, peeled & sliced
½ red chilli, deseeded & chopped
16 caper berries, halved (available from good delis)

Caramelised red onion & pink grapefruit
Heat the sunflower oil in a medium-sized saucepan and gently cook the onion and thyme for 5–6 minutes until tender. Add the sugar, balsamic vinegar and red wine and cook for a further 3–4 minutes, reducing to a viscous consistency. Allow to cool before adding the segmented grapefruit. Season to taste.

Spiced caper berries
Heat 1 tablespoon of sunflower oil in a small saucepan and gently cook all the spices for a couple of minutes. Next add 150 ml sunflower oil and allow to warm. Pour over the caper berries and allow to cool.

Cauliflower purée
Boil the milk in a medium-sized saucepan before adding the cauliflower florets and 50 g butter. Cover and cook on a steady heat for 10–12 minutes until tender. Pass through a sieve, discarding the milk, then blend the cauliflower, lemon juice, olive oil and 30 g melted butter together in a food processor. Season to taste and keep warm.

Seared Bere Island scallops
Prepare the scallops by pulling away the frilly membrane and black intestine and discarding the orange coral. Halve the scallops horizontally. Heat a frying pan to hot and heat the sunflower oil. Sear the halved scallops for 90 seconds each side, turning with a tongs. Check the seasoning before serving.

To serve
Arrange the hot cauliflower purée in the centre of each warm plate. Place the seared scallops about the purée. Add a spoonful of the caramelised red onion and grapefruit to each plate. Finally, spoon on some of the caper berries and infused oil.

West coast lobster with mango & buttermilk risotto, carrot & ginger froth, lobster oil

{serves 4}

West coast lobster
4 x ½ kilo lobsters (cooked chilled
 or cooked frozen will do)
salt

Mango & buttermilk risotto
2 shallots, peeled & diced
1 clove of garlic, peeled & crushed
50 g butter
100 g Arborio rice
330 ml fish stock (see page 211)
1 mango, peeled & diced
50 g Parmesan cheese, grated
50 ml buttermilk or 3 tablespoons
 crème fraîche
salt & freshly ground white pepper

Carrot & ginger froth
2 small carrots, peeled &
 finely diced
1 cm piece of root ginger,
 peeled & finely diced
2 shallots, peeled & finely diced
50 g butter
90 ml fish stock (see page 211)
90 ml cream
1 tablespoon white wine

Lobster oil
shells from the lobster
3 garlic cloves, unpeeled &
 lightly crushed
1 small bunch of rosemary
100 ml vegetable oil

Lobster oil
Preheat the oven to 150°C/300°F/gas mark 2. Break up the shells with a rolling pin and place them in a roasting tin with the garlic and rosemary. Bake for about 20 minutes until the shells are dry and lightly coloured. Place the shells in a heavy-based saucepan, add the oil and leave over a low heat for 4–5 hours until the oil is infused. The oil should be a light red colour with a sweet lobster taste.

Mango & buttermilk risotto
Fry the shallots and garlic gently in the butter until soft, add the rice and mix well. Gradually add the fish stock, ladle by ladle, ensuring that the rice absorbs all the liquid after each addition. The rice is cooked when all the liquid is absorbed and the rice is *al dente*. Add the mango, Parmesan cheese and buttermilk or crème fraîche. If the risotto is a little dry, add more buttermilk or crème fraîche. Adjust the seasoning and serve.

Carrot & ginger froth
Fry the carrots, ginger and shallots in the butter, but don't allow them to colour. Add the fish stock and simmer until a syrupy consistency is reached. Add 60 ml of the cream and the tablespoon of wine and reduce the sauce until thickened, then blend in a food processor and pass through a fine sieve. Season and add the remaining cream. Use a hand blender or a whisk to froth the mixture.

West coast lobster
Heat salted water in a large saucepan over a high heat until the water is boiling fast. This will ensure that the lobster is killed humanely and quickly. Place one lobster in the pan and cover. Cook for 5 minutes, or until the lobster is red, and remove. Reheat the water for each lobster, always making sure that the water is boiling fast. When cool, remove the meat from the shells and serve one claw and one whole tail per person.

To serve
Divide the risotto between four warm bowls. Place a lobster claw in the centre and curl a tail round it. Drizzle with the lobster oil and pour the froth over the claw.

Roast hake wrapped in Parma ham scented with lemon & herbs, Parmesan butter

{serves 4}

Roast hake wrapped in Parma ham scented with lemon & herbs
640 g fillet of hake, skinned, pin bones removed
1 tablespoon salt
1 lemon, washed
1 tablespoon flat leaf parsley, chopped
1 tablespoon coriander, chopped
½ clove of garlic, peeled & crushed
4 slices of Parma ham
salt & freshly ground white pepper
25 g butter
1 tablespoon olive oil

Parmesan butter
100 g broad beans, podded
salt
50 g butter, softened
20 g Parmesan cheese, finely grated
juice of ½ lemon
½ clove of garlic, peeled & crushed
1 tomato, skinned, deseeded & chopped
1 small bunch of mixed herbs (flat leaf parsley, chervil, chives), chopped
pinch of freshly ground black pepper

Garnish
1 recipe crisp sweet potato (see page 172)

Roast hake wrapped in Parma ham scented with lemon & herbs

Bring a medium-sized saucepan of water to the boil, add 1 tablespoon of salt and the lemon. Cover the saucepan and simmer the lemon for 1 hour to make a lemon confit. Cool the lemon, remove the skin and pith, and chop the flesh. Mix the chopped lemon with the parsley, coriander and garlic.

Lay a strip of clingfilm 65 cm x 25 cm on a work surface. Cover with a layer of slightly overlapping Parma ham. Lay the hake across the Parma ham and make a 1 cm incision left to right across its middle. Rub the lemon and herb mix into this and season with salt and pepper. Roll up the hake and Parma ham, securing with the clingfilm and tying both ends as tightly as possible. Refrigerate for 1 hour.

Preheat the oven to 190°C/375°F/gas mark 5. Remove the clingfilm and cut into four equal cylindrical portions. Heat an ovenproof frying pan. Heat the butter and olive oil in the pan and sear the ham-wrapped hake for 1 minute each side, then transfer the pan to the oven and roast for 10 minutes.

Parmesan butter

Blanch the beans in a medium-sized saucepan of boiling salted water for 1–2 minutes. Drain the beans and skin them, using a small, sharp knife. Stir all the ingredients together in a bowl.

Garnish

Make the crisp sweet potato from the Seared fillet of beef recipe on page 172.

To serve

Place a portion of cooked hake in the centre of each warm plate and top with a teaspoon of softened Parmesan butter. Insert a slice of crisp sweet potato into each piece of hake.

Pan-seared John Dory with ratatouille beurre blanc, caramelised baby fennel, basil mash & black olive tapenade

{serves 4}

Pan-seared John Dory
4 x 200 g fillets of John Dory
2 tablespoons olive oil
salt & freshly ground
 white pepper

Ratatouille beurre blanc
2 tablespoons olive oil
½ aubergine,
 chopped into 1 cm dice
½ courgette,
 chopped into 1 cm dice
1 red pepper, deseeded &
 chopped into 1 cm dice
1 tablespoon tomato paste

200 g cold butter, diced
1 shallot, peeled & finely diced
1 clove of garlic, peeled & crushed
100 ml dry white wine
salt & freshly ground
 white pepper

Caramelised baby fennel
4 baby fennel
25 g butter
25 g caster sugar
salt & freshly ground
 white pepper

Basil mash
4 Rooster potatoes, peeled & cut
 into even-sized chunks
25 g butter
50 ml cream
25 g basil, juiced in a fruit juicer

Black olive tapenade
100 g pitted black olives
25 g capers
2 cloves of garlic, peeled
75 g Parmesan cheese
25 ml extra-virgin olive oil

Black olive tapenade
Pulverise all the ingredients in a food processor. Transfer to a bowl and refrigerate until required.

Caramelised baby fennel
Plunge the baby fennel into a saucepan of simmering water and cook for 2–3 minutes. Melt the butter in a separate saucepan. Transfer the baby fennel to this saucepan, coat them in the melted butter and then add the sugar. Cook until the sugar melts and becomes golden brown. Season.

Basil mash
Boil the potatoes in a medium-sized saucepan until soft, then drain and mash them. In a separate saucepan heat the butter and cream and pour the mixture into the mash before stirring in the basil. Keep warm.

Ratatouille beurre blanc
Heat the olive oil in a medium-sized saucepan and cook the diced aubergine for 5 minutes, add the courgette and cook for a further 2 minutes, then add the red pepper and tomato paste and cook until tender. Season and allow to cool. To make the beurre

blanc, heat a little of the butter in a separate medium-sized saucepan and gently cook the shallot and garlic for 5 minutes until soft. Increase the heat, add the wine and reduce the sauce until it has almost evaporated. Lower the heat and slowly whisk in the diced cold butter a little at a time. Continue until all the butter has melted. (Keep stirring the butter when you are adding it so that it will not separate.) Remove from the heat and keep warm. Add the ratatouille to the beurre blanc. Season.

Pan-seared John Dory
Heat the oil in a heavy, non-stick frying pan. Season the fillets and place them in the frying pan skin side down. Cook until crisp and golden brown (2–3 minutes). Turn the fish over and turn the heat off. Leave the fillets in the pan for 1–2 minutes, when they will be cooked perfectly.

To serve
Arrange a baby fennel on each warm plate. Place the John Dory beside the baby fennel and cover it with ratatouille beurre blanc. Using two teaspoons, mould the tapenade mix into four quenelle shapes and place one on top of each John Dory.

Char-grilled swordfish steak, tomato purée, salsa verde, coral spring roll

{serves 4}

Char-grilled swordfish steak
4 x 150 g swordfish steaks
salt & freshly ground white pepper
juice of 1 small lemon
2 tablespoons olive oil

Tomato purée
1 tablespoon olive oil
1 clove of garlic, peeled & chopped
1 cm piece of root ginger,
  peeled & chopped
1 teaspoon white wine vinegar
1 teaspoon sugar
4 plum tomatoes, skinned,
  deseeded & chopped
2 teaspoons tomato paste
salt & freshly ground black pepper

Salsa verde
2 tablespoons mint,
  roughly chopped
2 tablespoons parsley,
  roughly chopped
2 tablespoons capers
4 anchovy fillets, roughly chopped
2 cloves of garlic, peeled &
  roughly chopped
2 teaspoons Dijon mustard
juice of 1 lemon
75 ml olive oil
salt & freshly ground black pepper

Coral spring roll
1 tablespoon sunflower oil
1 clove of garlic, peeled & crushed
2 shallots, peeled & finely diced
2 tomatoes, skinned, deseeded
  & chopped
1 teaspoon tomato paste
1 tablespoon white wine
salt & freshly ground white pepper
coral of 16 scallops, chopped
small bunch of basil leaves,
  chopped
12 sheets of spring roll pastry
1 egg, beaten

Tomato purée
Heat the olive oil in a small saucepan and cook the garlic and ginger gently until softened. Add the vinegar, sugar, tomatoes and tomato paste. Cook gently until it reaches a purée consistency. Season.

Salsa verde
Blend all the ingredients except the seasoning together in a food processor to a thick paste. Season with salt and pepper.

Coral spring roll
Heat the oil in a medium-sized saucepan and cook the garlic and shallots gently until softened. Add the tomatoes, tomato paste and white wine. Simmer for 5 minutes, season and cool. Add the coral and basil and mix. Lay out a sheet of spring roll pastry about 23 cm square on a board so that one of the corners points towards you. Brush around the edges with the beaten egg. Place a tablespoon of the coral mixture in a line near the top corner. Fold over the top corner and roll it towards you a little, then fold in the sides and continue to roll up. Repeat with the remaining filling and beaten egg to make 12 rolls. Lightly brush with the remaining egg and chill for about 30 minutes. Deep fry the rolls for 3–4 minutes until golden brown. Drain on kitchen paper.

Char-grilled swordfish steak
Preheat a griddle pan to hot. Season the swordfish with salt, pepper and lemon juice and brush with a little olive oil. Sear the steaks for 3–4 minutes each side until the flesh feels just firm but not hard.

To serve
Place a swordfish steak and three coral spring rolls on each of four warm plates with a spoonful of tomato purée and a spoonful of salsa verde.

Roast monkfish, langoustine glaze, shellfish, garden pea & saffron linguini, shellfish-scented oil

{serves 4}

Roast monkfish
4 x 160 g portions of monkfish,
  trimmed
salt & freshly ground white pepper
1 tablespoon olive oil

Langoustine glaze
1 tablespoon sunflower oil
1 lemongrass stalk, sliced
1 cm piece of root ginger,
  peeled & finely sliced
1 clove of garlic, peeled & sliced
3 basil stalks
rind of 1 lemon
1 tablespoon tomato paste
3 tablespoons white wine
1 tablespoon Pernod
750 ml langoustine stock
  (see page 211)
salt & freshly ground black pepper

Shellfish, garden pea & saffron linguini
Mussels
16 mussels
1 shallot, peeled & diced
1 clove of garlic, peeled & crushed
juice of 1 lemon
3 white peppercorns, crushed
1 bay leaf
2 tablespoons white wine

Langoustine glaze
Heat the sunflower oil in a large, heavy-based saucepan and gently cook the lemongrass, ginger, garlic, basil stalks and lemon rind. Stir in the tomato paste and add the wine and Pernod to deglaze the saucepan, ensuring that the concentrated flavours are retained and become part of the sauce. Next add the langoustine stock. Reduce for 25 minutes on a low heat until the liquid has a thick, syrup-like consistency. Pass through a sieve, retaining the liquid. Season with salt and pepper.

Shellfish, garden pea & saffron linguini
Cook the shellfish (mussels first): Heat a heavy-based saucepan until it's very hot. Add the mussels and all the other ingredients except the wine. Cook for 1 minute before adding the wine and covering with a lid. Check after 2 minutes to see whether all the mussels have opened and discard any that have not. Remove the mussels, strain them (reserving the cooking liquid) and leave them to cool. Repeat the procedure in a separate saucepan for the clams, discarding any that have not opened.

Garden peas: Bring a pot of salted water to the boil. Plunge the peas into the water and boil for 1½–2 minutes until all the peas are floating in the water. Drain them and drop them into a bowl of iced water, then drain them again.

Clams

16 clams
1 shallot, peeled & diced
1 clove of garlic, peeled & crushed
juice of 1 lemon
3 white peppercorns, crushed
1 bay leaf
2 tablespoons white wine

Garden peas

200 g garden peas
salt

Saffron linguini

30 g fresh Italian parsley
20 g fresh chervil
20 g fresh coriander
1 teaspoon saffron strands
½ teaspoon saffron powder
½ recipe pasta (see page 214),
* including herbs listed above*
* (see method)*
salt
150 ml cream

Shellfish-scented oil

250 g lobster or langoustine shells
3 sprigs of rosemary
3 cloves of garlic,
* unpeeled & lightly crushed*
150 ml sunflower oil

Saffron linguini: Preheat the oven to 80°C/170°F/gas mark ¼. Dry the parsley, chervil and coriander by placing them in a non-fan oven on a tray for 1–1½ hours until they are brittle. Remove the herbs from the oven, cool them, then put them into a plastic bag and shake. Discard the stalks.

When making the basic pasta recipe, add the saffron strands, saffron powder and dried herbs to the dough before mixing it in a food processor. Roll out the pasta to the thinnest setting on the pasta maker and allow it to dry for 10 minutes, then cut it into thin strips. Cook the linguini for 2 minutes in a large saucepan of boiling salted water, then drain the pasta and plunge it into ice-cold water, then drain it again. Reheat the linguini in a large saucepan of boiling salted water before serving.

Shellfish-scented oil

Preheat the oven to 150°C/300°F/gas mark 2. Break up the shells with the heel of a heavy knife and roast them with the rosemary and garlic for 20 minutes until the shells are dry. Place the cooked shells in a saucepan, add the sunflower oil and cook on a very low heat for 1 hour to allow the oil to infuse. Drain the oil, discarding the shells.

Roast monkfish

Preheat the oven to 200°C/400°F/gas mark 6. Heat the olive oil in an ovenproof frying pan. Season the monkfish and cook for 3 minutes on one side. Brush with langoustine glaze and roast the monkfish in the oven for 6–7 minutes.

To serve

Heat 150 ml cream and the reserved cooking liquid in a saucepan and warm up the linguini, peas and shellfish. Divide the linguini between four warm bowls. Place the roast monkfish on top and drizzle with shellfish-scented oil.

Steamed wild Irish salmon, whipped pea & garlic purée, saffron & roasted red peppers, chive dressing

{serves 4}

Steamed wild Irish salmon
4 x 150 g wild Irish salmon fillets,
*   skinned, each fillet diced into*
*   four even-sized pieces*
500 ml water
100 ml dry white wine
1 medium carrot,
*   peeled & finely diced*
1 stick of celery,
*   peeled & finely diced*
1 medium onion,
*   peeled & finely diced*
1 fennel bulb, finely chopped
4 lemongrass stalks,
*   trimmed, outer layers removed*

Whipped pea & garlic purée
200 g frozen/fresh garden peas
2 cloves of garlic, peeled & crushed
50 ml milk
salt & freshly ground white pepper

Saffron & roasted red peppers
2 red peppers, halved & deseeded
1 tablespoon olive oil
1 tablespoon vegetable oil
1 clove of garlic, peeled & crushed

2 cm piece of root ginger,
*   peeled & grated*
2 small shallots, peeled & diced
pinch of saffron strands
salt & freshly ground white pepper

Chive dressing
200 g natural yoghurt
1 tablespoon chives,
*   finely chopped*
juice of 1 lime
salt & freshly ground white pepper

Whipped pea & garlic purée
Boil the peas in a saucepan of simmering salted water for 3–4 minutes, then drain them and add the garlic. Add the milk and pulverise the mixture in a food processor until smooth. Season with salt and pepper.

Saffron & roasted red peppers
Place the peppers under a hot grill for 6–7 minutes until blackened. Peel the cooled peppers and cut them into 1 cm slices. Heat the olive oil and vegetable oil in a saucepan over gentle heat. Add the garlic, ginger, shallots and saffron and cook for 5–6 minutes until soft. Add salt and pepper and allow to cool before adding the red peppers.

Chive dressing
Spoon the yoghurt into a bowl and add the chopped chives, lime juice, salt and pepper. Combine all the ingredients together with a spoon. Allow to chill.

Steamed wild Irish salmon
Place the water, wine, carrot, celery, onion and fennel in the bottom of a steaming saucepan. Heat until the liquid is slightly simmering. Skewer the salmon with lemongrass and place it in the top half of the steamer. Cover and steam for 5–7 minutes or until the salmon is cooked.

To serve
Arrange the pea purée on each plate and place the salmon on top. Spoon the saffron and red peppers over the salmon. Finally, drizzle the chive dressing around the plate and serve.

Pan-seared ray wing on the bone, grenobloise

{serves 4}

Pan-seared ray wing on the bone
4 ray wings, trimmed (ask your
 fishmonger to do this)
salt & freshly ground black pepper
1 tablespoon sunflower oil

Grenobloise
50 g butter, clarified
1 tablespoon baby capers
1 sprig of chervil, roughly chopped
1 sprig of flat leaf parsley,
 roughly chopped
1 bunch of chives, roughly chopped

Garnish
2 lemons, peel & pith removed,
 each cut into 6 segments

Pan-seared ray wing on the bone
Heat the oil in a heavy, non-stick frying pan. Season the ray wings with salt and pepper and cook them for about 4–5 minutes each side. Remove from the frying pan.

Grenobloise
Clarified butter: Melt the butter in a small saucepan over low heat until it's completely liquid. Skim the foam from the surface and discard it. Let the butter settle for 1–2 minutes, then slowly pour the clarified butter into a small bowl, leaving the milky layer behind.

Sauce: When the fish has been removed from the frying pan, add the clarified butter, capers, chervil, parsley and chives. Allow the sauce to turn a nutty brown colour. Serve immediately.

To serve
Place the ray on warm plates and pour the grenobloise over it. Arrange three segments of lemon around each plate.

Pan-seared turbot with spinach purée, foie gras & mushroom tart, port wine jus

{serves 4}

Pan-seared turbot
4 x 150 g fillets of turbot
2 tablespoons olive oil
salt & freshly ground
 white pepper

Spinach purée
300 g spinach, washed
pinch of grated nutmeg
salt & freshly ground
 white pepper

Foie gras & mushroom tart
Shortcrust pastry
100 g plain flour
75 g unsalted butter, diced
2 egg yolks
2 tablespoons cold water
pinch of salt

Duxelle mix for tart
1 tablespoon olive oil
1 shallot, peeled & diced
1 clove of garlic, peeled & crushed
100 g mixed mushrooms,
 peeled & chopped
3 tablespoons port
3 tablespoons madeira
salt & freshly ground black pepper

Foie gras mix for tart
1 tablespoon olive oil
1 clove of garlic,
 peeled & chopped
1 sprig of thyme, chopped
60 ml cream
50 g foie gras
1 drop of truffle oil
1 egg yolk
salt & freshly ground
 white pepper

Port wine jus
100 ml port
100 ml jus (see page 212)

Foie gras & mushroom tart
Shortcrust pastry: Sift the flour into a large bowl. Using your fingertips, rub in the butter until the mix resembles breadcrumbs. Add one of the egg yolks and enough water to form a soft dough. The mix should come cleanly away from the bowl. Wrap the pastry in clingfilm and refrigerate for 30 minutes.

Preheat the oven to 200°C/400°F/gas mark 6. Grease four 8 cm tartlet tins. Roll out the pastry and line the tins. Lay a square of greaseproof paper on top of each pastry and fill with ceramic baking beans or dried beans and bake blind for 10 minutes. Allow to cool and glaze with the second egg yolk mixed with the salt.

Duxelle mix for tart: Heat the oil in a large saucepan and cook the shallot and garlic gently for 5 minutes until soft. Add the mushrooms and cook for a further 2 minutes over moderate heat. Add the port and madeira and reduce by half. Season with salt and pepper.

Foie gras mix for tart: Heat the oil in a large saucepan and cook the garlic and thyme gently for 3–4 minutes. Add the cream, increase the heat, bring the mixture to simmering point and remove the pan from the heat. Place the foie gras and truffle oil in a liquidiser and blend for 1 minute. Gradually add the warmed cream mixture and blend until smooth. Add the egg yolk and salt and blend for a further 2 seconds to combine. Pass through a fine sieve and add pepper.

Preheat the oven to 115°C/220°F/gas mark ¼. Place a spoonful of duxelle at the bottom of each tartlet case. Pour the foie gras mix into the tartlet case, filling it to the top. Bake the tart for 10 minutes.

Spinach purée
Plunge the spinach into a large saucepan of boiling water and boil for 30 seconds. Drain and refresh the spinach by plunging it into ice-cold water, then pulverise it in a food processor with a pinch of nutmeg. Add salt and pepper.

Pan-seared turbot
Heat the oil in a heavy-based frying pan set over medium heat. Add the turbot fillets and cook for 3 minutes each side. Season with salt and pepper.

Port wine jus
In a heavy-based saucepan heat the port and reduce it by half. Add the jus and heat through.

To serve
Place the cooked turbot on a small mound of spinach purée on each plate. Arrange the foie gras and mushroom tart beside the turbot. Finally, drizzle the port wine jus around the plate.

Breast of pheasant stuffed with chestnuts & smoked bacon, ballotine of thigh & wild mushrooms, juniper berry & madeira jus

{serves 4}

Breast of pheasant stuffed with chestnuts & smoked bacon
4 pheasant breasts, skinned
salt & freshly ground white pepper
12 sage leaves
8 slices of Parma ham
1 tablespoon olive oil

Chestnut & smoked bacon stuffing
2 tablespoons sunflower oil
200 g chestnuts, roasted, peeled & roughly chopped
1 shallot, peeled & finely chopped
1 sprig of thyme, finely chopped
1 clove of garlic, peeled & finely chopped
100 g smoked bacon lardons
150 g mashed potato (really dry)
salt & freshly ground black pepper

Ballotine of thigh & wild mushrooms
25 g butter
100 g wild mushrooms, cleaned & sliced
zest of 1 orange
4 juniper berries, cracked
4 pheasant thighs, boned & battened out, skin left on
salt & freshly ground white pepper

Roasted celeriac
50 g celeriac, peeled & cut into large dice
salt & freshly ground white pepper
2 tablespoons sunflower oil

Juniper berry & madeira jus
1 recipe jus (see page 212)
1 tablespoon sunflower oil
1 shallot, peeled & diced
1 clove of garlic, peeled & finely sliced
6 juniper berries, cracked
zest of 1 orange
3 tablespoons madeira

Breast of pheasant stuffed with chestnuts & smoked bacon
Chestnut & smoked bacon stuffing: Heat the sunflower oil in a medium-sized saucepan and cook the chestnuts gently with the shallot, thyme, garlic and bacon lardons for 2–3 minutes. Mix through the mashed potato and season to taste. Cool.

Breast of pheasant: Preheat the oven to 180°C/350°F/gas mark 4. Make an incision along the bottom of each pheasant breast and stuff it with the chestnut and bacon stuffing. Season the breasts. Place three sage leaves on each breast and wrap it in two slices of Parma ham. Heat the oil in an ovenproof frying pan and sear the breasts for about 2–3 minutes until golden brown, then roast for 20 minutes.

Ballotine of thigh & wild mushrooms
Roasted celeriac: Preheat the oven to 180°C/350°F/gas mark 4. Season the celeriac and place it in a roasting tin. Drizzle with the oil and cook for about 20 minutes or until the celeriac is brown and soft. Remove it from the oven and allow to cool, then break the celeriac into chunks lightly with a fork.

Ballotine: Heat the butter in a frying pan and fry the wild mushrooms for 4–5 minutes. Add the orange zest and cracked juniper berries and cook for 2–3 minutes. Cool. Add the celeriac chunks to the mixture and season. Lay the battened thighs end to end on a sheet of clingfilm and place the stuffing mixture along the centre of the thighs. Roll up the thighs tightly in clingfilm into a sausage shape. Tie each end with string and steam for 10 minutes in a steamer. Remove from the steamer and unwrap.

Juniper berry & madeira jus
Make the basic jus. Heat the oil in a small saucepan and fry the shallot, garlic, juniper berries and orange zest for 2–3 minutes, then add the madeira and reduce by half. Strain the mixture, add it to the basic jus and bring to the boil.

To serve
Place a pheasant breast on the centre of each warm plate with a ballotine of thigh at the side. Drizzle the juniper berry and madeira jus around the plate.

Seared loin of rabbit stuffed with Clonakilty black pudding, smoked sausage cassoulet, ceps dressing

{serves 4}

Seared loin of rabbit stuffed with Clonakilty black pudding
2 rabbit saddles, both fillets off the bone, sinew cut off & flaps battened out
salt & freshly ground black pepper
200 g pig's caul, washed & dried (available from good butchers)
1 tablespoon olive oil

Clonakilty black pudding mixture
100 g Clonakilty black pudding
1 chicken breast, diced
30 ml cream
salt

Smoked sausage cassoulet
200 g haricot blanc beans
1 tablespoon sea salt
1 duck leg
3 sprigs of thyme
2 cloves of garlic, peeled & sliced
100 g smoked bacon, fat removed, diced
1 onion, peeled & halved
1 carrot, peeled & left whole
1 stick of celery, left whole
1 bay leaf
1 tablespoon flat leaf parsley, chopped

1 litre chicken stock (see page 210)
1 Montpellier sausage, cut into 4 pieces
salt & freshly ground black pepper

Ceps dressing
½ litre chicken stock (see page 210)
1 tablespoon olive oil
1 shallot, peeled & finely diced
150 g ceps, cleaned & cut into small dice
salt & freshly ground black pepper

Smoked sausage cassoulet
Soak the beans overnight in a large bowl with three times the volume of water to beans. Sprinkle the sea salt over the duck leg with the thyme and 1 clove of garlic and marinate in a shallow dish overnight in the fridge. Wash off the salt the next day.

Preheat the oven to 160°C/325°F/gas mark 3. Heat a large frying pan to hot and seal the duck leg, fat side down, in a dry pan for 2–3 minutes, releasing the duck fat. Add the smoked bacon, onion, carrot, celery, garlic and herbs and cook in the duck fat for 2–3 minutes before adding the beans and chicken stock. Bring to simmering point and transfer to a large casserole dish. Cover and cook in the oven for 1½ hours, then add the quartered Montpellier sausage and cook for another hour or until cooked. Remove the bay leaf and thyme. Take out the duck leg, carrot, onion, celery and Montpellier sausage and slice them all into bite-sized pieces (removing the duck bone and skin). Return the chopped meat and vegetables to the cassoulet. Remove excess fat from the surface with a ladle or spoon. Season to taste.

Seared loin of rabbit stuffed with Clonakilty black pudding
Clonakilty black pudding mixture: Skin and crumble the black pudding into a food processor, add the chicken pieces, cream and salt and pulverise until smooth. Set aside in a bowl in the fridge until needed.

Seared loin of rabbit: Preheat the oven to 190°C/375°F/gas mark 5. Lay out the four rabbit fillets on a work surface and season them with salt and pepper. Divide the black pudding mixture between the fillets. Wrap the rabbit fillet over itself, covering the stuffing. Cut the pig's caul into four pieces and use it to wrap each of the rabbit fillets. Wrap the fillets in clingfilm and secure tightly. Bring a large saucepan of water to simmering point and poach for 3 minutes. Remove the clingfilm, heat the olive oil in an ovenproof frying pan and seal the rabbit for 2 minutes each side before transferring to the oven for a further 8–10 minutes. Slice each fillet into three pieces for serving.

Ceps dressing
Reduce the chicken stock by half in a saucepan. In a separate frying pan, heat the olive oil and fry the shallot gently for 1 minute before adding the ceps. Continue cooking for 2 minutes. Next add the reduced chicken stock and reduce again by a third. Season to taste.

To serve
Divide the cassoulet between four warm plates. Arrange the seared loins of rabbit beside it and spoon the ceps dressing around the plate.

Roast breast of duck with maple & black pepper glaze, carrot & cumin purée, thyme croquette & confit of carrot

{serves 4}

Roast breast of duck
4 x 200 g Barbary duck breasts

Maple & black pepper glaze
10 black peppercorns
3 coriander seeds
120 ml maple syrup
pinch of salt

Carrot & cumin purée
5 organic carrots, peeled &
* roughly chopped*
1 shallot, peeled & halved
1 clove of garlic,
* peeled & crushed*
1 teaspoon ground cumin

1 tablespoon water
2 tablespoons olive oil
salt & freshly ground
* white pepper*

Thyme croquette
1 tablespoon olive oil
1 shallot, peeled & diced
1 clove of garlic, peeled & crushed
2 sprigs of thyme, finely chopped
2 Rooster potatoes, peeled & diced
150 g plain flour, sifted
1 egg, beaten
100 ml milk
100 g soft white breadcrumbs,
* seasoned*
salt & freshly ground
* white pepper*

Confit of carrot
2 medium organic carrots,
* peeled & halved*
salt & freshly ground
* white pepper*
pinch of ground cumin
300 ml duck fat

Garnish
4 sprigs of thyme

Carrot & cumin purée
Preheat the oven to 180°C/350°F/gas mark 4. Place the carrots, shallot, garlic, cumin and water in a roasting tin. Stir in the olive oil. Cover with tinfoil and roast for 35–40 minutes until tender. Pulverise the carrot mixture in a food processor until smooth. Season with salt and pepper.

Confit of carrot
Place the carrots on a plate and sprinkle with salt, pepper and cumin. Cover and set aside for 1 hour. Gently warm the duck fat in a saucepan. Poach the carrots in duck fat for 15 minutes. Strain the carrots and retain the fat.

Maple & black pepper glaze
Crush the peppercorns and coriander seeds in a pestle and mortar. Place in a saucepan and heat the mixture until it begins to smoke. Add the maple syrup and heat through. Remove from the heat and allow to infuse for 1 hour before adding the salt.

Thyme croquette
Heat the olive oil in a saucepan and gently cook the shallot, garlic and thyme until soft. Set aside to cool. In a separate saucepan, boil the potatoes until soft, then drain and mash them. Add to the cooled shallot mixture. With floured hands, shape and mould the potato mixture into four balls about 5 cm wide.

Preheat the deep-fat fryer to 180°C/350°F. Line up three bowls, one containing the flour, the next the beaten egg and milk mixed together and the third the seasoned breadcrumbs. First roll the potato balls in flour, then, with your other hand, dip the floured potato ball in the egg wash. Using your dry hand, immerse the ball in the breadcrumbs and roll. Repeat the whole flour, egg wash and breadcrumbs process once so that the croquettes won't burst during cooking. Deep fry for 3–4 minutes until golden brown.

Roast breast of duck
Preheat the oven to 220°C/425°F/gas mark 7. Prepare the duck breasts by making criss-cross incisions in the skin with a sharp knife. With the skin side down, seal the breasts in a hot frying pan with no oil for 3 minutes until golden brown. Remove the breasts from the pan and transfer them to a roasting tin. Coat the breasts with maple and black pepper glaze and roast them in the oven, skin side down, for a further 8–10 minutes, depending on the thickness of the duck and the desired pinkness.

To serve
Arrange the carrot and cumin purée along with the thyme croquette and confit of carrot on half of each plate. On the other half, slice and fan the breast of duck and garnish each one with a sprig of thyme.

Roast crown of wild mallard, confit leg, spiced red cabbage, black cherry & cinnamon jus, parsnip mousseline

{serves 4}

Roast crown of wild mallard, confit leg
2 large wild mallard ducks
6 tablespoons Maldon sea salt
freshly ground white pepper
2 sprigs of rosemary, roughly chopped
2 sprigs of thyme, roughly chopped
675 g duck fat

Spiced red cabbage
25 g butter
1 teaspoon turmeric
1 teaspoon ground cumin
1 teaspoon ground coriander
2 tablespoons raisins
1 apple, cored & diced
1 cinnamon stick

1 whole star anise
1 shallot, peeled & diced
1 teaspoon soft brown sugar
1 litre red wine
½ head of red cabbage, shredded
salt & freshly ground black pepper

Black cherry & cinnamon jus
30 g butter
225 g black cherries, stoned
2 cinnamon sticks
2 shallots, peeled & finely diced
1 sprig of rosemary
zest of ½ orange
1 tablespoon sugar
6 tablespoons cherry brandy
2 tablespoons crème de cassis
juice of 1 orange

1 recipe jus (see page 212)
salt & freshly ground black pepper

Parsnip mousseline
4 medium parsnips, peeled, quartered, cored & cut into 6 mm dice
1 clove of garlic, peeled & crushed
2 sprigs of thyme
275 ml cream
70 g butter
salt & freshly ground white pepper

Confit leg
Remove the backbones from the ducks. (They can be used to make duck stock.) Trim the birds and remove the legs. You can ask your butcher to prepare the ducks if you prefer.

Marinate the duck legs overnight in the salt, pepper, rosemary and thyme. The next day, wash off the marinade and pat the legs dry. Melt the duck fat in a small saucepan, immerse the legs in the fat and cook slowly over a medium heat for 30–40 minutes until tender. Trim off any ragged edges of meat at the lower end of the leg, leaving about 3 cm of bone showing.

Spiced red cabbage
Heat the butter in a large saucepan and fry all the ingredients except the red wine, cabbage and seasoning for 3–4 minutes or until the shallots have softened. Add the red wine and bring to a simmer. Add the cabbage and cook slowly with the lid on for 40–45 minutes until tender. Season.

Roast crown of wild mallard
Preheat the oven to 180°C/350°F/gas mark 4. Season the crowns with salt and pepper. Heat a frying pan until smoking and cook the crowns, skin side down, for about 3–4 minutes each side until golden brown, then transfer them to a roasting tin, skin side up, and roast for about 25 minutes.

Black cherry & cinnamon jus
Melt the butter in a small saucepan, add the cherries, cinnamon, shallots, rosemary and orange zest and slowly cook until soft. Add the sugar and caramelise the mixture. Loosen the mixture with the cherry brandy, crème de cassis and orange juice, then simmer gently until it has reduced by half. Strain through a fine sieve, add the jus and reduce slowly to a sauce consistency. Season.

Parsnip mousseline
Place the diced parsnips in a small saucepan with the garlic, thyme, cream and butter. Cover and simmer gently for about 15 minutes until the parsnip is cooked. Remove the thyme and blend the mixture in a food processor. Season. Keep warm.

To serve
Pile some cabbage in the centre of each warm plate and place a roast crown on top with a confit leg to the side. Pipe a line of parsnip mousseline down the side of the plate and drizzle black cherry and cinnamon jus over the duck.

Char-grilled marinated rack of lamb, spiced root vegetables, pomme fondant, lemon & thyme jus

{serves 4}

Char-grilled marinated rack of lamb
2 x 400 g racks of lamb,
  French trimmed
  (ask your butcher to do this)
salt & freshly ground black pepper

Marinade
1 sprig of rosemary
1 clove of garlic, peeled & sliced
1 sprig of thyme
50 ml soy sauce
200 ml vegetable oil
½ teaspoon cracked peppercorns

Spiced root vegetables
2 tablespoons sunflower oil
2 shallots, peeled & diced
1 clove of garlic, peeled & sliced
1 teaspoon five spice powder
½ teaspoon ground coriander
½ teaspoon ground cumin
400 g root vegetables
  (turnip, carrot, celeriac,
  parsnip, fennel bulb), peeled,
  washed & cut into 1 cm dice
40 g butter, melted
10 g parsley, chopped

Pomme fondant
4 medium-large Rooster potatoes,
  peeled
25 g butter, melted
150 ml chicken stock (see page 210)
1 sprig of parsley, finely chopped
salt & freshly ground white pepper

Lemon & thyme jus
15 g butter
zest of 1 lemon
1 shallot, peeled & diced
1 clove of garlic, peeled & sliced
3 sprigs of thyme
juice of ½ lemon
1 tablespoon white wine
200 ml beef jus (see page 212)
salt & freshly ground black pepper

Char-grilled marinated rack of lamb
Mix all the marinade ingredients together in a bowl and marinate the lamb overnight. Preheat the oven to 190°C/375°F/gas mark 5. Remove the racks of lamb from the marinade. Heat a griddle pan until very hot and seal the lamb on the pan for 1 minute each side before transferring to the oven. Continue cooking for a further 7–8 minutes for rare, 10–12 minutes for medium and 15–18 minutes for well done. Remove from the oven and season. Keep warm. Slice the cutlets just before serving.

Pomme fondant
Preheat the oven to 190°C/375°F/gas mark 5. Trim the tops and bottoms from the potatoes until they are 5–6 cm high, then pare them down until they are slim barrel shapes (turned potatoes). Brush them with a little melted butter. Place the potatoes in a small, deep ovenproof dish and pour enough chicken stock over them to come half-way up the sides. Cook for 25 minutes until the potatoes are golden brown and tender. Remove from the dish and brush with more butter, then toss in parsley. Season and keep warm.

Spiced root vegetables
Heat the oil in a medium-sized saucepan and add the shallots, garlic and spices. Stir in the turnip, carrot and celeriac and colour them before adding the parsnip and fennel. Continue cooking over a medium heat for a further 15–17 minutes until the vegetables are tender. Toss in melted butter and parsley before serving.

Lemon & thyme jus
Melt the butter in a small saucepan and gently cook the lemon zest, shallot, garlic and thyme until soft. Add the lemon juice and wine and reduce by half. Next pour in the jus and reduce to a sauce consistency. Pass through a sieve, retaining the sauce, and season. Keep warm.

To serve
Spoon a pile of the spiced root vegetables into the centre of each plate. Arrange the cutlets around them so that the lamb bones are standing proud, spoon on the pomme fondant and drizzle the jus around the plate.

Roast loin of wild Irish venison, venison cutlet, candied pear, celeriac mousseline, beetroot jus & candied pecan

{serves 4}

Roast loin of wild Irish venison, venison cutlet
4 x 150 g loins of venison, trimmed
2 tablespoons olive oil
4 x 50 g venison cutlets
salt & freshly ground white pepper

Marinade
1 medium carrot, peeled & diced
1 stick of celery, diced
2 cloves of garlic, peeled & sliced
2 sprigs of rosemary
2 sprigs of thyme
150 ml red wine
40 ml red wine vinegar

Candied pear
4 Conference pears, peeled & cored
  with an apple corer
200 ml water
100 g caster sugar
1 sprig of thyme

Roast loin of wild Irish venison, venison cutlet
Marinate the venison: Cover the trimmed venison loins in a bowl with all the marinade ingredients. Cover with clingfilm and refrigerate for 24 hours.

Cook the venison: Drain the venison loins on kitchen paper to remove any excess marinade. Keep the marinade liquid, as you'll need it for the beetroot jus. Season the loins. Heat a tablespoon of oil in an ovenproof frying pan and seal the loins for 3–4 minutes before transferring them to the oven. Cook for a further 4–5 minutes for rare, 7–8 minutes for medium or 10–12 minutes for well done. Set the loins aside to rest.

Heat a tablespoon of olive oil in a frying pan and cook the cutlets for 2 minutes each side.

Beetroot jus
Roasted beetroot: Preheat the oven to 180°C/350°F/gas mark 4. Drizzle the beetroots with a tablespoon of olive oil and wrap them up in tinfoil. Place them in a roasting tin and roast for an hour until tender. Cool the beetroots, then peel them and retain the skins for the beetroot jus. Using a sharp knife, trim the beetroots into cylinders.

Jus: Heat 1 tablespoon of olive oil in a heavy-based saucepan and cook the shallot, carrot, celery, garlic, ginger and herbs gently for 5 minutes before adding the beetroot skins. Increase the heat and add the port, balsamic vinegar and sugar and cook for 2–3 minutes until the jus has a syrupy consistency. Next add the meat stock and cook it steadily until its volume has reduced by half. Pour in the venison marinade liquid and reduce by half again. Strain the jus through a muslin cloth, discarding the vegetables. Transfer the jus back to the saucepan and simmer. Add the beetroot cylinders. Season with salt and pepper.

Celeriac mousseline

1 tablespoon olive oil
1 shallot, peeled & diced
1 clove of garlic, peeled & crushed
1 sprig of thyme
200 g celeriac, peeled & diced
100 ml milk
100 ml cream
1 large Rooster potato, cooked,
  mashed & cooled
salt & freshly ground white pepper

Beetroot jus

4 medium beetroots
2 tablespoons olive oil
1 shallot, peeled & diced
1 medium carrot, peeled & diced
2 sticks of celery, diced
2 cloves of garlic, peeled & sliced
1 cm piece of root ginger, peeled &
  finely sliced
2 sprigs of rosemary
2 sprigs of thyme
skins from roasted beetroot, diced
75 ml ruby port
1 tablespoon balsamic vinegar

100 g brown sugar
150 ml beef or veal stock
  (see page 210)
venison marinade (after venison
  removed)
salt & freshly ground white pepper

Candied pecan

75 ml water
75 g caster sugar
25 g pecans

Celeriac mousseline

Heat the olive oil and gently cook the shallot, garlic and
thyme for 5 minutes before adding the diced celeriac.
Pour in the milk and cream to cover the celeriac and cook
for 10–12 minutes until tender. Transfer to a food
processor and pulverise. Add the mashed potato and
season with salt and pepper. Blend again. Keep warm.

Candied pear

Using a sharp knife, cut each pear into four cylinder
shapes. Heat the water, caster sugar and thyme in a
heavy-based saucepan until the sugar has dissolved and
bring to simmering point. Poach the pear cylinders in the
syrup for 2–3 minutes until tender, depending on the
ripeness of the pears. Using a perforated spoon, remove
the pears from the hot syrup and set aside. Reserve a
tablespoon of syrup to reheat the pears. For serving,
reheat the pear pieces in a small frying pan with the
tablespoon of syrup and cook them until they are
caramelised and golden brown.

Candied pecan

Place the water and sugar in a saucepan and boil steadily
for 5 minutes, bringing the syrup to the soft ball stage
(121°C/250°F). Add the pecans and cook for 1 minute
before carefully removing them with a perforated spoon.

To serve

Cut each venison loin into three pieces. Arrange the
venison, beetroot and sausage on four warmed plates.
Garnish with candied pecan and candied pear. Using a
piping bag, pipe the celeriac mousseline around the edges
of the plate.

Roast glazed rump of lamb with tomato & mint chutney, white onion mousseline, mushroom consommé

{serves 4}

Roast glazed rump of lamb
4 x 200 g lamb rumps
2 tablespoons olive oil
salt & freshly ground black pepper

Marinade
150 ml soy sauce
150 ml port
2 tablespoons rosemary, chopped
5 tablespoons honey
1 tablespoon balsamic vinegar
juice of 1 orange

Tomato & mint chutney
50 g brown sugar
50 ml red wine vinegar
400 g tin of tomatoes
1 bay leaf
salt & freshly ground
black pepper
1 tablespoon mint, chopped

White onion mousseline
25 g butter
1 large onion, peeled & sliced
1 clove of garlic, peeled & crushed
1 bay leaf
1 sprig of thyme
150 ml chicken stock (see page 210)
150 ml cream
salt & freshly ground
white pepper
1 medium potato,
cooked & mashed

Mushroom consommé
250 ml cold beef or veal stock
(see page 210)
1 medium carrot, peeled & diced
1 medium onion, peeled & diced
1 bay leaf
2 sprigs of rosemary
1 clove of garlic, peeled & crushed
1 egg white
100 g wild mushrooms, sautéed
(sliced if large)
salt & freshly ground
white pepper

Roast glazed rump of lamb
Combine all the marinade ingredients in a bowl. Add the lamb, cover and marinate overnight in the fridge. Preheat the oven to 190°C/375°F/gas mark 5. Heat the olive oil in a non-stick frying pan and seal the rumps of lamb. Season. Transfer to the oven and cook for about 8–10 minutes for medium-rare, 10–12 minutes for medium and 15–18 minutes for well done. Take the lamb out of the oven and leave to rest, covered, in a warm place for about 5 minutes.

Tomato & mint chutney
Place all the ingredients except the mint and the seasoning in a heavy-based saucepan and cook over a very low heat for 1 hour or until most of the liquid has evaporated. Remove the bay leaf. Add salt and pepper, allow to cool and add the mint.

White onion mousseline
Heat the butter in a saucepan and cook the onion and garlic over a gentle heat until they are translucent. Turn up the heat and add the bay leaf, thyme and chicken stock and reduce until the liquid has almost evaporated. Add the cream and continue to cook until the cream has reduced by half and the onion is cooked. Remove the bay leaf and thyme, then pulverise in a food processor. Add the salt, pepper and warm mashed potato. Keep warm.

Mushroom consommé
Place all the ingredients except the mushrooms and seasoning in a saucepan. Bring to boiling point, stirring constantly with a wooden spoon. Reduce the heat, stop stirring and simmer very slowly for 10 minutes. Remove surplus scum from the top of the stock with a ladle. Strain through damp muslin. Add the mushrooms and season.

To serve
Spoon the white onion mousseline into four warm bowls. Slice and arrange the rump of lamb on top. Pour the mushroom consommé around the lamb. Finally, top the lamb with a spoonful of tomato and mint chutney.

Seared fillet of beef with horseradish crust, flash-fried pak choi & chillies, crisp sweet potato & pickled walnut butter

{serves 4}

Seared fillet of beef with horseradish crust
4 x 150 g fillets of beef
1 tablespoon olive oil
salt & freshly ground
  black pepper
2 teaspoons creamed horseradish
25 g soft white breadcrumbs

Flash-fried pak choi & chillies
1 tablespoon sunflower oil
4 heads of baby pak choi,
  sliced crossways
2 red chillies,
  deseeded & finely diced
1 tablespoon honey
1 tablespoon soy sauce
1 tablespoon balsamic vinegar
salt & freshly ground
  black pepper

Crisp sweet potato
1 sweet potato
100 ml stock syrup (see page 215)

Pickled walnut butter
100 g salted butter
1 clove of garlic, peeled
1 sprig of thyme
salt & freshly ground white pepper
25 g pickled walnuts

Garnish
4 sprigs of watercress

Crisp sweet potato
Preheat the oven to 110°C/225°F/gas mark ¼. Peel and thinly slice the sweet potato (½ cm thick). Drop the slices into the stock syrup to coat. Arrange in a single layer on a baking sheet. Transfer to the oven and cook for 1 hour until crisp.

Pickled walnut butter
Blend the softened salted butter, garlic, thyme, salt and pepper with the pickled walnuts in a food processor. Transfer to greaseproof paper about 10 cm x 12 cm. Roll the paper around the butter to form a cylinder about 3 cm x 7 cm. Refrigerate until required.

Flash-fried pak choi & chillies
Heat the sunflower oil in a hot wok. Add the pak choi and chillies and cook for a couple of minutes. Next add the honey, soy sauce and balsamic vinegar. Season with salt and pepper.

Seared fillet of beef with horseradish crust
Preheat the grill to high. If you prefer medium to well-done steaks, preheat the oven to 190°C/375°F/gas mark 5. Heat the oil in a hot non-stick frying pan. Season the steaks and sear them in the pan for 5–7 minutes for rare. For medium or well-done steaks, transfer the seared steaks to the oven and cook for 5 minutes for medium or 10 minutes for well done, turning the steaks depending on their thickness.

Spoon the creamed horseradish over the steaks, cover with the breadcrumbs and brown under the grill.

To serve
Spoon the pak choi and chillies on to the centre of each warm plate and arrange a fillet on top. Slice the pickled walnut butter in four and allow to melt slightly on the hot fillets. Finally, garnish with the crisp sweet potato and a sprig of watercress.

Soy & honey glazed belly of pork confit, onion mash, glazed apricot, apple & cider froth

{serves 4}

Soy & honey glazed belly of pork confit
800 g piece of pork belly, bones removed, trimmed of excess fat
500 ml duck fat
50 ml chicken stock (see page 210)

Marinade
8 juniper berries, crushed
1 unpeeled orange, roughly chopped
120 g sea salt

Soy & honey glaze
200 ml soy sauce
3 tablespoons honey

Onion mash
50 g butter
1 medium onion, peeled & finely diced
2 large Rooster potatoes, boiled & mashed
salt & freshly ground white pepper

Glazed apricot
1 fresh apricot, stoned & quartered
50 ml stock syrup (see page 215)

Apple & cider froth
1 recipe froth (see page 213)
1 Granny Smith apple, stewed & puréed
100 ml cider

Soy & honey glazed belly of pork confit
Soy & honey glaze: Bring the soy sauce to the boil in a heavy-based saucepan, then reduce the heat until it's lightly simmering. Skim any impurities that rise to the surface. When the soy is thick enough to coat the back of a spoon heavily, strain it through a fine sieve. Add the honey and stir well over a low heat until it comes together. Taste and add more honey if required.

Marinade: Cover the pork belly with the marinade ingredients and marinate overnight in a covered, deep earthenware container in the fridge. Remove from the marinade the next day, wash the meat and pat dry with kitchen paper. Preheat the oven to 150°C/300°F/gas mark 2. Melt the duck fat, pour it over the pork belly and roast the meat for 2½ hours. Remove the pork belly, now pork confit, from the duck fat and place between two baking trays. Lay a heavy weight on top to flatten the confit. Cool.

Preheat the oven to 180°C/350°F/gas mark 4. Cut the pork confit into four equal portions. Heat a dry frying pan and seal the confit, skin side down, in the pan for 3–4 minutes, then put it in a roasting tin, skin side up. Brush the pork confit with the chicken stock, then with the soy and honey glaze, and roast in the oven for 5 minutes.

Preheat the grill to medium. Brush the pork confit with the chicken stock and soy and honey glaze again. Place under the grill, skin side up, for 2 minutes.

Onion mash
Heat the butter in a medium-sized saucepan and add the diced onion. Cook over a gentle heat until the onions are soft but not brown. Add the mashed potato and season. Keep warm.

Glazed apricot
Preheat the grill to medium. Glaze the apricot quarters with the stock syrup and grill until the apricot is golden. Serve at room temperature.

Apple & cider froth
Make the basic froth recipe, but add the apple purée and half the cider with the first addition of cream and add the remaining cider at the end with the rest of the cream.

To serve
Spoon the onion mash on to four warm plates. Arrange the soy and honey glazed pork confit beside it. Drizzle with the apple and cider froth and, finally, garnish with the glazed apricot.

Roast cutlet of veal, white onion Tarte Tatin, pine nut paste, port wine beurre rouge & gremolata

{serves 4}

Roast cutlet of veal
4 x 250 g veal cutlets
salt & freshly ground white pepper
1 tablespoon olive oil

White onion Tarte Tatin
4 medium white onions
250 g puff pastry (see page 214 or
* use frozen)*
1 sprig of rosemary, finely chopped
1 clove of garlic, peeled & crushed
1 tablespoon balsamic vinegar
1 tablespoon port
50 g caster sugar
50 g unsalted butter, melted

Pine nut paste
100 g pine nuts, toasted & cooled
25 g Parmesan cheese, grated
5 basil leaves
½ clove of garlic, peeled & chopped
1 tablespoon olive oil
salt & freshly ground black pepper

Port wine beurre rouge
1 recipe beurre rouge,
* substituting 150 ml port for*
* 150 ml red wine*
* (see page 213)*

Gremolata
50 g Parmesan cheese,
* roughly grated*
½ clove of garlic, peeled &
* finely chopped*
1 tablespoon olive oil
zest & juice of ½ lemon
2 small bunches of parsley,
* chopped*
Maldon sea salt & freshly
* ground black pepper*

White onion Tarte Tatin
Preheat the oven to 190°C/375°F/gas mark 5. Peel the onions right down until they are 5 cm wide. Cut off the tops and bottoms, making them 2½ cm high. Roll out the pastry to ½ cm thickness and, using a 10 cm cutter, make four 10 cm circles. Cover the bottom and sides of the onion with the pastry. Mix the rosemary, garlic, balsamic vinegar, port, sugar and melted butter together and divide between the four cups of a muffin tin. Place the pastry-covered onions into the cups with the covered pastry side up. Bake for 20 minutes until the pastry is golden brown. Use two spoons to remove the Tarte Tatins for serving.

Pine nut paste
Blend all the ingredients except the salt and pepper in a food processor until they form a paste. Season.

Port wine beurre rouge
Make the basic beurre rouge recipe, substituting port for red wine.

Gremolata
Mix all the ingredients except the salt and pepper together in a bowl and season.

Roast cutlet of veal
Preheat the oven to 190°C/375°F/gas mark 5. Season the cutlets. Heat the olive oil in a frying pan and seal the cutlets for 1 minute each side. Transfer to the oven and cook for a further 12 minutes.

To serve
Arrange a Tarte Tatin on each plate and lay a veal cutlet beside it. Put a spoonful of pine nut paste on each plate. Sprinkle the gremolata over each veal cutlet. Finally, drizzle the port wine beurre rouge around each plate.

Seared veal liver with whipped cheese & onion potatoes, crisp cured bacon, onion gravy

{serves 4}

Seared veal liver
600 g veal liver
2 tablespoons sunflower oil
salt & freshly ground black pepper

Whipped cheese & onion potatoes
3 large Rooster potatoes, peeled &
  cut into chunks
1 tablespoon sunflower oil
½ medium onion, peeled & sliced
100 g smoked Applewood cheese,
  grated
salt & freshly ground white pepper

Crisp cured bacon
1 teaspoon vegetable oil
4 rashers of streaky bacon

Onion gravy
65 g butter
1 medium onion, peeled &
  finely sliced
1 tablespoon white wine
500 ml jus (see page 212)
salt & freshly ground black pepper

Whipped cheese & onion potatoes
Boil the potatoes in a saucepan of salted water until tender, then drain and mash them. Meanwhile, heat the sunflower oil in a frying pan and cook the sliced onion gently for 8–10 minutes until translucent. Mix the mashed potatoes, grated cheese and sautéed onion together. Season with salt and pepper and keep warm.

Crisp cured bacon
Preheat the oven to 180°C/350°F/gas mark 4. Grease a baking tray with the vegetable oil and lay the rashers flat on the tray without overlapping. Grease the underside of another tray and place it on top. Cook for 15–18 minutes until crisp.

Onion gravy
Melt 40 g of the butter in a frying pan and cook the onion gently for 8–10 minutes until translucent. Add the white wine and reduce it by half. Next add the jus and simmer gently until the sauce has a coating consistency. Skim with a spoon and remove from the heat. Mix in the remaining butter and season to taste.

Seared veal liver
Slice the veal liver 1 cm thick with a long, straight-edged knife. Heat the oil in a large frying pan until it's hot and quickly sear the veal liver for 90 seconds each side, turning with a tongs. Season and serve immediately.

To serve
Pile the potatoes into the centre of each of four warm plates. Place the seared veal liver on top, pour over the onion gravy and finally place the crisp cured bacon on top.

Chilled char-grilled vegetables, red pepper jelly & chutney

{serves 4}

Chilled char-grilled vegetables
Char-grilled vegetables
1 aubergine, sliced ½ cm
  thick lengthways
1 red pepper, quartered & deseeded
1 yellow pepper,
  quartered & deseeded
1 green pepper,
  quartered & deseeded
1 courgette, topped & tailed,
  sliced lengthways
1 red onion, peeled &
  cut into 8 segments
5 tablespoons olive oil
salt & freshly ground black pepper

Basil pesto
6 sprigs of basil
1 clove of garlic,
  peeled & left whole
75 g Parmesan cheese, grated
75 g pine nuts, toasted & cooled
200 ml olive oil
salt & freshly ground black pepper

Red pepper jelly
2 red peppers, roasted,
  peeled & deseeded
½ clove of garlic, peeled & sliced
salt & freshly ground white pepper
2 leaves of gelatine
200 ml water

Red pepper chutney
1 tablespoon olive oil
1 clove of garlic, peeled & sliced
1 red onion, peeled & finely sliced
½ teaspoon ground cumin
1 sprig of thyme
1 bay leaf
2 red peppers, roasted, peeled,
  deseeded & roughly chopped
1 tablespoon caster sugar
2 tablespoons red wine
1 tablespoon red wine vinegar
salt & freshly ground black pepper

Red pepper jelly

Pulverise the roasted red peppers with the garlic in a food processor. Season with salt and pepper. Soak the gelatine leaves for 3–4 minutes in a bowl of ice-cold water. Heat the roasted red pepper purée in 200 ml water. Drain the gelatine leaves and dissolve them in the heated purée. Pass through a fine sieve and allow to set for 2–3 hours.

Red pepper chutney

Heat the olive oil in a medium-sized saucepan and gently cook the garlic, onion, ground cumin, thyme and bay leaf for 3–4 minutes until soft. Add the red peppers and caster sugar and cook for 1–2 minutes until syrupy. Add the red wine and red wine vinegar and reduce until all the liquid has evaporated (about 5 minutes). Remove the bay leaf and thyme. Season and cool.

Chilled char-grilled vegetables

Char-grilled vegetables: Pour the olive oil into a shallow dish and toss the vegetables in it. Season with salt and pepper. Heat a griddle pan to hot. Char the aubergines for 2 minutes each side and remove, cook the pepper for 3 minutes each side and remove and, finally, cook the onion segments and courgettes for 2 minutes each side.

Basil pesto: Blend all the ingredients except the salt and pepper in a food processor. Season to taste.

Assembly: Roughly chop the courgettes, peppers and onions. Add 3 tablespoons of basil pesto and mix. Cut the aubergine slices in half. Lay four 8 cm ring moulds on a small tray and layer the sandwich as follows: half a slice of aubergine, 1 tablespoon of pesto vegetables, half a slice of aubergine, 1 tablespoon of pesto vegetables, topping off with half a slice of aubergine. Refrigerate until needed.

To serve

Arrange the chilled char-grilled vegetables on four cooled plates. Serve with a spoonful each of the red pepper chutney and red pepper jelly.

Ricotta & basil gnocchi, French beans with sweet mustard, pine nut tapenade, Parmesan froth

{serves 4}

Ricotta & basil gnocchi
50 g 00 or strong white flour
30 g semolina
100 g baked potato,
  peeled & mashed
20 g Ricotta cheese
1 egg
10 basil leaves, finely shredded
salt
1 tablespoon plain flour

French beans with sweet mustard
150 g French beans,
  topped & tailed

Sweet mustard
4 teaspoons home-made
  mayonnaise (see page 212)
1 teaspoon wholegrain mustard
½ clove of garlic, peeled &
  finely chopped
1 teaspoon honey
salt & freshly ground white pepper

Pine nut tapenade
100 g pine nuts, toasted & cooled
40 g Parmesan cheese
3 sprigs of basil

2 tablespoons olive oil
6 black olives
1 tablespoon non pareil
  (baby) capers
½ clove of garlic, peeled &
  chopped
salt & freshly ground black pepper

Parmesan froth
1 recipe froth (see page 213)
60 g Parmesan cheese, finely grated

Garnish
4 caper berries (available from
  good delis)
2 teaspoons olive oil
2 cherry tomatoes, halved

Ricotta & basil gnocchi
Sift the flour with the semolina into a large bowl and add the potato. Next add the Ricotta, egg, basil leaves and a pinch of salt, and mix to form a stable mixture. Sprinkle the tablespoon of flour on to the work surface, roll out the mixture to form a cylinder and divide it into 16 pieces. Shape the pieces into 16 tiny dumplings and depress each one lightly with a floured fork. Bring a large saucepan of salted water to the boil and poach the gnocchi for 5–6 minutes. Drain well. To reheat for serving, plunge the gnocchi into boiling salted water for 30 seconds.

French beans with sweet mustard
French beans: Plunge the French beans into a saucepan of boiling salted water and cook for 2 minutes. Drain the beans, refresh them in ice-cold water, then drain them again. Keep warm.

Sweet mustard: Mix all the ingredients except the seasoning together in a bowl with a spoon. Season to taste.

Pine nut tapenade
Place all the ingredients except the seasoning in a food processor and blend roughly. Season to taste.

Parmesan froth
Make the froth following the basic froth recipe and add the finely grated Parmesan.

Garnish
Preheat the oven to 170°C/325°F/gas mark 3. Place the halved tomatoes in a roasting tin, drizzle with the olive oil and cook for 15 minutes.

To serve
Divide the French beans between four warm plates. Spoon over the sweet mustard and place four gnocchi on each plate. Carefully place a spoonful of pine nut tapenade on each plate before drizzling with the Parmesan froth. Garnish with a caper berry and half a roasted tomato.

Tempura of organic vegetables with oven-dried aubergine, chilli jam & aïoli

{serves 4}

Tempura of organic vegetables
Organic vegetables
4 x 35 g cauliflower pieces
4 x 15 g broccoli pieces
4 x baby carrots, peeled & trimmed
4 x baby courgettes, topped & tailed
1 red pepper, quartered & deseeded
2 tablespoons plain flour
salt & freshly ground white pepper

Tempura batter
80 ml iced water
100 g cornflour, sifted

Oven-dried aubergine
25 g sugar
100 ml water
1 aubergine

Chilli jam
150 ml red wine vinegar
150 ml red wine
100 g sugar
1 cm piece of root ginger, peeled
 & grated
8 red chillies, deseeded & finely
 diced

Aïoli
½ recipe aïoli (see page 212)

Oven-dried aubergine
Preheat the oven to 100°C/200°F/gas mark ¼. Dissolve the sugar in the water and bring the mixture to the boil in a medium-sized saucepan, then remove the pan from the heat. Allow the water and sugar to cool slightly and transfer to a shallow container. Slice the aubergine as thinly as possible, using a sharp serrated knife. Dip the sliced aubergine into the water and sugar and lay the slices on a non-stick silicone baking mat. Bake for 45–55 minutes until dry.

Chilli jam
Place all the ingredients except the chillies in a small saucepan. Cook over gentle heat for 20 minutes. Remove from the heat, add the chopped chillies and allow to cool.

Aïoli
Make the basic aïoli recipe given on page 212, using half quantities.

Tempura of organic vegetables
Tempura batter: Add the water to the cornflour in a bowl and whisk until a batter consistency is achieved.

Organic vegetables: Preheat the deep-fat fryer to 170°C/340°F. Bring a medium-sized saucepan of water to simmering point. Plunge the cauliflower, broccoli and carrots in the water and cook for 2 minutes. (The courgettes and red pepper don't need to be precooked.) Drain the vegetables and refresh in a bowl of ice-cold water. Toss all the organic vegetables in a shallow dish with the flour, shaking off the excess. Dip the vegetables in the tempura batter, shaking off the excess. Deep fry for 2–3 minutes until golden brown, then drain the tempura and transfer them to a tray lined with kitchen paper. Season with salt and pepper. Keep warm.

To serve
Arrange the aubergine and organic vegetables in the centre of each plate. Put a spoonful of the aïoli at the side and drizzle the chilli jam about the plate.

Tomato plate: tartelette, sorbet, Bloody Mary & salad with crisp fried onions

{serves 4}

Tomato tartelette
4 plum tomatoes, skinned
250 g puff pastry
  (see page 214 or use frozen)
1 sprig of rosemary, finely chopped
1 clove of garlic, peeled & crushed
1 tablespoon balsamic vinegar
1 tablespoon port
50 g caster sugar
50 g unsalted butter, melted
salt & freshly ground black pepper

Tomato sorbet
1 plum tomato, skinned
1 clove of garlic, peeled & crushed
¼ cucumber, peeled & chopped
½ red pepper, deseeded & chopped
½ red chilli, deseeded & chopped
1 sprig of basil
300 ml tomato juice
40 ml vodka
60 ml stock syrup (see page 215)
salt & freshly ground black pepper

Bloody Mary
30 ml vodka
120 ml tomato juice
pinch of salt
1–2 drops Tabasco
2–3 drops Worcestershire sauce

Salad with crisp fried onions
1 medium onion, peeled & finely
  sliced
1 tablespoon plain flour
1 tablespoon balsamic vinegar
3 tablespoons olive oil
salt & freshly ground black pepper
50 g assorted salad leaves

Tomato sorbet

Blend the tomato, garlic, cucumber, red pepper, chilli and basil in a food processor. Pass through a sieve before adding the tomato juice, vodka and stock syrup. Season to taste. Transfer to an ice-cream maker and churn until frozen. Alternatively, pour the mixture into a shallow container and freeze to a slush. Whisk well every hour so the sorbet becomes light and fine grained.

Tomato tartelette

Preheat the oven to 190°C/375°F/gas mark 5. Trim the tops and bottoms of the skinned tomatoes until they are 2½ cm high. Roll out the pastry to ½ cm thickness and make four circles, using a 10 cm cutter. Cover the bottom and sides of the tomato with the pastry. Mix the rosemary, garlic, balsamic vinegar, port, sugar, melted butter and seasoning together and divide between four greased cups of a muffin tin. Place the pastry-covered tomatoes into the cups with the pastry side up. Bake for 20 minutes until the pastry is golden brown. Use a spoon to remove them for serving.

Bloody Mary

Mix all the ingredients with some crushed ice in a cocktail shaker before dividing between four chilled glasses.

Salad with crisp fried onions

Preheat a deep-fat fryer to 170°C/340°F. Toss the sliced onion in a little flour and shake off the excess. Deep fry until golden brown and crispy and drain on kitchen paper. Mix the balsamic vinegar, olive oil, salt and pepper together to make a dressing. Toss the salad leaves in the dressing.

To serve

Place the dressed salad leaves on chilled plates and scatter with the deep-fried onions. Arrange the tomato tartelette beside the salad before scooping on the tomato sorbet. Serve with a glass of Bloody Mary.

Wild mushroom risotto with black truffles & baby spinach, slow oven-roasted plum tomato

{serves 4}

Wild mushroom risotto with black truffles & baby spinach

250 g seasonal wild mushrooms, cleaned with a small brush to remove grit, sliced, trimmings retained for stock
2 tablespoons sunflower oil
2 shallots, peeled & diced
½ tablespoon fresh thyme leaves
1 clove of garlic, peeled & crushed
300 g Arborio rice
1 litre mushroom stock (see right)
80 g baby spinach leaves, washed
2 tablespoons crème fraîche

2 tablespoons fresh tarragon leaves
salt & freshly ground white pepper
10 g black truffle shavings, made using a vegetable peeler

Mushroom stock

1 tablespoon olive oil
1 shallot, peeled & diced
½ clove of garlic, peeled & crushed
10 tarragon leaves
trimmings from fresh wild mushrooms
25 g dried wild mushrooms, soaked in 250 ml water for 15–20 minutes

Slow oven-roasted plum tomato

2 large ripe plum tomatoes
1 teaspoon rock salt
pinch of cracked black pepper
½ teaspoon fresh thyme leaves
1 clove of garlic, peeled & sliced

Garnish

4 sprigs of Italian parsley

Slow oven-roasted plum tomato

Preheat the oven to 80°C/170°F/gas mark ¼. Using a small, sharp knife, cut the core from the stalk end of each tomato. Halve the tomatoes lengthways and place them on a roasting tin with the cut side up. Sprinkle each with the rock salt, pepper, thyme and slivers of garlic. Place in the oven and cook for 1¼ hours. Transfer to another dish to cool.

Wild mushroom risotto with black truffles & baby spinach

Mushroom stock: Heat the olive oil in a medium-sized saucepan and cook the shallot, garlic and tarragon gently for 5 minutes. Stir in the mushroom trimmings and cook for a further 2 minutes. Add the soaked wild mushrooms, including the liquid in which they were soaked. Bring the volume of liquid up to 1 litre by adding water. Bring to the boil, reduce the heat and simmer for 1 hour. Pass through a sieve and top up with water if necessary to bring the volume back to 1 litre.

Risotto: Heat 1 tablespoon of sunflower oil in a heavy-based saucepan. Add the shallots, thyme and garlic and cook on a low heat for a few minutes. Add the rice and stir until it is coated with the oil. Add the hot mushroom stock, ladle by ladle, allowing each to be absorbed before adding the next. Continue cooking until all the liquid is absorbed but the rice still retains a bite. (This should take about 15–18 minutes.) In a separate saucepan cook the fresh wild mushrooms in the remaining tablespoon of sunflower oil and add them to the rice. Stir in the baby spinach leaves and allow them to wilt in the rice mixture. Stir in the crème fraîche, tarragon, salt and pepper. Finally, garnish with the black truffle shavings.

To serve

Divide the wild mushroom risotto between four warm bowls or plates. Place the oven-roasted tomatoes on top and garnish with a sprig of Italian parsley.

Chilled summer fruits risotto with natural yoghurt, warm orange & cardamom syrup

{serves 4}

Chilled summer fruits risotto with natural yoghurt
150 g Arborio rice
1 dessertspoon sunflower oil
570 ml water
1 vanilla pod, split
50 g sugar
240 ml milk
1 dessertspoon natural yoghurt
150 g strawberries
300 g raspberries

Warm orange & cardamom syrup
200 ml orange juice
8 cardamom pods
100 g granulated sugar
2 oranges, peeled, segmented
  & chopped

Garnish
4 teaspoons natural yoghurt
100 g strawberries
100 g raspberries

Chilled summer fruits risotto with natural yoghurt
Heat the sunflower oil in a medium-sized saucepan. Add the Arborio rice, stir, coating the rice with the oil, and cook gently for 3 minutes. Meanwhile heat the water in a separate saucepan. Add the water to the rice ladle by ladle, stirring constantly. With a knife, scrape the seeds from the vanilla pod into the rice mixture, then add the split pod. Continue to stir, allowing the rice to simmer until all the water is absorbed (12–15 minutes) and the rice is cooked. Add the sugar, milk and natural yoghurt and mix. Remove the vanilla pod and cool. Transfer to a bowl and gently mix in the strawberries and raspberries. Refrigerate.

Warm orange & cardamom syrup
Place the juice, cardamom pods and granulated sugar in a medium-sized saucepan. Heat the mixture gently until the sugar has dissolved, increase the heat and reduce by half. Remove the pods, allow to cool slightly and add the orange pieces.

To serve
Place an 8 cm ring mould in a cool bowl. Using a spoon, fill the mould with the chilled risotto and top with a teaspoon of natural yoghurt. Remove the ring mould and repeat the process with the other three bowls. Arrange the berries around the risottos and drizzle the warm orange and cardamom syrup over them.

Terrine of summer berries, clotted cream, lemon custard

{serves 8}

Terrine of summer berries
250 g blueberries
250 g blackberries
550 ml raspberry coulis
 (raspberry purée)
2 tablespoons water
8 slices of white bread,
 crusts removed
4 leaves of gelatine
pinch of ground cinnamon or
 1 whole star anise (optional)

Clotted cream
8 dessertspoons clotted cream
 (available from any good
 food store)

Lemon custard
275 ml cream
275 ml milk
zest of 1 lemon
6 egg yolks
100 g caster sugar

Terrine of summer berries
Line a 23 cm x 12 cm loaf tin with a double wrapping of clingfilm in a criss-cross fashion, ensuring that it covers all the sides, leaving an excess to cover the top later. Using half of the coulis and 2 tablespoons of water, soak the bread in a wide tray. Soak the gelatine leaves in ice-cold water in a bowl for 3–4 minutes until soft, then drain off the excess water. Heat the remaining coulis in a saucepan and cook the blueberries for 1 minute before adding the blackberries, then remove the saucepan from the heat. Stir the soaked gelatine leaves into the hot berry mixture. At this stage, add the ground cinnamon or star anise if you are using it. The addition of spice works extremely well with the fruit. If you use star anise, remember to remove it after it has infused. Line the loaf tin evenly with the soaked bread, one slice thick. Half-fill the mould with the berry mixture and place a layer of soaked bread on top. Add the remaining berry mixture and finally a last layer of bread. Wrap with the excess clingfilm and refrigerate for 3–4 hours before serving.

Lemon custard
Put the cream and milk in a heavy-based saucepan, add the lemon zest and bring to the boil. Beat the egg yolks and sugar in a bowl until the mixture is pale and thick. Pour a little of the hot cream into the egg yolks and stir. Return this mixture to the remainder of the hot cream and cook over a low heat, stirring constantly, until it coats the back of a wooden spoon. At this point, remove the saucepan from the heat, strain the mixture and chill it.

To serve
Remove the terrine from the loaf tin and slice it into eight. Place a slice of the terrine on each chilled plate, drizzle some lemon custard around the slices and top each with a spoonful of clotted cream.

Assiette of peach: sundae, sorbet, brûlée & tart

{serves 6}

Peach sundae
6 raspberries

Peach compote
4 white peaches, stoned &
 finely diced
25 ml peach schnapps
30 g caster sugar

Vanilla ice cream
500 ml milk
300 ml cream
1 vanilla pod
5 egg yolks
160 g caster sugar

Vanilla ice cream
500 ml milk
300 ml cream
1 vanilla pod
5 egg yolks
160 g caster sugar

Peach froth
½ peach compote recipe
300 ml cream
50 ml milk

Peach sorbet
270 g granulated sugar
750 ml water
juice of 1 lemon
icing sugar (if needed)

Peach purée
450 g peaches, peeled, stoned
 & quartered
110 g caster sugar
juice of 1 lemon

Peach sundae
Vanilla ice cream: Place the milk, cream and vanilla pod in a heavy-based saucepan over gentle heat, allowing the vanilla to infuse. Heat until almost boiling or until the skin begins to shiver. In a separate bowl beat the egg yolks and sugar until the mixture is pale and thick. Pour a little of the hot cream mixture into the egg mixture and stir. Return this mixture to the remainder of the hot cream and cook over a low heat, stirring constantly, until it coats the back of a wooden spoon. Remove the saucepan from the heat, cool the custard and pass it through a sieve. Churn in an ice-cream maker for 30 minutes or until frozen. Alternatively, transfer the mixture to a shallow container, place in the freezer and stir it every hour until it has set.

Peach compote: Place all the ingredients in a small saucepan and heat gently until the peaches soften. Remove from the heat, cool and refrigerate. Half of the compote is used in the peach sundae and the other half is used in the peach froth.

Peach froth: Mix all the ingredients together and froth in a blender.

Assembly: Spoon a little of the compote into a shot glass, place a raspberry on top, then a small ball of ice cream, and finish with the peach froth.

Peach sorbet
Peach purée: Put the peaches in a medium-sized saucepan with just enough sugar to cover the fruit. Cook over a gentle heat for 10–15 minutes or until a knife will pierce the fruit easily. Remove the peaches and reduce the cooking liquid until it starts to thicken and become syrupy, but don't let it get brown. Remove from the heat, allow to cool and add the lemon juice. Liquidise the fruit and the cooking liquid in a food processor.

Sorbet: Put the sugar, water and lemon juice in a medium-sized saucepan and bring to the boil. Cool. Mix with the purée and add some icing sugar if the sorbet needs it. Churn in an ice-cream maker until set or transfer it to a shallow container, place in the freezer and whisk, using a balloon whisk or a large fork, every hour until it has set.

Peach brûlée
Preheat the oven to 100°C/200°F/gas mark ¼. Follow the method for the ice-cream recipe until the mixture coats the back of a wooden spoon. Strain. Place three raspberries in the bottom of each of six small ramekin dishes and pour in the brûlée mixture. Place the filled ramekins in a deep ovenproof dish, half filled with boiling water, and cook for 25–30 minutes or until set. Allow to cool and chill overnight.

Peach brûlée
125 ml milk
375 ml cream
1 vanilla pod
6 egg yolks
100 g caster sugar
18 raspberries

Peach tart
18 raspberries

Sweet pastry
110 g butter
55 g icing sugar, sifted
2 egg yolks
210 g plain flour, sifted
ice-cold water (if needed)
25 g butter, melted

Pastry cream
300 ml milk
1 vanilla pod
3 egg yolks
60 g caster sugar
45 g plain flour, sifted

Peach tart

Sweet pastry: Cream the butter and icing sugar until smooth, then add the egg yolks gradually. Turn the mixer to its lowest speed and spoon in the flour in stages. Add a little ice-cold water if needed. As soon as the mixture clings together as a crumbly dough, remove it and knead it lightly by hand. Wrap the dough in clingfilm and rest it in the fridge for at least 2 hours.

Preheat the oven to 170°C/325°F/gas mark 3. Lightly grease six 4–5 cm tartlet tins with the melted butter. Roll the pastry out ½ cm thick on a lightly floured board and line the tins. Press the pastry into the sides and make sure that there are no holes. Prick the bases lightly with a fork. Cover and refrigerate for 20 minutes. Place a square of non-stick baking parchment in each tartlet, add some ceramic baking beans or dried beans and bake blind for 8–10 minutes, then remove the beans and parchment and bake for another 3–4 minutes or until the base is dry and golden brown. Cool on a wire rack.

Pastry cream: Boil the milk and vanilla pod in a medium-sized saucepan. Whisk the egg yolks and sugar together in a bowl until light in colour, then stir in the flour. Remove the vanilla pod, add the boiled milk to the egg mixture and whisk, using a wire hand whisk. Pour the mixture back into the saucepan and cook gently, stirring constantly, until it is thick enough to coat the back of a wooden spoon. Take care not to overheat. Transfer to a bowl, cool and refrigerate.

Assembly: Pipe some pastry cream into each tart and place three raspberries on top.

To serve
Place the shot glass containing the sundae at the side of a large cooled plate. Arrange a peach brûlée and a peach tart on each plate with a teaspoon of sorbet at the side.

Organic carrot plate: bavarois, cake & sorbet

{serves 8}

Carrot bavarois
2 organic carrots, peeled & diced
1 cardamom pod
1 bay leaf
zest of ½ orange
1 dessertspoon honey
50 ml orange juice
2 leaves of gelatine
2 egg yolks
40 g caster sugar
100 ml cream, semi-whipped
33 cm x 23 cm home-made
  sponge cake (see page 215)
50 ml stock syrup (see page 215)

Carrot cake
350 g plain flour
2 teaspoons baking powder
1 teaspoon salt
1 teaspoon ground cinnamon
400 g caster sugar
200 ml vegetable oil
2 teaspoons vanilla extract
2 eggs
2 organic carrots, peeled & grated
75 g sultanas
50 g walnuts, chopped

Cream cheese frosting
200 g cream cheese
250 g icing sugar
50 g soft butter
1 teaspoon vanilla extract

Carrot sorbet
500 ml carrot juice
375 ml orange juice
125 ml water
1 large organic carrot, peeled &
diced
250 g caster sugar
2 dessertspoons liquid glucose

Carrot bavarois
Preheat the oven to 180°C/350°F/gas mark 4. Place the carrots, cardamom pod, bay leaf, orange zest and honey in a covered roasting tin in the oven. Roast for 50 minutes. Remove the cardamom pod and bay leaf. Blend to a purée and pass this through a sieve, using a little of the orange juice if necessary. Warm the orange juice, soak the gelatine in it to dissolve, and add to the carrot purée.

Whisk the egg yolks and caster sugar in a heatproof bowl over a saucepan of simmering water until the mixture is pale and creamy. Allow it to cool, then fold it into the carrot purée. Stir in the semi-whipped cream. Line a tray with the sponge soaked with stock syrup and pour the carrot bavarois on top. Place in the fridge and allow to set.

Carrot cake
Preheat the oven to 180°C/350°F/gas mark 4. Sieve the flour, baking powder, salt and ground cinnamon into a bowl. In a separate bowl whisk together the caster sugar, vegetable oil, vanilla extract and eggs. Stir this mixture into the dry ingredients. Fold in the carrots, sultanas and walnuts. Transfer to a greased 33 cm x 23 cm swiss roll tin and bake for 50–60 minutes. Remove the cake from the tin and allow it to cool.

Cream cheese frosting: Cream all the ingredients together in a bowl for 3–4 minutes, then spread the frosting over the carrot cake.

Carrot sorbet
Bring all the ingredients to the boil in a large saucepan and simmer for 40 minutes. Blend the mixture and pass it through a sieve. Transfer to an ice-cream maker and churn until frozen. Alternatively, pour the mixture into a shallow container and freeze to a slush. Whisk well so that the sorbet becomes very light and fine grained. Freeze until firm.

To serve
Arrange a 6 cm square of carrot bavarois and a slice of carrot cake on each chilled plate and put a spoonful of carrot sorbet at the side.

Pineapple Tarte Tatin with coconut ice cream

{serves 4}

Pineapple Tarte Tatin
4 slices of fresh pineapple, 1 cm
  thick, core removed, outer skin
  removed
110 g granulated sugar
110 g butter
300 g puff pastry
  (see page 214 or use frozen)

Coconut ice cream
275 ml milk
6 egg yolks
75 g caster sugar
150 ml cream, lightly whipped
½ tin of coconut milk

Garnish
icing sugar, sifted

Coconut ice cream
Put the milk in a saucepan and bring it to the boil. Whisk the egg yolks and sugar together. Remove the milk from the heat and pour on to the egg mixture, whisking continuously. Pour the mixture back into the saucepan and return to the heat, stirring continuously, until the mixture thickens and coats the back of a spoon. Do not boil. Remove the custard from the heat and cool. Strain. Fold in the cream and coconut milk. Pour into an ice-cream maker and churn. Alternatively, transfer the mixture to a shallow container, place in the freezer and stir it every hour until it has set.

Pineapple Tarte Tatin
Preheat the oven to 200°C/400°F/gas mark 6. Melt the sugar in a large, ovenproof frying pan until caramelised. Add the butter and combine, then add the pineapple to the caramel. Roll out the puff pastry to ½ cm thickness and shape to fit the pan. Remove the pan from the heat and place the pastry on top. Bake for 25 minutes. When the tart is cooked, remove it from the oven, place a plate on top of the pan, cover it with a cloth and turn the tart upside down. Remove the pan and cool the tart.

To serve
Dust the Tarte Tatin with icing sugar and place a slice on each chilled plate. Place a scoop of coconut ice cream beside it. Dust with some icing sugar.

Classic vanilla crème brûlée, lemon curd ice cream

{serves 6}

Classic vanilla crème brûlée
2 vanilla pods
850 ml cream
250 ml milk
12 egg yolks
200 g caster sugar
12 teaspoons demerara sugar

Lemon curd ice cream
Ice cream
juice of 2 lemons
zest of 1 lemon
400 ml crème brûlée custard from
  the crème brûlée recipe on the left

Lemon curd
60 ml lemon juice
135 g icing sugar
20 g butter
1 egg
4 egg yolks

Garnish (optional)
1 recipe chocolate tuile
  (see page 202)

Classic vanilla crème brûlée

Preheat the oven to 120°C/225°F/gas mark ¼. Slit the vanilla pods, scrape out the seeds and mix them with the cream. Bring the cream, milk, vanilla seeds and vanilla pods to the boil in a large saucepan. Meanwhile whisk the egg yolks and caster sugar in a heatproof bowl over a saucepan of simmering water until the mixture is pale and creamy. When the cream mixture starts to boil, slowly pour it on to the egg and sugar mixture, stirring all the time. Transfer the mixture back into the saucepan the cream was boiled in and continue cooking on a gentle heat until the custard coats the back of a wooden spoon. Pass the custard through a sieve and discard the vanilla pods.

Once the custard has thickened, remove it from the stove. Use 1 litre of mix to fill six 7 cm ramekin dishes. (Set the remaining 400 ml aside for the lemon curd ice cream.) Place the filled ramekin dishes in a deep ovenproof dish, half filled with boiling water. Cook in the oven for 40–50 minutes, or until the custards have lightly set. The custard is set when, if tipped, it comes away slightly from the edge of the ramekin dish. Cool until firm.

Sprinkle each chilled custard with 2 teaspoons of demerara sugar. Caramelise either by using a blowtorch or placing under a hot grill.

Lemon curd ice cream

Ice cream: Add the juice of 2 lemons and the zest of 1 lemon to the remaining 400 ml of crème brûlée custard while it is still hot. Allow the custard to cool, then strain it. Churn in an ice-cream maker, adding the lemon curd just before it freezes. Alternatively, transfer the mixture to a shallow dish and place in the freezer. Stir every hour until it has set. Stir in the cooled lemon curd just before it has completely set.

Lemon curd: In a large heatproof bowl over a saucepan of simmering water, heat the lemon juice, icing sugar and butter. Add the egg and egg yolks, stirring constantly, until the curd is thick and creamy (about 20 minutes). Allow to cool.

Garnish
Make the chocolate tuile from the Sticky fudge & pecan parfait recipe on page 202.

To serve
Place a crème brûlée on each cooled plate and arrange a scoop of lemon curd ice cream beside it. Insert a chocolate tuile at the side of the crème brûlée if you wish.

Îles flottantes: slow-cooked meringue, blood orange & chocolate salad, crème anglaise

{serves 4}

Slow-cooked meringue
3 egg whites
100 g caster sugar
600 ml milk

Blood orange & chocolate salad
2 blood oranges, peeled &
segmented
25 g dark chocolate shavings

Crème anglaise
1 recipe crème anglaise
(see page 215)

Slow-cooked meringue
Whisk the egg whites until stiff with an electric whisk in a large mixing bowl. Add half the caster sugar, whisk and add the remaining sugar and beat until stiff and glossy.

Bring the milk to simmering point in a medium-sized saucepan. Using two tablespoons, make the meringue mixture into smooth oval shapes. Gently place the spoonfuls of meringue into the hot milk and poach them for 2 minutes each side until set. Once set, remove the meringues carefully with a perforated spoon and put aside to drain well. Continue shaping, poaching and draining until all the mixture is used.

Crème anglaise
Make the crème anglaise given on page 215.

To serve
Divide the poached meringues between four bowls. Pour the crème anglaise around the meringues to suggest they are floating. Place the oranges on top of the meringues and scatter with the chocolate shavings.

Raspberry & aged sherry trifle, cracked black pepper cookie

{serves 6}

Raspberry & aged sherry trifle
6 tablespoons Lustau Old East
  India sherry
450 g raspberries

Sponge
25 g butter, melted
4 eggs
110 g caster sugar
110 g plain flour, sifted
30 ml sunflower oil

Pastry cream
300 ml milk
1 vanilla pod
3 egg yolks
60 g caster sugar
45 g plain flour, sifted

Jelly
500 g sugar
600 ml red wine
zest of 1 lemon
zest of 1 orange
7 leaves of gelatine

Chantilly cream
600 ml cream
25 g icing sugar
1–2 drops of vanilla extract

Cracked black pepper cookie
25 g butter, melted
450 g butter
225 g caster sugar
1 egg, beaten
440 g self-raising flour, sifted
5 g cracked black pepper
  (depending on personal taste)

Garnish
6 mint leaves

Cracked black pepper cookie
Preheat the oven to 170°C/325°F/gas mark 3. Brush a baking tray with 25 g melted butter and line with non-stick baking parchment. Cream 450 g butter and 225 g sugar together. Add the egg and mix. Add the flour and black pepper. Once all the ingredients are combined, place in a piping bag and pipe out fingers about 5 cm long. Bake for 8–10 minutes until golden. Remove from the oven and place on a wire rack. Cool.

Raspberry & aged sherry trifle
Sponge: Preheat the oven to 180°C/350°F/gas mark 4. Brush a 25 cm x 38 cm baking tray with melted butter and line it with non-stick baking parchment. Whisk the eggs and sugar together in a bowl until light and fluffy. Fold in the flour and then the oil. Spread the mixture out evenly and thinly on the tray and bake for 5–6 minutes or until golden. Once the sponge is cool, turn it out on to a clean cutting board and cut out six circles to fit six small ramekin dishes. Place the sponge circles in the ramekins and add a little sherry to each one. Refrigerate until the jelly is ready.

Pastry cream: Boil the milk and vanilla pod in a medium-sized saucepan. Whisk the egg yolks and sugar together in a bowl until light in colour, then stir in the flour. Remove the vanilla pod, add the boiled milk to the egg mixture and whisk, using a wire hand whisk. Pour the mixture back into the saucepan and cook gently, stirring constantly, until it is thick enough to coat the back of a wooden spoon, but take care not to overheat the mixture. Transfer to a bowl and cool. Refrigerate.

Jelly: Bring the sugar, red wine, lemon and orange zest to the boil. Put the gelatine leaves in a bowl of ice-cold water for 3–4 minutes, remove them, shake off the excess liquid and place in a bowl. Pour the boiling red wine mixture over the gelatine, stirring until it has completely dissolved. Allow to cool. Place some raspberries neatly on top of each sponge and cover the fruit with jelly, saving some berries for the garnish. Refrigerate overnight. The next day, spoon some pastry cream on top of each trifle and level with a knife. Refrigerate for a couple of hours before serving.

Chantilly cream: Put the cream into a chilled bowl and whisk, using a balloon whisk, for about 2 minutes until the cream starts to thicken. Add the icing sugar and vanilla extract and whisk until the mixture is very fluffy and forms soft peaks – be careful not to overbeat.

To serve
Using a teaspoon, spoon some Chantilly cream on to each trifle. Place a trifle (in its ramekin dish) on each cooled dessert plate. Lay a black pepper cookie at the side. Garnish with some berries and a mint leaf.

Cappuccino parfait with apple beignets & apricot preserve

{serves 8}

Cappuccino parfait
4 eggs, separated
100 g caster sugar
1 vanilla pod
3 tablespoons espresso coffee
400 ml cream, semi-whipped

Apple beignets
120 g plain flour, sifted, plus
* 2 tablespoons for coating*
50 g caster sugar
3 eggs, separated
120 ml milk
2 eating apples, peeled,
* cored & thinly sliced*

Apricot preserve
50 g caster sugar
40 g water
40 ml white wine
zest of ½ orange
120 g fresh apricots, halved,
* pitted & sliced*

Cappuccino parfait
Whisk the egg yolks and half the caster sugar in a large heatproof bowl over a saucepan of simmering water until the mixture is pale and creamy. Scrape the vanilla seeds from the pod into the egg and sugar mixture and add the halved vanilla pod, cut lengthways. Add the espresso and allow the mixture to cool. Remove the vanilla pod. Fold in the cream. In a separate bowl whisk the egg whites and add the remainder of the sugar. Add to the egg and cream mixture. Line a 23 cm x 12 cm loaf tin with clingfilm, pour in the parfait mixture and freeze.

Apricot preserve
Combine the sugar, water, wine and orange zest in a large, heavy-based saucepan. Stir over medium heat until the sugar dissolves. Add the apricots and simmer for about 5 minutes until the apricots are tender. Leave for 5 minutes before transferring to a bowl and chilling.

Apple beignets
Place the flour, sugar, egg yolks and milk in a bowl and mix with a wooden spoon. In a separate bowl whisk the egg whites and fold into the egg and flour mixture. Preheat the deep-fat fryer to 180°C/350°F. Toss the apple slices in the flour and then dip them into the batter, shaking off any excess. Deep fry for 1–2 minutes until the beignets are cooked and golden brown. Drain well on kitchen paper.

To serve
Remove the parfait from the freezer and slice it with a warm, sharp knife. Arrange on cooled plates. Spoon on the apricot preserve and serve with the apple beignets.

Banana & chocolate feuilletine, black rum & toffee ice cream, Crème de bananes sabayon

{serves 8}

Banana & chocolate feuilletine
Puff pastry
300 g puff pastry (see page 214 or
  use frozen)

Chocolate ganache
60 ml cream
50 g butter
150 g 71% dark chocolate

Black rum & toffee ice cream
Toffee sauce
200 g brown sugar
50 ml water
75 g butter
75 ml cream

Black rum ice cream
1 recipe crème anglaise
  (see page 215)
35 ml black rum

Crème de bananes sabayon
3 egg yolks
50 g caster sugar
50 ml Crème de bananes liqueur

Garnish
2 bananas, finely sliced
2 tablespoons brown sugar

Banana & chocolate feuilletine
Puff pastry: Preheat the oven to 180°C/350°F/gas mark 4. Roll out the puff pastry to ½ cm thickness. Using an 8 cm pastry cutter, cut out eight discs. Place on a greased baking tray and bake for 25 minutes. Allow the pastry to cool.

Chocolate ganache: Melt the chocolate in a heatproof bowl over a saucepan of simmering water. Boil the cream and butter in a small saucepan. Pour the cream and butter mixture over the melted chocolate and whisk. Transfer the mixture to a baking tray lined with greaseproof paper, ensuring that the ganache is 2 cm thick. Chill the ganache until it's cool, then use a 3 cm pastry cutter to make eight discs and set them aside.

Black rum & toffee ice cream
Toffee sauce: Bring the brown sugar and water to the boil in a large saucepan, making caramel. Add the butter and allow it to melt before adding the cream. Bring the mixture to the boil and simmer it for 3 minutes, then allow it to cool.

Black rum ice cream: Churn the crème anglaise and black rum in an ice-cream maker. Alternatively, transfer the mixture to a shallow container and place in the freezer, whisking every hour. When the ice cream has almost frozen, fold in the cooled toffee sauce.

Crème de bananes sabayon
Put the egg yolks, caster sugar and Crème de bananes in a heatproof bowl and set it over a saucepan of simmering water. Whisk the mixture until it is pale and creamy and the whisk leaves its mark on the sabayon.

To serve
Preheat the oven to 180°C/350°F/gas mark 4. Preheat the grill to hot. Divide the puff pastry discs in two horizontally and place a disc of ganache in the centre of each. Place the pastries in the oven for 5 minutes to warm through and soften the ganache. When warm, place the sliced bananas on top of the pastries and sprinkle with brown sugar. Caramelise under the grill for 1 minute. Serve with the black rum and toffee ice cream on top of the banana and chocolate feuilletine. Drizzle the Crème de bananes sabayon around the plate.

Banana Bakewell tart, praline sauce, cinnamon ice cream

{serves 8}

Banana Bakewell tart
Sweet pastry
115 g butter
115 g caster sugar
1 egg, beaten
265 g plain flour, sifted

Frangipane
100 g butter
100 g caster sugar
2 eggs, beaten
100 g ground almonds
25 g plain flour, sifted

Tart
1 egg yolk
20 ml milk
4 bananas
15 g nibbed almonds

Praline sauce
20 g flaked almonds
100 g caster sugar
250 ml water
1 teaspoon liquid glucose
35 ml black rum

Cinnamon ice cream
600 ml cream
200 ml milk
2 cinnamon sticks
9 egg yolks
160 g caster sugar

Cinnamon ice cream
Bring the cream, milk, and cinnamon sticks to the boil in a large saucepan. Meanwhile whisk the egg yolks and caster sugar in a heatproof bowl over a saucepan of simmering water until the mixture is pale and creamy. When the cream starts to boil, slowly pour it on to the egg and sugar mixture, whisking all the time. Transfer the mixture back into the large saucepan and continue cooking on a gentle heat until the custard coats the back of a wooden spoon. Cool, pass through a sieve and discard the cinnamon sticks. Churn in an ice-cream maker or transfer the ice cream to a shallow dish, place in the freezer and stir every hour until it has set.

Banana Bakewell tart
Sweet pastry: Cream the butter and sugar with an electric mixer in a bowl until the mixture is smooth, then add the egg gradually. Turn the mixer to its lowest speed and spoon in the flour in stages. As soon as the mixture clings together as a crumbly dough, remove it and knead it lightly by hand. Wrap the dough in clingfilm and refrigerate.

Frangipane: Using an electric mixer, cream the butter and sugar in a bowl until the mixture is smooth. Gradually add the eggs. Stop the electric mixer and mix in the ground almonds, using a wooden spoon. Finally, fold in the flour until the frangipane is smooth.

Tart: Preheat the oven to 160°C/325°F/gas mark 3. Beat the egg yolk and the milk with a fork to make an egg wash. Lightly grease a 28 cm flan tin and roll out the sweet pastry to line the tin. Press the pastry well into the sides and make sure that there are no holes. Cover with clingfilm and refrigerate the pastry case for 20 minutes. Remove the pastry case from the fridge, slice the bananas and arrange the slices over the bottom of the pastry case. Spoon on the frangipane and smooth it over with a palette knife. Brush the frangipane with the egg wash and sprinkle it with nibbed almonds. Bake for 30–35 minutes.

Praline sauce
Toast the almonds and allow them to cool. Put the almonds into a freezer bag and smash them with a rolling pin. In a heavy-based saucepan, make a caramel by boiling the sugar, 150 ml water and liquid glucose steadily for 5 minutes. Remove from the heat and add 100 ml water and the rum. Allow the caramel to cool and add the crushed toasted almonds.

To serve
Place a slice of tart in the centre of each chilled plate, drizzle the praline sauce around it and top with a scoop of cinnamon ice cream.

Baked orange & cardamom sponge pudding, natural yoghurt ice cream, orange fondue

{serves 8}

Baked orange & cardamom sponge pudding
150 g unsalted butter plus 1
  tablespoon for pudding moulds
150 g caster sugar plus 2
  tablespoons for pudding moulds
zest & juice of 2 medium oranges
seeds from 5 cardamom pods,
  removed from pods & crushed
4 egg yolks
200 g plain flour
1 tablespoon baking powder

Natural yoghurt ice cream
375 ml cream
125 ml milk
6 egg yolks
100 g caster sugar
125 ml natural yoghurt

Orange fondue
juice of 4 oranges (500 ml)
zest of 1 orange
250 ml water
200 g sugar

Natural yoghurt ice cream
Heat the cream and the milk in a heavy-based saucepan until the mixture almost reaches boiling point. In a separate bowl beat the egg yolks and sugar until the mixture is pale and thick. Pour a little of the hot cream mixture into the egg yolks and stir. Return this mixture to the remainder of the hot cream and cook over a low heat, stirring constantly, until it coats the back of a wooden spoon. At this point, remove the pan from the heat, strain the mixture, then chill it and add the natural yoghurt. Churn the mixture in an ice-cream maker for 30 minutes. Otherwise, transfer it to a shallow container, place in the freezer and stir it every hour until it has set.

Baked orange & cardamom sponge pudding
You will need eight 7 cm pudding moulds. Preheat the oven to 150°C/300°F/gas mark 2. Liberally butter and sugar each pudding mould. Beat the butter and sugar together in a bowl until the mixture is pale. Add the zest and the cardamom seeds and continue beating for 10 minutes. In a separate bowl whisk the egg yolks and orange juice together and pour into the creamed mixture. Sieve the flour and baking powder together, then gently fold them into the butter and egg mixture. Divide the mixture between the pudding moulds and bake in the oven for 20–25 minutes.

Orange fondue
Place all the ingredients in a heavy-based saucepan. Bring to the boil and simmer for 25 minutes until halved in volume. Allow to cool.

To serve
Remove the puddings from their moulds and turn them upside down on to warm plates. Drizzle the orange fondue around and finally top with a scoop of natural yoghurt ice cream.

Sticky fudge & pecan parfait with macerated berries, chocolate tuile

{serves 8}

Sticky fudge & pecan parfait
Pecan brownie
1 recipe pecan brownie
  (see page 209)

Parfait
6 egg yolks
175 g caster sugar
300 ml Bailey's liqueur
80 g 71% dark chocolate
570 ml cream, semi-whipped
80 g pecan brownie (see above),
  cut into small dice

Macerated berries
100 g raspberries
100 g blackberries
100 g strawberries
400 ml stock syrup
  (see page 215)
1 tablespoon kirsch

Chocolate tuile
100 g icing sugar
70 g butter, melted
1 tablespoon honey
25 g cocoa
75 g plain flour, sifted
1 egg white, lightly beaten

Sticky fudge & pecan parfait
Make the pecan brownie from the Pecan brownie with chocolate butterscotch sauce recipe on page 209. Whisk the egg yolks, sugar and Bailey's in a heatproof bowl over a saucepan of simmering water until the mixture holds the mark of the whisk. Remove from the heat and whisk until it is cold. Melt the chocolate in a separate heatproof bowl over a saucepan of simmering water. Fold in the melted chocolate and semi-whipped cream, then add the diced brownie. Pour the mixture into eight small ramekin dishes and freeze.

Chocolate tuile
Preheat the oven to 180°C/350°F/gas mark 4. Blend all the ingredients in a food processor until you have a smooth mixture. Line a baking sheet with a silicone mat or non-stick baking parchment. Spread out the mixture to form circles about 15 cm diameter, allowing some room for expansion. Bake in the oven for 7–8 minutes. Remove the tuiles from the tray with a palette knife while they are still hot and curve them round a rolling pin to form rounded shapes. Allow the tuiles to cool.

Macerated berries
Soak the berries for 1 hour at room temperature in the stock syrup and kirsch.

To serve
Turn the parfaits out and place one in the centre of each chilled plate. Top with a chocolate tuile and spoon the macerated berries, with a little of their soaking liquor, around the parfait.

Passion fruit & white chocolate délice, watermelon & star anise consommé

{serves 4}

Passion fruit & white chocolate délice
*150 ml passion fruit purée
  (available from good delis)
50 ml water
175 g caster sugar
2 leaves of gelatine
100 g white chocolate
25 ml cream
3 egg whites*

Topping
*2 leaves of gelatine
100 ml passion fruit purée
50 g caster sugar*

Watermelon & star anise consommé
*500 g watermelon
3 whole star anise
75 g caster sugar
20 ml Pernod or Ricard*

Passion fruit & white chocolate délice

Boil the water with 25 g of the caster sugar in a small saucepan to make a syrup. Soak the gelatine leaves in a bowl of ice-cold water for 3–4 minutes, then remove them and shake off the excess liquid. Add to the syrup to melt the gelatine. Whisk the syrup into the passion fruit purée. Melt the white chocolate with the cream in a heatproof bowl over a saucepan of simmering water. In a separate bowl whisk the egg whites to soft peak stage and add the remaining 150 g sugar. Fold the white chocolate mix into the passion fruit mixture and, finally, fold in the egg whites. Lay clingfilm over a baking tray and place four 7 cm ring moulds on the tray. Fill the moulds with passion fruit mousse and allow them to set for 1 hour in the fridge.

Topping: Soak the gelatine leaves in a bowl of ice-cold water for 3–4 minutes. Heat the passion fruit purée and sugar together. Drain the gelatine leaves, squeezing out the excess water, and add them to the heated passion fruit purée. Allow the purée to cool but not set, then pour it on top of each passion fruit and white chocolate délice mould. Leave the délices to set for 45–50 minutes.

Watermelon & star anise consommé

Scoop the flesh from the watermelon, remove the seeds and blend the flesh in a food processor. Transfer the mixture to a saucepan and bring it to the boil with the star anise and the sugar. Simmer for 5 minutes. Strain the watermelon liquid twice, ensuring that it is quite clear. Allow the liquid to cool and add the alcohol.

To serve

Remove the passion fruit and white chocolate délices from their moulds and transfer them to four cooled bowls. Spoon the watermelon and star anise consommé around them.

Warm chocolate fondant tart, balsamic strawberries, milk chocolate sorbet

{serves 6}

Warm chocolate fondant tart
Pastry
75 g 71% dark chocolate
195 g butter
75 g caster sugar
245 g plain flour, sifted
60 g cocoa, sifted
1 egg, lightly beaten
1 egg yolk

Fondant filling
140 g 71% dark chocolate
140 g butter
3 eggs
3 egg yolks
170 g caster sugar
60 g plain flour, sifted

Balsamic strawberries
12 strawberries, washed,
* hulled & quartered*
1 tablespoon good-quality
* balsamic vinegar*

Milk chocolate sorbet
330 g milk chocolate
1 teaspoon dark rum
1 litre water
80 g powdered milk
120 g caster sugar
50 g liquid glucose

Garnish
mint leaves

Warm chocolate fondant tart
Pastry: Melt the chocolate in a heatproof bowl over a saucepan of simmering water. Cream the butter and sugar in a separate bowl until light in colour, then mix in the flour and cocoa. Beat in the egg and egg yolk slowly, then beat in the melted chocolate. Turn the pastry out on to a floured work surface and knead into a ball, working quickly so that the chocolate doesn't melt. Wrap the dough in clingfilm and leave to rest in the fridge for at least 2 hours.

Fondant filling: Melt the chocolate and butter in a heatproof bowl over a saucepan of simmering water. Lightly whisk the eggs, egg yolks and sugar together in a separate bowl until pale and fluffy. Add the melted chocolate and butter to the eggs, mixing continuously. Fold in the flour and mix gently until fully combined. Cool and refrigerate.

Tart: Preheat the oven to 170°C/325°F/gas mark 3. Grease six 8 cm tartlet tins with a little melted butter. It is also a good idea to line the base with non-stick baking parchment to prevent the pastry sticking to the base. Roll out the pastry to ½ cm thickness and line the tins, allowing the pastry to overhang a little, as it will shrink during baking. Chill in the fridge for 20 minutes. Cover each tartlet with a square of greaseproof paper and weigh the greaseproof down with ceramic baking beans or dried beans. Bake blind for 8–10 minutes, then remove the paper and beans and bake for a further 5 minutes or until the base is dry. Remove from the oven.

Turn the temperature up to 190°C/375°F/gas mark 5. Once the pastry has cooled, pipe the fondant filling into the pastry cases, using a piping bag. Bake for about 8–10 minutes or until set.

Milk chocolate sorbet
Place the chocolate and rum in a heatproof bowl. Heat the water, powdered milk, sugar and glucose in a medium-sized saucepan until the sugar and milk powder have dissolved. Bring to the boil, pour the mixture over the chocolate and rum, and stir until the chocolate has melted. Allow to cool and refrigerate overnight. The next morning, blend the mixture with a hand blender, then churn it in an ice-cream maker until the mixture reaches sorbet consistency. Alternatively, transfer the mixture to a shallow dish, place in the freezer and stir every hour until it has set.

Balsamic strawberries
Cut the strawberries into quarters and toss in a bowl with the vinegar.

To serve
Serve the warm tarts on chilled plates with a spoonful of balsamic strawberries and a mint leaf. Place a tablespoon of milk chocolate sorbet at the side.

Tasting of chocolate: chocolate dome, tartelette, Bailey's ice cream, chocolate tuile

{serves 6}

Chocolate dome
Chocolate crisp base
100 g milk chocolate
100 g feuilletine
  (continental wafers), crushed

Chocolate mousse
4 egg yolks
50 g caster sugar
100 g 71% dark chocolate, melted
150 ml cream, semi-whipped

Chocolate glaze
100 ml cream
50 g 71% dark chocolate, melted

Tartelette
Pastry
120 g unsalted butter
50 g caster sugar
2 egg yolks
150 g plain flour, sifted
50 g cocoa, sifted

Filling
40 g butter
200 ml cream
175 g 71% dark chocolate

Bailey's ice cream
600 ml cream
200 ml milk
9 egg yolks
160 g caster sugar
1 tablespoon Bailey's liqueur

Chocolate tuile
1 recipe chocolate tuile
  (see page 202)

Chocolate dome
Chocolate crisp base: Melt the chocolate in a large saucepan. Add the feuilletine and mix well. Roll the mixture between two layers of greaseproof paper with a rolling pin until wafer thin, then refrigerate. Cut out six 7 cm circular discs to fit the base of the mousse.

Chocolate mousse: Whisk the egg yolks with the caster sugar in a heatproof bowl over a saucepan of simmering water until the mixture is pale and creamy. Remove from the heat. Add the melted dark chocolate and allow the mixture to cool before adding the semi-whipped cream. Transfer the mixture to six clingfilmed 7 cm dome moulds. Place a circle of chocolate crisp on top and freeze the domes. When the domes have frozen, turn them upside down, allowing the chocolate crisps to become the bases.

Chocolate glaze: Boil the cream in a saucepan. Melt the chocolate in a separate bowl and pour the cream into it. Whisk the mixture until it is smooth and pour it over the chocolate domes.

Tartelette
Pastry: In a large bowl beat the butter and sugar until creamy. Add the egg yolks before mixing in the combined flour and cocoa. Grease one 28 cm springform tin or six 10 cm springform tins. Line the tins with the rolled-out pastry and leave them to rest in the fridge for 30 minutes. Preheat the oven to 150°C/300°F/gas mark 2. Lay a square of greaseproof paper on top of each pastry and fill with ceramic baking beans or dried beans. Bake for 15 minutes and allow the pastry shell to cool.

Filling: Bring the butter and cream to the boil in a large saucepan. Melt the chocolate in a separate bowl, pour the cream into the chocolate and mix well. Pour the mixture into the chocolate pastry shell. Cool, transfer the tartelette to the fridge and allow it to set.

Bailey's ice cream
Bring the cream and milk to the boil in a saucepan. Meanwhile whisk the egg yolks and caster sugar in a heatproof bowl over a saucepan of simmering water until the mixture is pale and creamy. When the cream and milk mixture starts to boil, slowly pour it on to the egg and sugar mixture, whisking all the time. Transfer the mixture back into the large saucepan and continue cooking over gentle heat until the custard coats the back of a wooden spoon. Cool and pass through a sieve. Churn in an ice-cream maker, adding the Bailey's just before the ice cream has set. Alternatively, transfer the mixture to a shallow dish, place in the freezer and stir every hour until it has almost set. Stir in the Bailey's and freeze the ice cream.

Chocolate tuile
Make the chocolate tuile from the Sticky fudge & pecan parfait recipe on page 202.

To serve
Slice the tartelette into six and place on cooled plates. Arrange a chocolate dome beside each one and lay a chocolate tuile on top. Place a scoop of Bailey's ice cream at the side.

Pistachio-crusted dark & white chocolate mousse, Black Crimson grape compote

{serves 6}

Dark chocolate mousse
200 g 71% dark chocolate
50 g unsalted butter
1 gelatine leaf
40 ml Tia Maria
450 ml double cream,
  semi-whipped
½ recipe Italian meringue
  (see below)

Italian meringue for both mousses
150 g caster sugar
75 ml water
5 egg whites

White chocolate mousse
200 g white chocolate
50 g unsalted butter
1 gelatine leaf
40 ml Tia Maria
450 ml double cream, semi-
  whipped
½ recipe of Italian meringue
  (see left)

Pistachio crust
200 g caster sugar
60 ml water
200 g pistachio nuts

Black Crimson grape compote
300 g seedless Black Crimson
  grapes
zest of 1 lemon
zest of 1 orange
50 g caster sugar
40 seedless Black Crimson grapes,
  peeled with a sharp knife

Dark chocolate mousse

Italian meringue: Put the sugar and water in a heavy-based saucepan and heat until the sugar has dissolved. Meanwhile, in a separate bowl, whisk the egg whites to soft peaks. Once the sugar has dissolved, boil the syrup for about 7 minutes until it reaches hard ball stage (121°C/250°F). Remove from the heat. Slowly pour the syrup into the bowl containing the egg white. Continue whisking until the meringue is tepid. Keep the meringue for the two mousses.

Mousse: Make the dark chocolate mousse first. Melt the dark chocolate and butter in a heatproof bowl over a pot of simmering water. Soak the gelatine leaf in a bowl of ice-cold water for 3–4 minutes. Heat the Tia Maria gently so that it is hot enough to melt the gelatine. Remove the gelatine leaf from the water and shake off the excess liquid. Transfer it to the hot Tia Maria and whisk to melt the gelatine. Fold the Tia Maria and gelatine into the chocolate and butter mix, then fold in a third of the cream and half the Italian meringue mix and, finally, fold in the remaining cream.

Half-fill six 8 cm ring moulds with dark chocolate mousse on a clingfilmed baking tray. Transfer the mousses to the fridge and allow them to set for 30 minutes.

White chocolate mousse

Repeat the procedure for the dark chocolate mousse, using white chocolate instead of dark and the second half of the Italian meringue. Fill the ring moulds to the top with the white chocolate mousse and leave them to set in the fridge.

Pistachio crust

Cook the sugar and water for 5–6 minutes in a heavy-based saucepan to make a caramel. Add the pistachio nuts. Pour the mixture on to a greased baking tray and cool. When it has cooled, transfer it to a food processor and pulse until the mixture has the texture of coarse breadcrumbs. Don't overprocess it into dust.

Black Crimson grape compote

Blend 300 g Black Crimson grapes, the citrus zests and the sugar in a food processor. Bring the mixture to the boil in a heavy-based saucepan and simmer until reduced by half. Cool, pass through a sieve and add the peeled grapes.

To serve

When the chocolate mousses have set, remove them from the ring moulds. (You can use a blowtorch around the rings if they prove difficult to remove.) Using a palette knife, cover the sides of the mousse with the pistachio crust. Transfer to cooled plates and drizzle the Black Crimson grape compote around.

Pecan brownie with chocolate butterscotch sauce, buttermilk ice cream

{serves 4}

Pecan brownie
100 g 71% dark chocolate
150 g butter, melted
250 g caster sugar
3 eggs, beaten
2 drops of vanilla extract
175 g plain flour, sifted
100 g pecan nuts, chopped

Buttermilk ice cream
500 ml cream
180 ml buttermilk
8 egg yolks
130 g caster sugar

Chocolate butterscotch sauce
150 g brown sugar
100 ml cold water
50 g butter, diced
350 ml cream
75 g 71% dark chocolate

Pecan brownie
Preheat the oven to 170°C/325°F/gas mark 3. Melt the chocolate in a heatproof bowl over a saucepan of simmering water. Combine the melted chocolate and butter in a large mixing bowl. Add the sugar, eggs and vanilla extract and mix until combined. Add the flour and pecans. Fold all the ingredients together in the mixing bowl until they are well combined. Line a 22 cm square tin with buttered greaseproof paper. Bake for 30 minutes. Allow to cool before removing the brownies from the tin. Cut the brownies into four squares.

Buttermilk ice cream
Heat the cream and buttermilk in a heavy-based saucepan until the mixture almost reaches boiling point. In a separate bowl beat the egg yolks and sugar until the mixture is pale and thick. Pour a little of the hot cream mixture into the egg yolks and stir. Return this mixture to the remainder of the hot cream and cook over a low heat, stirring constantly, until it coats the back of a wooden spoon. At this point, remove the saucepan from the heat, chill the mixture and strain it. Churn the mixture in an ice-cream maker until it has frozen. Alternatively, transfer it to a shallow container, place in the freezer and stir every hour until it has set.

Chocolate butterscotch sauce
Bring the sugar and water to the boil and continue to cook until the sugar caramelises. Add the diced butter and cream, bring to the boil and simmer for 3–4 minutes. Add the chocolate and stir until the sauce is smooth.

To serve
Preheat the oven to 170°C/325°F/gas mark 3. Place the pecan brownies in an ovenproof dish, drizzle with 4 tablespoons of chocolate butterscotch sauce, cover with tinfoil and heat in the oven for 5 minutes or until hot. Remove the brownies from the dish and place one in the centre of each plate. Cover each with another tablespoon of hot chocolate butterscotch sauce and serve with a scoop of buttermilk ice cream.

Beef or veal stock

This quantity makes about 1½–2 litres.

2 kg beef or veal bones
1 bay leaf
2 parsley stalks
1 sprig of thyme
40 g butter
1 large onion, unpeeled,
* roughly chopped*
3 medium carrots, roughly chopped
2 medium leeks, roughly chopped
2 sticks of celery, roughly chopped
60 g mushroom trimmings,
* roughly chopped*
1 tomato, roughly chopped
1 clove of garlic, unpeeled
3 white peppercorns
8 litres water

Preheat the oven to 200°C/400°F/ gas mark 6. Arrange the bones on a roasting tin and roast for 1 hour. Tie the bay leaf, parsley and thyme together with string to make a bouquet garni. Melt the butter in a large saucepan and colour the onion, carrots, leeks and celery in the butter before adding the roasted bones (drained of excess fat), the bouquet garni, mushroom trimmings, tomato, garlic and peppercorns. Add the water, bring to the boil and skim scum from the surface using a ladle. Reduce the heat and simmer very gently, uncovered, for 8–9 hours, skimming scum from the surface. Pass through a muslin-lined colander into a large bowl, discarding any solids. Cool, cover and refrigerate. The stock will keep for 5 days in the fridge. Stock can be frozen in ice-cube trays and stored in plastic bags in the freezer.

Chicken stock

This quantity makes about 1½ litres.

3 raw chicken carcases, skin &
* fat removed*
1 bay leaf
1 parsley stalk
1 sprig of thyme
2½ litres water
1 large carrot, trimmed
* & quartered*
1 medium leek, roughly chopped
2 sticks of celery, roughly chopped
1 large onion, unpeeled, roughly
* chopped*
3 white peppercorns

Tie the bay leaf, parsley stalk and thyme together with string to make a bouquet garni. Place the chicken carcases in a large saucepan and cover with water. Bring to the boil and skim any scum from the surface with a ladle. Add all the other ingredients and simmer the stock, uncovered, very gently for 4 hours. Strain the stock through a muslin-lined colander. Discard the bones, vegetables and herbs. Cool and refrigerate in a covered container. The stock will keep for more than a week in the fridge. Stock can be frozen in ice-cube trays and stored in plastic bags in the freezer.

Duck stock

This quantity makes about 500 ml.

600 g duck bones
200 ml red wine
1½ litres water
1 sprig of thyme
1 bay leaf
2 parsley stalks
1 small carrot, peeled &
* roughly chopped*
1 small onion, peeled &
* roughly chopped*
1 stick of celery, roughly chopped
1 sprig of sage
1 sprig of rosemary
2 juniper berries, crushed
½ clove of garlic, peeled
* & crushed*
2 tablespoons olive oil
30 dried mushrooms, soaked for
* 20 minutes*
2 white peppercorns

Preheat the oven to 200°C/400°F/gas mark 6. Place the bones in a roasting tin and roast until they are really brown. Remove the bones from the oven and transfer them to a large saucepan. Deglaze the roasting tin with the wine and add this to the saucepan with the water. Bring to the boil and remove scum from the surface with a ladle.

Tie the thyme, bay leaf and parsley together with string to make a bouquet garni. Place the vegetables, sage, rosemary, juniper berries and garlic in a roasting tin and drizzle with the oil. Roast in the oven for about 20 minutes until the vegetables are soft and brown, but not burnt. Add the vegetables and herbs to the stock with the bouquet garni, dried mushrooms and peppercorns. Simmer gently, uncovered, for 4 hours. Strain the stock through a muslin-lined sieve. Discard the bones, vegetables and herbs. Cool and refrigerate in a covered container. The stock will keep for 2–3 days in the fridge. Stock can be frozen in ice-cube trays and stored in plastic bags in the freezer.

Fish stock

This quantity makes about
1½ litres.

1.5 kg fish bones (sole, turbot or
  whiting), washed
40 g butter
1 medium onion, peeled &
  roughly chopped
1 bay leaf
4 white peppercorns
10 parsley stalks
juice of ½ lemon
1½ litres water

Melt the butter in a large
saucepan. Add the onion, bay leaf,
peppercorns, parsley stalks, lemon
juice and bones and cook gently
for 5 minutes. Add the water,
bring the stock to the boil and
skim. Lower the heat and simmer
for 20 minutes. Strain and use at
once or cool and refrigerate in a
covered container for no more
than 1 day. Stock can be frozen in
ice-cube trays and stored in plastic
bags in the freezer.

Langoustine stock

This quantity makes about 2 litres.

3 kg prawn shells
75 g butter
2 medium onions, peeled &
  roughly chopped
2 medium carrots, peeled &
  roughly chopped
2 sticks of celery, roughly chopped
2 medium leeks, roughly chopped
1 fennel bulb, roughly chopped
200 ml white wine
100 ml brandy
1 lemongrass stalk
1 bay leaf
8 white peppercorns
20 g parsley stalks
2 tablespoons tomato paste
5 litres water

Preheat the oven to 150°C/300°F/
gas mark 2. Roast the prawn shells
until golden brown. Heat the
butter in a large saucepan and
cook the vegetables until they are
golden brown. Add the wine to
deglaze the saucepan, then add
the roasted prawn shells and
flambé with the brandy by pouring
the brandy into the saucepan and
lighting it. (Pour the brandy from
a separate container, not the
bottle, use a long match, and be
prepared for a whoosh of flame.)
Add the lemongrass, bay leaf,
peppercorns, parsley stalks,
tomato paste and cold water. Bring
to the boil and simmer gently for 2
hours, skimming any scum from
the surface with a ladle. Pass
through a muslin-lined colander
into a large bowl, discarding any
solids. Cool, cover and refrigerate.
The stock will keep for 2–3 days in
the fridge. Stock can be frozen in
ice-cube trays and stored in
plastic bags in the freezer.

Vegetable stock

This quantity makes about
1¼ litres.

40 g butter
1 large onion, unpeeled, roughly
  chopped
2 carrots, roughly chopped
4 sticks of celery, roughly chopped
2 leeks, roughly chopped
1 parsnip, roughly chopped
25 g dried mushrooms, soaked
  for 20 minutes
1 tomato, roughly chopped
1 clove of garlic, peeled & sliced
1 bay leaf
1 sprig of thyme
5 white peppercorns
3 parsley stalks
pinch of salt
2 litres water

Melt the butter in a large saucepan
and gently colour the onion,
carrots, celery, leeks and parsnip
before adding all the other
ingredients. Bring to the boil,
reduce the heat and simmer,
uncovered, for 30 minutes.
Remove the saucepan from the
heat and let it sit for another 30
minutes. Strain the stock through
a fine sieve to remove all the
solids. Cool completely before
refrigerating in a covered
container. The stock should be
used within 2 days. Stock can be
frozen in ice-cube trays and stored
in plastic bags in the freezer.

Jus

20 g butter
1 shallot, peeled & chopped
1 clove of garlic, peeled & chopped
1 stick of celery, roughly chopped
1 carrot, unpeeled, roughly
  chopped
1 bay leaf
1 sprig of thyme
1 tablespoon sugar
1 tablespoon balsamic vinegar
200 ml ruby port
200 ml red wine
1½–2 litres beef or veal stock
  (see page 210)

Melt the butter in a large saucepan and gently cook the shallot, garlic, celery, carrot, bay leaf and thyme for about 5 minutes. Add the sugar and cook for 2–3 minutes to caramelise. Add the balsamic vinegar, port and red wine and reduce by half. Next add the stock and reduce to a sauce consistency. Pass through a muslin-lined sieve, cool and refrigerate in a covered container. The jus should keep for about 5 days in the fridge. It can also be frozen in ice-cube trays and stored in plastic bags in the freezer.

Mayonnaise

2 egg yolks
1 tablespoon Dijon mustard
1 tablespoon white wine vinegar
salt & freshly ground white pepper
300 ml olive oil

Combine the egg yolks, mustard, vinegar and seasoning in a food processor. Blend these for 1 minute before slowly drizzling in the olive oil. Continue to add the oil slowly until the sauce reaches a thick mayonnaise consistency. Adjust the seasoning. Refrigerate. Mayonnaise will keep for 2 days in the fridge.

Aïoli

4 cloves of garlic, peeled & crushed
2 egg yolks
250 ml olive oil
salt & freshly ground white pepper
1 tablespoon lemon juice

Combine the garlic with the egg yolks in a food processor. Blend these for 1 minute before slowly drizzling in the olive oil. Continue to add the oil slowly until the aïoli has taken on the consistency of mayonnaise. Season with salt and pepper, then add the lemon juice and taste again. Refrigerate. Aïoli will keep for 2 days in the fridge.

Beurre blanc

2 shallots, peeled & finely chopped
20 ml white wine vinegar
40 ml dry white wine
60 ml fish stock or water
20 ml cream
175 g unsalted butter, diced

Put the shallots in a small saucepan with the wine vinegar, wine and stock or water. Bring to the boil and simmer until nearly all the liquid has evaporated. Add the cream and reduce a little. Reduce the heat and add the butter, whisking briskly, until all the butter is incorporated into the sauce and the sauce has thickened. Serve at once.

Beurre rouge

2 red onions, peeled & finely
  chopped
150 ml red wine
85 ml chicken stock (see page 210)
85 ml red wine vinegar
½ teaspoon sugar
pinch of salt
100 g unsalted butter, diced

Put the onions in a medium-sized saucepan with the wine, chicken stock, wine vinegar, sugar and salt. Bring to the boil, reduce to a simmer and cook until the onions are soft. Reduce the heat and add the butter piece by piece, whisking vigorously, until all the butter is incorporated into the sauce and the sauce has thickened. Serve at once.

Froth

90 ml vegetable stock
90 ml cream
salt & freshly ground white pepper
50 g butter, diced

Bring the vegetable stock to the boil in a medium-sized saucepan and simmer until it has reduced by half. Add 60 ml of the cream and reduce again by half. Season and pass through a sieve. Add the remaining cream and, using a balloon whisk or hand-held blender, whisk in the butter and froth the mixture until you have a good foam. Spoon the foam on to the plate when you are ready to serve.

Pasta

500 g 00 flour, sifted
3 eggs
6 egg yolks
pinch of salt
1 tablespoon olive oil

Place the flour in a food processor. Add the eggs and egg yolks and process until the dough just starts to form a ball. Next add the salt and olive oil and combine. Shake a little flour on a work surface and knead the ball of dough by hand for 5 minutes until it's smooth, adding more flour if it sticks. Wrap the dough in clingfilm and rest it in a cool place for 1–2 hours.

Puff pastry

500 g strong white flour, sifted
5 g salt
500 g unsalted butter
1 teaspoon lemon juice
250–300 ml cold water

Place the flour in a large bowl and add the salt. Rub 50 g of the butter into the flour, then the lemon juice and enough water to make a soft dough that does not stick to the bowl. Knead to a smooth dough. Roll the dough into a ball and wrap in clingfilm. Refrigerate for 30 minutes.

Cut a cross in the ball of dough, then pull out the four corners in the shape of a star, leaving the centre about 15 mm thick. Roll out each corner to a quarter the thickness of the centre.

Knead the rest of the butter and place it in the centre of the paste. Fold over the corners and enclose the butter completely, excluding any air. Fold the pastry in three and roll it out in the opposite direction to the way it was rolled previously, then fold in three again. Wrap the dough in clingfilm and refrigerate for 30 minutes.

Repeat the rolling and folding procedure twice more. Rest the pastry for 1 hour before using.

Risotto

50 g butter
1 small onion, peeled & finely diced
300 g Arborio rice
1 litre chicken stock (see page 210)
salt & freshly ground white pepper

Melt the butter in a medium-sized saucepan and cook the onion gently for 5 minutes until tender. Add the rice, stir, and cook for another 3 minutes. Meanwhile heat the stock in a separate saucepan. Add the hot stock to the rice ladle by ladle, stirring constantly. Continue to stir, allowing the rice to simmer until all the stock is absorbed (15–18 minutes) and the rice is cooked. Season to taste.

Stock syrup

450 g sugar
570 ml water
80 g liquid glucose

Place all the ingredients in a large saucepan. Stir, without heating, until the sugar has dissolved, then bring the mixture to the boil. Take off the heat and cool.

Sponge cake

4 medium eggs, beaten
110 g caster sugar
1 tablespoon vegetable oil
110 g self-raising flour, sifted

Preheat the oven to 180°C/350°F/ gas mark 4. Whisk the eggs and sugar together in a bowl until light and fluffy and add the oil. Fold in the flour gently and pour the mixture into a 28 cm round cake tin. Bake for 25 minutes until golden brown. Cool on a wire rack.

Crème anglaise

300 ml cream
100 ml milk
1 vanilla pod, halved lengthways
4 egg yolks
80 g caster sugar

Bring the cream, milk and vanilla pod to the boil in a large saucepan. Meanwhile whisk the egg yolks and caster sugar in a heatproof bowl over a large saucepan of simmering water until the mixture is pale and creamy. When the cream starts to boil, pour it slowly over the egg and sugar mixture, whisking all the time. Transfer the mixture back into the saucepan the cream was heated in and continue cooking on gentle heat until the custard coats the back of a wooden spoon. Pass the custard through a sieve. Scrape the seeds from the vanilla pod into the custard, then discard the pod. Cool.

L'ECRIVAIN

guide to matching wine & food

To help you choose wines that will complement the recipes in the book, we have given a very general outline of the most popular grape varieties below. Wines made from the same grape varieties can vary tremendously, depending on the country and region where they're grown. Wines from warmer climates tend to be richer and fuller bodied than wines from cooler areas. Wine suggestions for the recipes are given with page numbers. Sometimes more than one wine can go with a recipe – it all depends on personal preference.

The 'Old World' refers to Europe and the 'New World' covers North and South America, Australia, New Zealand and South Africa.

Wines	Food match

Dry whites

Chardonnay

The best-known white grape variety, Chardonnay styles vary dramatically, depending on whether the wine has been matured in oak barrels or stainless steel vats. Unoaked Chardonnay, such as Chablis, has a mineral steeliness and quite high acidity, with green apple and citrus flavours and aromas. Oaked Chardonnay comes from southern Burgundy (Chassagne-Montrachet, Meursault, Puligny-Montrachet), California, Australia, Chile and South Africa. Aromas are bold, rich, buttery and nutty, with sweet vanilla tones. Acidity is lower in these wines. The palate is rich and creamy, with ripe melon and nut flavours.

Oaked: cheese, poultry, white fish, lobster, salmon, shellfish, veal
Roasted celeriac soup (page 97)
Caesar salad (page 111)
Terrine of smoked mackerel (page 118)
Ballotine of salmon (page 112)
Roast hake wrapped in Parma ham (page 150)
Roast monkfish, langoustine glaze (page 154)
Char-grilled swordfish steak (page 153)
Burgundy: *West coast lobster with mango & buttermilk risotto (page 146)*
Poached fillet of brill (page 148)
Pan-seared turbot (page 160)
New World: *Dublin Bay prawn risotto (page 107)*
Terrine of red mullet (page 119)
Steamed wild Irish salmon (page 156)

Unoaked: cheese dishes, simply cooked fish, shellfish
Deep-fried Dublin Bay prawns in ketaifi pastry (page 104)
Sally Barnes's natural smoked haddock risotto (page 120)
Chablis: *Bere Island scallops (page 144)*

Chenin Blanc

A steely, dry wine with high acidity. The palate has flavours of apples, apricots and honey with nutty overtones. The best examples are found in the Loire, e.g. Savennières, where wines develop fantastic complexity with ageing. South Africa produces some good examples for earlier drinking.

Goats' cheese, fish, poultry, shellfish, risotto
Chilled goats' cheese parfait (page 138)
Ravioli of goats' cheese (page 137)
Bere Island scallops with mussel & clam orzo (page 144)
Seared Bere Island scallops (page 145)
Seared loin of rabbit stuffed with Clonakilty black pudding (page 162)

Gewürztraminer

Striking aromas of lychees, roses and Turkish Delight. Flavours are flowery and spicy, with lychees, ginger and cinnamon. Acidity is low and wines are best drunk young. The best examples are from Alsace, Austria and Germany.

Spicy food, pâtés
Cream of spiced parsnip & coriander (page 94)
Cream of sweet potato (page 95)
Marinated native oysters (page 103)
Seared duck foie gras (page 130)

Pinot Gris/Pinot Grigio

Spicy aromas with a floral background. Flavours on the palate are rich, peachy and spicy in Alsace, Germany and Austria, with medium acidity. Wines are drier, lighter, crisper and not so aromatic in northern Italy. The best examples come from Alsace, Germany, Austria and Italy; new plantings reflect Pinot Grigio's growing popularity in California.

Aperitif, sole, vegetables
Alsace Pinot Gris: *Tempura of organic vegetables (page 180)*
Italian Pinot Grigio: *Pan-seared John Dory (page 152)*
Pan-seared ray wing on the bone (page 158)

Wines	Food match

Dry whites {cont.}

Riesling

One of the most underrated grapes, Riesling is an ideal food wine because of its naturally high acidity. Dry Rieslings from Germany, Alsace and Austria are aromatic and flowery, with citrus aromas and a mineral edge. Grapefruit and citrus flavours dominate the palate. New World Rieslings (Australia, New Zealand) are higher in alcohol, are more full bodied and have richer fruit, very often with a strong lime element.

Fish, duck, goose, ham, salmon
Dublin coddle soup (page 96)
Smoked fish & wild salmon fish cake (page 113)
Wholegrain mustard & whiskey cured wild Irish salmon (page 116)
Deep-fried cod in light potato & onion batter (page 149)
Soy & honey glazed belly of pork confit (page 173)
Alsace: *Crispy beignets of crab (page 110)*

Sauvignon Blanc

Aromatic grape with high acidity. Grassy aromas, gooseberries, sometimes hints of asparagus. High acidity on the palate and delicious flinty flavours, gooseberry and citrus. Best Old World examples are from the Loire (Sancerre, Pouilly-Fumé), Bordeaux (white Graves) and Rueda in Spain. The best New World Sauvignons are from New Zealand, South Africa and the Margaret River area of Australia. Fumé Blanc is the Californian version.

Goats' cheese, tomato sauce, crab, fish, shellfish, smoked salmon
Spider crab & tomato consommé (page 100)
Prawn bisque (page 101)
Carpaccio of scallop (page 108)
Crisp roll of crab, goats' cheese & pine nuts (page 109)
Deep-fried Dublin Bay prawns in ketaifi pastry (page 104)
Frank Hederman's beech smoked salmon (page 114)
Terrine of wild Irish smoked salmon with crab, Mascarpone cheese & horseradish (page 117)
Chilled goats' cheese parfait (page 138)
Pan-seared ray wing on the bone (page 158)
Tomato plate (page 181)

Sémillon

Often blended with Sauvignon Blanc in Bordeaux. Waxy, toasty aromas, low acidity. Richly textured, with honey and nuts, Sémillon produces full-flavoured wines that are often oaked. Young Australian oaked examples are richer in fruit, with apricot and mango flavours. Very long-lived. The best examples come from Australia's Hunter Valley and Bordeaux.

Shellfish, fish, poultry
White Graves: *Crisp roll of crab, goats' cheese & pine nuts (page 109)*
Seared peppered rare tuna loin (page 122)
Pan-seared ray wing on the bone (page 158)

Wines	Food match

Dry reds

Cabernet Sauvignon & blends

A Bordeaux grape, but now planted worldwide. Aromas of blackcurrants, black fruits and cedar in the Old World, eucalyptus and mint in the New. Very tannic, benefits from ageing in oak barrels. The best examples hail from Bordeaux, California, Australia, South Africa and Chile, and are often blended, mainly with Merlot and Cabernet Franc. Benefits from long ageing.

Hard cheese, red meats, duck, venison
Roast breast of duck (page 163)
Roast crown of wild mallard (page 164)
Roast loin of wild Irish venison (page 166)
Char-grilled marinated rack of lamb (page 165)
Roast glazed rump of lamb (page 170)

Merlot

Soft, ripe and plummy, with damson and fruit cake aromas. A fleshy wine, with flavours of fruits of the forest, plums and damsons, it has soft tannins and a delicious, velvety texture. The best examples come from St Emilion and Pomerol, where it is often blended with Cabernet Sauvignon, and California. Also found in Australia, South Africa and Chile.

Duck, lamb, game
Char-grilled marinated rack of lamb (page 165)
Roast glazed rump of lamb (page 170)
California: *Roast crown of wild mallard (page 164)*
St Emilion: *Breast of pheasant stuffed with chestnuts & smoked bacon (page 161)*
Roasted veal kidney (page 136)

Pinot Noir

A pale wine, but with plenty of aroma and fruit. Depending on where it comes from, aromas are of strawberries, black cherries and violets. When aged, it takes on nuances of mushrooms and truffles – even a whiff of the farmyard. Pinot Noir has a silky, velvety texture and flavours of black cherries, strawberries and sometimes a little spice. Although it's a less tannic grape variety than Cabernet Sauvignon, it benefits from long ageing. Best examples from Burgundy; also found in California (Carneros), Oregon, South Africa and New Zealand.

Salmon, tuna, meaty white fish, duck, game, goose, beef, ham, roast poultry, veal, mushrooms
Carpaccio of aged Angus beef (page 132)
Roasted farmyard quail (page 125)
Roasted wood pigeon (page 126)
Roasted white asparagus wrapped in Parma ham (page 140)
Poached fillet of brill (page 148)
Roast hake wrapped in Parma ham (page 150)
Roast monkfish, langoustine glaze (page 154)
Pan-seared turbot with spinach purée (page 160)
Wild mushroom risotto (page 182)

Wines	Food match

Dry reds {cont.}

Sangiovese
One of Italy's stars. Aromas of cherries and cold tea, with flavours of cherries and plums. Acidity is high, as are tannins; wines age very well. The most outstanding wines are Chianti and Brunello di Montalcino; Sangiovese is blended with Cabernet Sauvignon in Supertuscan wines. Also found in California.

Pasta dishes, beef, pork, turkey, veal
Roasted plum tomato & red pepper soup (page 98)
Roasted farmyard quail (page 125)
Ravioli of goats' cheese (page 137)
Chilled char-grilled vegetables (page 176)
Ricotta & basil gnocchi (page 177)
Tomato plate (page 181)

Syrah/Shiraz
Known as Syrah in the Old World and Shiraz in the New. Spicy, black fruit aromas with leather developing in mature wines. Flavours are intense and even tarry – blackberries, spice, chocolate. Firm tannins often need time to soften. The best examples come from the northern Rhône (Hermitage, Côte-Rôtie). It is blended in the southern Rhône (Châteauneuf-du-Pape); in the New World, Australia and South Africa produce excellent Shiraz.

Duck, goose, game, turkey, beef, wild mushrooms
Shiraz: *Assiette of duck (page 128)*
Boudin of Clonakilty black pudding (page 134)
Roast loin of wild Irish venison (page 166)
Seared fillet of beef with horseradish crust (page 172)
Southern Rhône: *Crisp organic salad Landaise (page 127)*
Seared loin of rabbit stuffed with Clonakilty black pudding (page 162)

Tempranillo
Spicy aromas with cooked strawberries and a hint of tobacco, but with a certain complexity. Acidity and tannin are on the low side; wines are broad, rich and expressive and can be drunk young (*crianza*), when they are light and fruity, or older (*reserva* or *gran reserva*), when wines from the best years develop a wonderful complexity and maturity. Mainstay of Rioja and Ribera del Duero, but widespread in the rest of Spain; known as Tinta Roriz in Portugal.

Game, poultry, lamb, mushrooms, truffles
Terrine of teal & swede (page 124)
Pressed ham hock (page 131)
Char-grilled marinated rack of lamb (page 165)
Roast glazed rump of lamb (page 170)
Seared veal liver with whipped cheese & onion potatoes (page 175)
Wild mushroom risotto (page 182)

Rosé
Dry rosé wines are flexible when it comes to food. Good examples have plenty of red fruit on the palate and lively acidity. Rosé is made all over the world.

Aperitif, shellfish, fish, poultry, cold meats
Smoked fish & wild salmon fish cake (page 113)
Pressed ham hock (page 131)
Roasted white asparagus wrapped in Parma ham (page 140)
Roast monkfish, langoustine glaze (page 154)

Wines	Food match

Sweet wines
Chenin Blanc
Very susceptible to botrytis, which intensifies sweetness and flavour. With honey and barley sugar aromas, flavours are of peach, barley sugar and marzipan. Chenin Blanc has a wonderful backbone of acidity, which keeps the wine fresh and light. Wines will improve and mature for decades. Best examples are from the Loire Valley – Vouvray, Coteaux du Layon, Bonnezeaux, Quarts de Chaume.

Fruit-based puddings, white chocolate
Chilled summer fruits risotto (page 183)
Terrine of summer berries (page 184)
Classic vanilla crème brûlée (page 192)
Passion fruit & white chocolate délice (page 204)

Riesling
Wonderful ageing ability due to its very high acidity and fruit extract. Young Riesling has citrus and grapefruit aromas, but the best Rieslings are mature, when they develop a definite whiff of kerosene and take on honey and apricot nuances. The palate is full of peach, honey, apricot and passion fruit. Length is memorable. Best examples are late-harvest wines from Germany, Austria and Alsace.

Foie gras, fruit-based puddings, custards, ice cream
Cappuccino parfait with apple beignets (page 197)
Classic vanilla crème brûlée (page 192)
Austrian or German: *Terrine of summer berries (page 184)*
Pineapple Tarte Tatin (page 191)

Sémillon
Usually blended with Sauvignon Blanc and Muscadelle; wines are often affected by botrytis. Honeysuckle and orange aromas and deliciously waxy, creamy flavours of honey, nectarines and marmalade. Acidity is balanced due to the presence of Sauvignon Blanc. These wines can live for many years. Best examples from Bordeaux, e.g. Sauternes, Barsac, Monbazillac. The most famous sweet wine in the world, Château d'Yquem, is a Sauternes.

Blue cheese, foie gras, custard puddings
Sauternes: *Assiette of peach (page 186)*
Organic carrot plate (page 190)
Îles flottantes (page 194)
Baked orange & cardamom sponge pudding (page 201)

Tokaji
Famous sweet Hungarian wine made with the Furmint grape, which is high in sugar, acidity and fruit. It is also very susceptible to noble rot, which adds complexity. Wonderful ageing potential. Apricot, orange and marzipan flavours, with nutty spiciness veering to cinnamon in aged examples, vibrant acidity and a long, smoky finish.

Blue cheese, foie gras, Christmas pudding, rich desserts
Raspberry & aged sherry trifle (page 196)
Banana & chocolate feuilletine (page 198)
Banana Bakewell tart (page 200)

Wines	Food match

Fortified wines
Port
Tawny: Aged in wood, normally a blend of several vintages. Tawny in colour, it has a silky texture and a lovely spicy, nutty character.

Stilton, Cheddar, chocolate desserts, nuts, or on its own after dinner
Pecan brownie with chocolate butterscotch sauce (page 209)
Pistachio-crusted dark & white chocolate mousse (page 208)
Tasting of chocolate (page 206)

Late-bottled vintage: Wine from a single year, aged in cask and bottled after 4–6 years. Prunes, plums, spice and Christmas cake flavours. Good examples give vintage port a run for its money.

Vintage: Wine from the best vineyards, made only in 'declared' (excellent) years. Aged in bottle rather than cask, it throws a deposit of sediment and has to be decanted. Blackberries, black cherries, mulberries and figs, with an abundance of cinnamon and fruit cake. Tannins can be firm in youth, but become yielding and velvety with age.

Sherry
Manzanilla: Pale in colour, delicate, with a salty, nutty tang.

Aperitif, tapas

Fino: Pale, light. Rounded, very dry, almond and yeast aromas, almonds and marzipan flavours, nutty finish.

Aperitif, tapas

Amontillado: Caramel, walnuts, fig and apricot aromas. Rich palate, figs, baked caramel, layered and concentrated. Nutty finish.

Dry: consommé, olives, almonds, tapas
Sweet: trifle
Dry amontillado: *Chicken & wild mushroom consommé (page 99)*
Sweet amontillado: *Raspberry & aged sherry trifle (page 196)*

Oloroso: Burnt sugar and fig aromas. Sweet, rich, figgy, soft toffee palate. Long, harmonious, rich finish.

Chocolate, custard desserts, trifle
Raspberry & aged sherry trifle (page 196)
Pecan brownie with chocolate butterscotch sauce (page 209)
Sticky fudge & pecan parfait (page 202)
Tasting of chocolate (page 206)

Pedro Ximénez: Dark and luscious, burnt toffee and spice aromas. Treacle toffee palate, very sweet, dark chocolate, a little spice.

Chocolate, fudge; excellent poured over ice cream
Pistachio-crusted dark & white chocolate mousse (page 208)
Warm chocolate fondant tart (page 205)

Wines

Food match

Champagne & sparkling wine
Non-vintage champagne
Champagne is made only in the Champagne area of France from Pinot Noir, Chardonnay and Pinot Meunier. Non-vintage champagne varies according to which grape varieties are used, but, when young, it has fresh citrus aromas that develop a toastiness with age. With its crisp acidity and lively fruit flavours, non-vintage champagne is versatile with food.

Brut (dry): aperitif, oysters, smoked salmon
Dublin Bay prawn plate (page 106)
Chilled goats' cheese parfait (page 138)
Deep-fried cod in light potato & onion batter (page 149)
Rosé: aperitif, shellfish
Dublin Bay prawn plate (page 106)
Demi-sec: fruit desserts
Chilled summer fruits risotto (page 183)

Vintage champagne
Made only in the best years, vintage champagne is richer than non-vintage, with delicious biscuity aromas. Champagne's vibrant acidity balances the rich fruit and biscuit flavours of the palate.

Lobster, smoked salmon
Frank Hederman's beech smoked salmon (page 114)
Seared Bere Island scallops (page 145)
West coast lobster with mango & buttermilk risotto (page 146)

Cava
Cava, from the Penedès region of Spain, is made in the same way as champagne, but uses different grape varieties – Macabéo, Parellada and Xarel-lo. Cava has a different aroma from champagne, with hints of burnt earth. It's crisp and clean, with flavours ranging from lemon to biscuit. Lively acidity.

Aperitif, shellfish, Asian cuisine
Baked rock oysters with bacon & cabbage (page 102)
Soy & honey glazed belly of pork confit (page 173)

Prosecco
From the Veneto region of Italy, a light, easy-drinking sparkling wine with fruity aromas and flavours.

Aperitif, shellfish
Dublin Bay prawn plate (page 106)

Asti
Italy's most popular sparkling wine comes from Piedmont. Light, off-dry, fruity, it must be drunk young and fresh.

Aperitif, light desserts
Assiette of peach (page 186)
Chilled summer fruits risotto (page 183)

New World sparkling wine
'Traditional-method' (same method as champagne) sparkling wine is made in all the New World countries, but the most successful examples come from New Zealand and California, with Australia and South Africa hard on their heels.

Aperitif, shellfish, fish
Pan-seared ray wing on the bone (page 158)
Wild mushroom risotto (page 182)

English sparkling wine
The chalky soils of champagne are also found in south-east England, where some very respectable sparkling wines are being produced. Nyetimber is the outstanding example.

Aperitif, shellfish, smoked salmon, poultry
Dublin Bay prawn plate (page 106)
Frank Hederman's beech smoked salmon (page 114)
Chilled goats' cheese parfait (page 138)
Deep-fried cod in light potato & onion batter (page 149)

Recipe index